Innocent I. Asouzu

Ibuaru̩

Studies in African Philosophy

Series Editors

volume 6

LIT

Innocent I. Asouzu

IBUARỤ

The Heavy Burden of Philosophy Beyond African Philosophy

LIT

Bibliographic information published by the Deutsche Nationalbibliothek
The Deutsche Nationalbibliothek lists this publication in the Deutsche Nationalbibliografie; detailed bibliographic data are available in the Internet at http://dnb.d-nb.de.

ISBN 978-3-03735-170-3 (Schweiz)
ISBN 978-3-8258-0538-8 (Deutschland)

A catalogue record for this book is available from the British Library

Dufourstr. 31
CH-8008 Zürich
Tel. +41 (0) 44-251 75 05
Fax +41 (0) 44-251 75 06
e-Mail: zuerich@lit-verlag.ch
http://www.lit-verlag.ch

LIT VERLAG Dr. W. Hopf
Berlin 2007
Auslieferung/Verlagskontakt:
Fresnostr. 2
D-48159 Münster
Tel. +49 (0)251–62 03 20
Fax +49 (0)251–23 19 72
e-Mail: lit@lit-verlag.de
http://www.lit-verlag.de

Distributed in the UK by: Global Book Marketing, 99B Wallis Rd, London, E9 5LN
Phone: +44 (0) 20 8533 5800 – Fax: +44 (0) 1600 775 663
http://www.centralbooks.co.uk/acatalog/search.html

Distributed in North America by:

Transaction Publishers
New Brunswick (U.S.A.) and London (U.K.)

Transaction Publishers
Rutgers University
35 Berrue Circle
Piscataway, NJ 08854

Phone: +1 (732) 445 - 2280
Fax: + 1 (732) 445 - 3138
for orders (U. S. only):
toll free (888) 999 - 6778
e-mail:
orders@transactionspub.com

Introduction

The main title of this book, *ibuarụ,* is a composite word drawn from the Igbo language and is constituted of the two words, *ibu* (load) and *arụ* (heavy). Hence, *ibuarụ* means "heavy load" or "heavy burden". In this sense, this book is dealing with one of the heaviest loads or burdens of philosophy, which can be located in the tendency for philosophers to approach their subject matter with unintended ethnocentric mindset. This is the *phenomenon of unintended ethnocentric commitment,* which is the philosophical *ibuarụ* or heavy burden. This phenomenon surfaces mostly in those cases where philosophy is understood as culture-relevant inquiry. The title *ibuarụ* is in so far suggestive because the means needed to address this burden has much to do also with *ibu* or load. To unburden such constraints entails the acquisition of the spirit of *ibuanyidanda* or a complementary mindset. In the expression *ibu anyi danda,* we affirm that all burdens become bearable and manageable when all stakeholders complement their efforts. We do this in the transferred sense, because we are committed to the insight that those ants called *danda* can lift and manage excruciating heavy loads (*ibu*) when they complement their efforts. Here, we can even say *ibu arụ anyi danda* or no heavy burden is insurmountable for *danda,* the ant. Therefore, all matters of unintended ethnocentric commitment, as the *ibuarụ* or heavy burden militating against philosophical investigation, have to be handled within a complementary horizon to be manageable.

Many seem to assume that ethnophilosophy, with some of its major constraints, is a typical problem of African philosophy. Here they may be wrong. The phenomenon of unintended ethnocentric commitment goes to demonstrate that most philosophical inquiries and methodologies often have an ethnocentric undertone that gives them ethnophilosophic character. This is that tendency for philosophers and scientists to pursue their subject matter with ethnocentric mindsets. Thereby, they seek to project and protect their specific cultural legacies, often at the risk of being exclusivist, though unintentionally. In this form, one can say that there is often traces of ethnophilosophy of the unintended ethnocentric type in most things that are paraded as "scientific philosophy". When this happens the universal and comprehensive character of philosophy as a science is immediately put into serious doubt. Contrary to the assumption of many, this ethnocentric heavy burden is not restricted to ethnophilosophy of the African type. Rather, it is something that goes beyond African philosophy itself. For this reason, one can say that this phenomenon of unintended ethnocentric commitment is something that has not received the serious attention it deserves. This work will try to show how this *ibuarụ* can impinge on scientific objectivity, invalidate good intentions, and even make mutual coexistence among peoples very difficult. Some of the major difficulties which this *ibuarụ* presents become evident in the major themes handled in this work. These are themes that have to deal with our understanding of science, our choice of method of inquiry and the types of conclusions ensuing from our reflection. Other themes are those that have to deal with issues of meaning, understanding, nature of language, origin and nature of ideas and concepts etc. Since philosophy, as cultural science, can be seen as a tool of self-affirmation, often against those inquirers researchers identify as outsiders or foreigners, we see how, due to the intrusion of unintended ethnocentric commitment, scientific inquiry can easily be degraded to a tool of folk's ideological manoeuvres.

Since the publication of my book "The Method and Principles of Complementary Reflection in and Beyond African philosophy" there have been numerous reactions to it. Going through these reactions, it quite striking how widespread this phenomenon of ethnocentric commitment is. I shall formulate my replies bearing this important point in mind. Prof. Kimmerle wrote a lengthy critical review of my book in June 2005. His review bore the title "critical review of the book *The Method and Principles of Complementary Reflection in and beyond African Philosophy"*. My reply to his review followed immediately thereafter and both appeared as internet publications in June 2005 (www.frasouzu.com). I consider Prof. Kimmerle's contribution in so far significant as he is one of the main proponents of a philosophy of culture whose tenets can build a harmonious whole with complementary reflection. This notwithstanding, I discovered that one of the main problems saddling Kimmerle's reaction to my work is methodological. Whereas the version of intercultural philosophy that he espouses lays much emphasis on the relative position of the human person in history, complementary reflection seeks to show how the human person can be grasped within a more comprehensive relative-absolute bracket. Over and above all, Kimmerle's reaction to my work shows traces of unintended ethnocentric commitment and such that often misled him to some inaccurate interpretations of my position.

For the present book, Prof. Kimmerle has requested me to publish his review as ”reaction on 'The Method and Principles of Complementary Reflection in and beyond African Philosophy' referring mainly to its meaning in African philosophy”. Whereas I have reproduced in this book Prof. Kimmerle's "reaction" to my book without modification, I have adjusted my reply to reflect the positions of other scholars who have equally reacted to my work. To some of these scholarly replies and reviews belong the inputs of Prof. Oguejiofor of Nnamdi Azikiwe University, Nigeria and Prof. Udo Etuk of University of Uyo, Nigeria. Prof. Jürgen Hengelbrock of the University of Bochum, Germany made available his critical comment to me in the form of E-mail correspondents, a part of which I have published in this work with his permission. Prof. DDr. Franz Gmainer-Pranzl of the University of Salzburg, Austria wrote a lengthy critical review of my book in "Polylog. Zeitschrift für Interkulturelles Philosophieren". From the United States of America, Ralph Dumain has equally undertaken a lengthy review of "Method and Principles" ((http://www.autodidactproject.org/my/blog-culture-0612.html). Since his review is still in the making at his blog, I shall restrict myself to some of the insights that are now public in that blog.

I am aware that many essays and scientific project inspired by complementary reflection are going on. I shall consider for reply, in this book, those works that have been published or documented officially as scientific works mostly from the graduate level and above. I have selected the work of Esu, Thomas Ejemot on "The Dialectics in Asouzu's Complementary Reflection and The Principle of Contradiction. A Critique", written under the supervision of Prof. Andrew Uduigwomen, because of its usefulness in elucidating some important points raised by other critics. Besides, this book gives me the opportunity to clarify certain issues that have been raised so far in symposia, conferences and seminars concerning complementary reflection. My gratitude goes many who have shown interest in complementary reflection as a very important philosophical trend in contemporary African philosophy. Their good will has helped to sustain my efforts. Most quotations in this book are taken from the Lit-Verlag 2005 international edition of my book "The Method and Principles of Complementary Reflection in and Beyond African Philosophy", except where otherwise indicated.

Innocent I. Asouzu
Azumini, Ndoki
9 April 2007
website: http://www.frasouzu.com
E-mail: frasouzu@frasouzu.com

A. Reaction to Innocent Asouzu's Approach to African Philosophy and the Context of Other Interpretations by Heinz Kimmerle, Zoetermeer

In the following remarks I want to give a critical review of the book The Method and Principles of Complementary Reflection in and beyond African Philosophy, written by Innocent Izuchukwu Asouzu, a Catholic priest and Professor of Philosophy at the University of Calabar in the Igbo-region of Nigeria. This book has first been published in July 2004 with Calabar University Press and re-published in 2005 as volume 4 of the series 'Studies in African Philosophy' with LIT-Verlag at Münster in Germany (ISBN 3-8258-8578-x). When numbers between brackets are given, they refer to pages of the new edition. In his 'Comments to the Lit-Verlag edition' the author reports that the earlier publication had certain shortcomings ('oversights' and 'avoidable errors'), which the new edition 'endeavours to address'. (15)

In his book Asouzu presents a fresh approach to African philosophy, which has an incisive impact on the discussions about this particular kind of philosophy. First of all it is underlined that African philosophy has to be regarded as philosophy precisely in the same way as the philosophies of any other region of the world: 'Arab philosophy, Greek philosophy, Asian philosophy, Indian philosophy, Japanese philosophy … American philosophy, European philosophy' and other philosophies. (52) The specificity of African philosophy, with its primarily oral practice and tradition and its particular cultural ambience, is worked out by Asouzu from the perspective of the Igbo community. He comes to generalisations, which are valid for the big majority of peoples living in Africa south to the Sahara. As the key notion and the paradigm of thought of African philosophy in this sense is introduced 'complementary reflection'.

The special conditions of partly nomadic living peoples in Africa south to the Sahara like the Masai, Hausa, or Fulani, and of groups with different historical backgrounds on this continent like the Pygmies, San or Khoi Khoi are not taken into consideration in detail. Although it is not discussed at length, one can say that the northern parts of Africa, which have a primarily Arabic cultural ambience since about the 10th or 11th century, are not excluded. 'Besides the ancient Egyptian heritage', Asouzu refers to the 'highly intellectualised and sophisticated climate of thought' in this region, which 'produced such brilliant minds of the third century Alexandrian school as Tertullian, Clement, and Origen'. (275) African philosophy in this broad context is part and parcel of the philosophies of the world as a whole, and it contributes to the contents and the potential of problem solving reflections all over the world. Therefore, the paradigm of complementary reflection has its meaning 'in and beyond African philosophy'.

In Azouzu's book complementary reflection has mainly three different aspects. Firstly, there is 'ontological complementarity'. Reality is regarded as an all-embracing whole, in which all units form together a dynamic play of forces, which are in harmony with each other, by completing and supporting one another. The harmony of this play of forces does not exist without dangers, but it can maintain its balance against the influence of counter-forces, which try to disturb or undermine it. 'The worldview of the traditional African shows, in a very natural way, strong moment[s] of the transcendent ontological categories of unity, totality, universality, comprehensiveness, wholeness and future referentiality as authentic dimensions of thoroughgoing complementarism'. (150)

Secondly, complementarity can be found in society. What is true for the units of reality as a whole is also and in a more conscious manner valid for the members of society. They do not leave alone somebody, who is in danger or in need, but in the family or in the larger community, which is regarded as an 'extended family', this person will find support. There are limits to this kind of harmony between human beings in society. Envy and hatred between them do occur, even sacrifice of human beings are real sometimes and somewhere. Personal interest and the personal existential situation are the causes of these limits. However, completing and supporting one another is and remains the main attitude of the members of African societies, so that the principle of 'caring is sharing' forms the predominant feature of them. The ant is the example of strength by cooperation and mutual support, as it is expressed in the 'Igbo work song', in which the following verse is repeated many times: 'Bunu bunu oo ibu anyi danda' ('Lift the load, lift the load, nothing is impossible for the ant'). (118)

Thirdly, 'personal complementarity' is taken into consideration. Every person represents this paradigm because his or her permanent and transcendent flow of consciousness connects the present life to the former life of the ancestors and to the own afterlife in the land of spirits. Thus the understanding of reality and all its different units turns out to transcend personal life by embedding it into a spiritual whole of a cosmic process, which develops in time and space. To every person the possibility is offered that he or she can participate in what is called in the Igbo-language: 'Jide ka iji' ('Joy of being'), which permeates the cosmos as a whole, society with its structure of extended families, and personal life. (148) When a person is referred to by 'using the impersonal pronoun it', this gives expression to the fact that one is speaking of the human being in its totality that 'can never be conceptualised in a fragmented mode, but as complementary units that form a whole'. (159)

The 'complementary approach to reality' is not exactly 'anthropocentric or human-centred' as it is sometimes described. Ontologically it is 'rather comprehensive': 'to be is to be in a relationship of mutual joyous complementary service'. (156/7) There is a special accent on being part of the community, and certain metaphysical and mythological ideas about the influence of the spirits occur in the worldview of African people. Also a misuse of these ideas for 'ideological manipulation' cannot be denied. Nevertheless the 'theoretical technical reason' of the African mindset and also a widespread pragmatic attitude in solving everyday problems have to be argued for.

Asouzu knows about complementary reflection from his own personal history and experience as a member of a family within the Igbo people. In the Section 'Dedication and Acknowledgement' the reader gets thoroughly informed about this personal background. Asouzu participates in this particular knowledge by learning from his ancestors and from the fellow members of his people and also by listening to his language, especially to proverbs, sayings or maxims.

This knowledge is spread in the society as a whole. Nevertheless it is concentrated in persons like himself, summarising and critically evaluating what is handed down and communicated to them. These persons can be elders, office bearers, priests, healers or ordinary people. At any rate, it can be attributed to certain individuals in the present situation and in the history of the Igbo community, although Asouzu does not and/or cannot give their names. In this sense, he speaks about 'the anonymous Igbo philosopher'. (142-148, passim) The 'experience of transcendent complementary unity of consciousness joins' this thinker 'to his milieu'. This can be regarded as an advantage. For, 'the thinker and his environment reinforced themselves mutually'. On the other hand must be admitted: 'Due to the symbiotic relationship between the ideas of these thinkers and their environment, their thoughts did not attain the level of refinement, freshness and dynamism it would (or could) otherwise have attained'. (212; addition in the quotation between brackets by me, HK)

By the reformulation of the method and principles of complementary reflection Asouzu tries to avoid the limits and the negative aspects of the teachings of the anonymous Igbo philosopher. In respect of the 'ontological reflection' the conditions for overcoming the negative forces in the world and for stabilising harmony are sorted out. This kind of reflection includes a certain type of logic, which 'seeks to explore missing links in a comprehensive, total and universal' way of thought. Thus 'it presupposes the acquisition of an inclusive comprehensive logical mindset as opposed to a disjunctive logical mindset'. (355) And it has an impact on the 'ethical reflection', which is not only related to the questions of right or wrong, but also to those of beauty and ugliness in an aesthetic sense (369), and to the 'the joy and sadness of human action', as they are incorporated in the joyful being of cosmic and natural harmony. (361) Above all, this ontology has a religious foundation. For, 'the ontological joy of being is transcendent in the sense that it is something that has to do with the foundation of our being outside ourselves' in the land of spirits. In connection with that, 'the search for this ultimate foundation of our existence takes very concrete and acute shape in religious experiences where this one true, absolute, and transcendent being is clearly identified in different cultures under diverse names. Some of these names are Chukwu, God, Mu'umba, Udali ...Olodumare, Onyankupon ... Allah, Yahwe' and others. (438/9)

It is a remarkable contribution to the history and the specific problems of philosophy in the Western world that complementary reflection leads to a possibility of 'overcoming the subject-object dichotomy'. It turns out not to be adequate to 'raise a thoroughgoing subjectivism' or 'a thoroughgoing objectivism' to 'a universal methodological principle'. On the one hand, scepticism and relativism, which undermine every true statement, would follow from that. And on the other hand dogmatism and imposed orthodoxy could not be avoided. In the way of thought, which is suggested by Asouzu, 'we see how a transcendent complementary unity of consciousness belongs to the same region as (or is in correspondence with) the transcendent categories of being'. (474-481; addition in the quotation between brackets by me, HK)

Not all dimensions of complementary reflection can be reviewed here. In a final analysis Asouzu comes back to a perspective of the first part of his book: the 'African paradigm' forms an answer to the 'global imperative' of political peacekeeping and social justice. The promise of a New World Order can become true by using complementary reflection instead of thinking in oppositions and in terms of friend and enemy. (51-60) In the 'new global family' nobody 'can be understood without reference to other members of the family'. And everybody has the right to be helped in a situation of danger or of need. The 'differences in age, in sex, in nationality, in religion, in language, in ethnicity, in tribe, in race, in culture, in ideologies' are expressions of a multidimensional reality. They can and must be seen as enrichment for each other in 'building a viable and meaningful human family'. (481/2)

In his Preface to Asouzu's book, Obi Oguejiofor from the Seminary at Enugu in Nigeria declares it as an advantage and as 'a clear indication of its originality' that this book 'does not dwell on discussions of theories and contentions about past writers', but 'charts its unique course in contriving a special theory'. (13) And this special theory, one could add, is based on the author's personal knowledge of authentic African traditions in the Igbo community and on dealing with them in his own philosophical thinking. This is a reasonable judgment of Asouzu's approach to African philosophy and its meaning in the context of world-philosophy.

Nevertheless I am of opinion that his approach becomes clearer and more concrete, that it gets sharper contours, if it is embedded into the context of other interpretations of African philosophy. Of course, in certain connections Asouzu is in discussion with other African and non-African philosophers. He is referring especially to well known and also to less famous Nigerian thinkers and theorists, more in particular from Igboland. References to Achebe, Bodunrin, Eboh, Eze, Okolo, Serequeberhan, Sodipo or Unah are important and often enlightening, those to Aligwekwe, Arazu, Iwe, Okadigbo, Ugorji or Uwalaka add something to the list of authors, who have already been quoted in many other books on African philosophy. From the Nigerian environment I miss names as Gbadegesin, Oluwole or Momoh. Absolutely essential contributions to African philosophy as those of Senghor, Nkrumah, Hountondji, Odera Oruka, Wiredu or Gyekye are only mentioned incidentally and not always judged carefully enough. For instance, Wiredu's project of 'conceptual decolonisation' is taken as 'a typical example' of a 'reactionary mindset'. (265) Actually Wiredu endeavours with this project to include original African thought into the worldwide philosophical work of today. To decolonise the mind does not mean to go back to traditional ways of thought, but to make them active and influential in present debates.

Odera Oruka does not refrain from giving the names of 12 Kenyan traditional philosophers from different peoples: Mwitani Masero (Utonga), Njuhi Muthoni (Kikuyu), Simiyu Chaungo (Luhyia), Oruka Rang'inya (Luo), and others. (Sage Philosophy, Leiden a.o.: Brill 1990) And he presents more in detail the politician and philosopher Oginga Odinga. His Philosophy and Beliefs (Nairobi: Initiatives 1992) He calls them 'sages', like Hampaté Bâ had done in his book, written in French, with regard to his own teacher Tierno Bokar. (La vie et l'enseignement de Tierno Bokar. Le sage de Bandiagara, Paris: Seuil 1980) As a follow up to that, Yacouba Konaté is looking for great names of sages further back in history and at the same time is he investigating the connection between the work of the sages and the origin of proverbs with philosophical contents. ('Le syndrome Hampaté Bâ ou comment naissent les proverbes', in: Quest. An International African Journal of Philosophy 8,2; 1994, p. 23-44) Thus it becomes clear how the philosophical impact of language can originate and why proverbs can be regarded as philosophical texts in the primarily oral African traditions. (H. Kimmerle, 'The philosophical text in the African oral tradition', in: Kimmerle/Wimmer (eds), Philosophy and democracy in intercultural perspective, Amsterdam/Atlanta, GA: Rodopi 1997, p. 43-56)

In his book An essay on African philosophical thought. The Akan conceptual scheme (Cambridge: University Press 1987) Gyekye refers to the names and the dates of interviews with Akan 'wise persons' (anyansafo) whom he regards as traditional philosophers. We learn from Asouzu and also from other African philosophers (Tschiamalenga Ntumba and Mabe) that sagacity cannot only be found with a certain group of persons. But is there in general such a recognisable group of 'wise persons' in African traditional communities? Are there persons among the Igbo people who could be identified as sages? Except his mention of Oruka's research, Asouzu refers to Ogotemmeli, a blind hunter and wise person of the Dogon, by quoting the (not quite correct) story, which Masolo tells about him. (African Philosophy in Search of Identity, Bloomington/ Indianopolis: Indiana University Press 1994) And he knows about the work of Hallen and Sodipo who have discussed epistemological questions with traditional healers among the Yoruba. (Hallen/Sodipo, Knowledge, belief and witchcraft. Analytic experiments in African philosophy, London: Ethnographica 1986) (134-36) Odera Oruka contests that Ogotemmeli and the persons who have been interviewed by Hallen and Sodipo may be called 'sages' in the sense of the word as he understands it. Is such a rather strict understanding possible? And what about philosophical sagacity which is possessed by other people than the sages? These questions arise when Asouzu refers to 'the anonymous Igbo philosopher'.

Complementary reflection of living in society makes it necessary to look at 'African communalism' and 'sense of community' as they are worked out by Senghor, Nkrumah, Nyerere and others. (87) However, the theoretical project of these authors, especially in connection with the movement of Negritude, is not discussed clearly enough by Asouzu. The historical context of reassuring African culture of its own value is not part of his judgment. And these authors are brought together with quite a different current in the emerging self-consciousness of African philosophy. I mean the representatives of ethnophilosophy, Tempels, Kagame, Mbiti and others, whose work was fiercely contested by Hountondji and Towa. It is true that communalism, by which a somehow idealistic picture of the African sense of community is drawn, has a limited meaning compared to complementary reflection of societal relations. It could help to show this by a more detailed argumentation. Actually the broader ontological context of complementarity in society, embedding it into a cosmic dimension, is closer to ubuntu than to communalism. Here again a discussion of conformities and differences would give sharper contours to the meaning of complementary reflection. According to Ramose ubuntu refers to the relations between human beings, completing and supporting each other, and at the same time to the forces of the universe, which are unfolded and come to self-consciousness in human thinking and speaking (African Philosophy Through Ubuntu, Harare: Mond Books 1999).

That traditional African philosophy has been practised mainly in oral forms of tradition and communication does not mean being in any way less important, less elaborate or less thoughtful than philosophies, which prefer written forms of tradition and exchange of ideas. I agree also with Asouzu that there is no strict contradiction between orality and literacy in the practice of philosophy. (146-148) In this respect the new concept of writing which is developed by Derrida, putting it exactly on the same level as the oral use of language, can be very helpful (De la grammatologie, Paris: Minuit 1967). Nevertheless it is worth-wile to work out the special possibilities and strong aspects of primarily oral forms of philosophising. Oluwole has pioneered in this field relying also on the philosophical impact of oral literature, especially of the Ifa-corpus in the Yoruba tradition. (Philosophy and Oral Tradition, Lagos: ARK Publications 1999) And a lot can be expected for the contribution of African philosophy to solving the problems of philosophy all over the world by bringing together and harmonising both forms of philosophising, and by combining the strong aspects of them, as Mabe has suggested (Schriftliche und mündliche Formen philosophischen Denkens in Afrika, Diss. habil., TU Berlin 2003).

In her book: Witchcraft, Reincarnation and the God-Head (Lagos: Excel Publishers 1992) Oluwole argues more cautiously than Asouzu and with reference to the restrictions of reliable knowledge in Western philosophy, especially in Kant's Critique of Pure Reason, when she speaks of the belief in supernatural powers, the existence of God and the coming back of persons from the invisible world of spirits to the visible world of people living now. Her argumentation runs, roughly speaking, like this: If finite human beings cannot have reliable, scientifically proved knowledge, whether these dimensions of thought have a correspondence in reality, the option that there is such a correspondence (as preferred in the African worldview) is in the same way possible as the other one that there is not such a correspondence (as preferred in the Western way of thought). According to Oluwole the developments in the most advanced forms of science, particularly in microphysics, strengthen the African position. Like Achebe, to whom Asouzu refers several times, Oluwole strongly affirms that in African thought 'nothing is absolute'. (126) Therefore, she would contest that 'the worldview of the traditional African shows ... strong moment[s] of the transcendent ontological categories of unity, totality, universality, comprehensiveness, wholeness and future referentiality as authentic dimensions of thoroughgoing complemetarism', (150) which is a core argument in Asouzu's book.

The predominant 'future relatedness' of Igbo thought, of which Asouzu speaks repeatedly (150-51, 181 a.m.o.), is also different from Mbiti's thesis that the past is the most relevant dimension of time in African thought. (African religions and philosophy, London 1969) Although Mbiti's statement that in African languages no anticipation of future events farther away than about two years can be expressed, has been contested heavily by Hountondji, Odera Oruka,Gyekye and others, these authors do not deny that there is a predominantly backward orientation in the African way of thought.

Therefore, Asouzu's report about the future relatedness of the anonymous Igbo philosopher is in sharp contrast to most of the other philosophies of African peoples we know about. One could say, it adds a radically new aspect to the African philosophies of time. However, the close and concrete connection of time and space as 'integral dimensions of the unity of consciousness' and in the same way of 'the aspects of processes observable in nature' and of the 'aspects of the spiritual immaterial world' in Asouzu's text (175-177) is very much in accordance with the unity of time and space in the philosophy of Bantu-languages, which is worked out by Kagame. (Sprache und Sein. Die Ontologie der Bantu Zentralafrikas, Brazzaville/ Heidelberg 1985)

To Asouzu's ideas about 'building a viable and meaningful human family', can be added Odera Oruka's conception of a 'parental earth ethics'. In this conception the African sense of family is also extended to humanity as a (concrete) whole. And within the human family different roles and obligations can be determined. The human rights should be made more complete by the right to an existence minimum for every human being, which includes eating, clothing and housing. The former colonising countries, which are now, not independently from their colonising past, the rich countries of the world, have clear ethical obligations to share with the former colonised and now poor countries. In a future related perspective it is wise, if the rich countries now more effectively share with the poor parts of the world, for in the long run the relations between dominant and dominated parts of the world never remain the same, as history teaches us. ('Ecophilosophy and the Parental Earth Ethics', in: Graness/Kresse (eds), Sagacious Reasoning. Henry Odera Oruka in memoriam, Frankfurt/M. a.o.: Peter Lang 1997, p. 119-131, 'Philosophie der Entwicklungshilfe. Die Frage des Rechts auf ein menschliches Minimum, in: polylog. Zeitschrift für interkulturelles Philosophieren 6, 2000, p. 6-16)

In a final judgment I would say that Asouzu's book presents a new approach to African philosophy as a whole and gives valuable details about African philosophy of a certain region. He argues himself that this kind of regional differentiations of African philosophy are useful and necessary. (121-22 a.m.o.) This is in line with his general claim for differentiation and multidimensionality. (450 a.m.o.) Without reducing the renewing value of Asouzu's approach to African philosophy in general, we can add his conception to those of other regional African philosophies. Besides the knowledge we have about thought systems of African peoples in the literature of cultural anthropologists, we know about Luba and other Bantu philosophies by the works of Tempels and Kagame, about Fulani and Toucouleurs philosophies by Tierno Bokar and Hampaté Bâ, about Dogon philosophy by Ogotemmeli, about Luo, Lyhsia and other Kenyan philosophies by Odera Oruka, about Akan and Ga philosophies by Abraham, Wiredu, Gyekye and Kudadjie, about Gikuyu philosophy by Wanjohi, about Yoruba philosophy by Hallen/Sodipo, Oluwole and Gbadegesin. And fortunately now we know more about Igbo-philosophy by Asouzu.

B. My reply to critics, anchored around Heinz Kimmerle, Zoetermeer's "Reaction".

For the sake of clarity, I have built my reply around some identifiable themes deduced from the critical reaction of Kimmerle and other critics. To these belong:

1. - On some important challenges of unintended ethnocentric intrusions - *ibuarụ* -
2.- On the similarities between ethno-philosophy and unintended ethnophilosophic commitment
3. - On unintended ethnocentric commitment and the nature of a philosophical question
4.- On patchwork philosophical approaches and unintended ethnocentric commitment
5. - On how complementary reflection relates to other philosophies of culture
6. - On intellectual protectionism and the heavy philosophical burden (*ibuarụ*) of non-interference
7.- On the "Tempelsian damage" as the special *ibuarụ* of African philosophy
8. On radicalisation of the "Tempelsian damage" in the rediscovery of encrypted phenomena and ideas of science in Africa
9.- On the restricting character of two major forms of reduction
10.- On the principle of judicious interference and some of its challenges
11.- On the raw primary and complementary cognitive ambiences
12.- On encrypted phenomena as pragmatic cognitive postulates
13. - On encrypted phenomena and context of understanding
14.- On encrypted phenomena in their dynamism and pseudo-legitimate transformation strategies
15.- On encrypted phenomena, confluxing role of the subject and basic epistemological problems
16.- On encrypted phenomena and context of explanation
17- On decoding the encrypt, complementary noetic propaedeutic and effective legal system
18.- On encrypted rationality, complementary rationality and

1. On some important challenges of unintended ethnocentric intrusions - *ibuarụ* -

The first major task of this book is to illustrate in practical terms what is implied by unintended ethnocentric commitment. In this way, the type of unintended ethnocentric mindset with which most inquirers embark on their work would become clearer. This is mostly the case in those inquiries that require some sort of reference to those we identify as outsiders or foreigners. I consider ethnocentric intrusion in inquiry one of the commonest problems, which go quite unnoticed in most investigations that are culture-bound, as we have this in various variants of philosophy of culture. It is for this reason that it easily militate, not only against scientific objectivity, but more so, against scientific progress generally, due to its dogmatic type of conservatism and intolerance. What is interesting about this phenomenon is that it is often an unintended act. This is mostly why in spite of the avowed goodwill to do science in an unbiased objective manner many scientists find themselves taking sides in very crucial matters in a way that betrays their folk ideological commitment. Such biases result mostly from long years of exposure to certain climates of thought or some forms of idiosyncrasies that can give the inquirer some false notions about himself and the world generally. This is applicable, not only to those African philosophers who see philosophy as an avenue for projecting their African identity, but more so, to inquirers from other regions of the world who tend to see something "specific" about their own conceptual schemes. Where unintended ethnocentric commitment is prevalent, we are confronted with a situation where the mind can be a victim of long years of bad habits and prejudices, which have come to sediment as accepted ways of seeing the world and doing things. When this happens, those accepted dogmas deriving from long years of biases tend to resist change, no matter how hard we try. To show how widespread this heavy burden or *ibuarụ* holds sway, I have chosen to make reference to sources outside of African philosophy, by discussing two vanguards of intercultural philosophy. Heinz Kimmerle and Jürgen Hengelbrock are two eminent European philosophers who today belong to those rare Western philosophers that show deep commitment towards understanding other paradigms of philosophy beyond what has come to be known as Western philosophy. Over and above all, their commitment to African philosophy marks them out as people who are exploring new ways of doing philosophy beyond their ethnic locations. In what they characterise as "an encounter" one can see how, in spite of their declared goodwill, they, like many, are subject to the challenges arising from unintended ethnocentric commitment. Theirs is still very striking because each, inadvertently, seeks to reclaim Hegel's infamous title as German African number one commentator. As if this is not embarrassing enough, they embark on a variant of "philosophy of stolen legacy" that can safely be characterised as "copycat philosophy". This is what unintended ethnocentric commitment can cause, as the heavy burden of philosophy or *ibuarụ*.

i) "Infamous contest" for Hegel's legacies and "copycat philosophy" as instances of unintended ethnocentric commitment (*ibuarụ*)

What I designate as the 'infamous contest" is contained in an "encounter" between two philosophers, Heinz Kimmerle and Jürgen Hengelbrock. This "encounter" is constituted of two essays written by each. Both essays were published at the internet (http://home.concepts-ict.nl/~kimmerle/ceheng.htm).

a) The first essay has the title:
"The stranger between oppression and superiority Close encounter with Heinz Kimmerle - Jürgen Hengelbrock"

b) The second essay as response has the title:

"You cannot free yourself from Hegel! An encounter with Heinz Kimmerle Response to Jürgen Hengelbrock by Heinz Kimmerle"

Due to their implicit dogged efforts to reclaim Hegel's title as German number one African commentator, I have used the expression "the infamous contest" merely to highlight the unintended ethnocentric character of this "encounter".

In this published internet "encounter", both writers unite in questioning the reasonableness of the arrogance characteristic of the attitude of many so-called Western scholars who assume that philosophy is best practiced in western languages and categories of thought, and within what is regarded as philosophy's traditional natural habitat. Notwithstanding their goodwill and good dispositions towards an egalitarian type of trans-cultural philosophy, where the interest of every culture should be equally represented, their ideas take a swipe most especially when it comes to taking a clear stand as to the status of African philosophy.

In this regard, Hengelbrock never tires of giving the impression, that that brand of philosophy and philosophising practiced in Africa can at best be subsumed under the category of "African thinking" or "wisdom" and not philosophy. He came to this conclusion when he argues, "Undoubtedly we find philosophical elements or views of life in African proverbs, myth, pedagogical and religious narrations, as well as in the proverbs and tales of my Westfalian country. But I think we don't need to speak about philosophy here. It would be better to speak about wisdom." Even Aristotle, in spite of his elitist discriminating way of thinking, was more generous in his assessment of the mythological thinkers of his time. Here, he avers "And a man who is puzzled and wonders thinks himself ignorant (whence even the lover of myth is in a sense a lover of Wisdom, for the myth is composed of wonders); therefore since they philosophized order to escape from ignorance, evidently they were pursuing science in order to know, and not for any utilitarian end. And this is confirmed by the facts; for it was when almost all the necessities of life and the things that make for comfort and recreation had been secured, that such knowledge began to be sought." (Book A, 1). If these mythological thinkers qualify as philosophers in the eyes of Aristotle, what more some of those trained professional African philosophers of our time whose works by every standard can not be said to be a preoccupation with myths, in the debased sense, as Hengelbrock uses the term? Theirs no doubt, in the eyes of Hengelbrock, belongs to a type of philosophy comparable only to those of "Westfalian country" "Originell" or eccentrics individuals.

It is in keeping with this mode of reasoning that Kimmerle also finds it expedient, when discussing the works of individual African thinkers, to do so mostly within the bracket of "thought systems of African peoples". He came to this conclusion however based on other reasons; and surprisingly in countering Hengelbrock's tendency to reject what is generally presented, even today, as African philosophy as philosophy per se.

In this matter, Kimmerle passionately advocates a special type of African philosophy with focus on symbols, wise sayings, proverbs, myth, etc, as is widely also advocated by a brand of African hermeneutics of culture, whose position leaves much to be desired on account of its ethnocentric undertone.

What is obvious is that both Kimmerle and Hengelbrock disagree to agree that African philosophy can be reduced to a special type of philosophy that concerns itself merely with symbols, wise sayings, proverbs and myths. Even if Kimmerle's advocacy is based on what has come to be characterised as near absence of written philosophical texts in traditional African societies, his penchant to see African philosophy often from the background of ethnology, colours his understanding of African philosophy generally. Just like most African philosophers who have the tendency to equate African philosophy with tradition, such approaches give the impression that African philosophy can be equated with wise-sayings, myths, folklore, proverbs. In this case, to think of African philosophy entails extracting it from these carriers of philosophical ideas. That is to say, African philosophy is an event that happened sometime in the past and is located somewhere and as such, it needs to be extracted or recouped. This form of advocacy easily forgets that African philosophers from time immemorial and even today have their styles and methods, which may differ or even supersede these fixed cultural carriers of meaning. It is precisely on this point that Hengelbrock, understandably, takes Kimmerle to task but appears to use this as a cover-up mechanism to subject the merits of the whole corpus of African philosophical reflection, both past and present, to very serious doubt. It is on account of this type of what he perceives as Kimmerle's reduction of African philosophy to myths and symbols, a position quite in conformity with his mode of thinking, that Hengelbrock dares accuse Kimmerle of being a modern incarnate of Hegel's contempt for African philosophy. That is to say, one who does not believe that Africans have another type of philosophy other than myth.

There is no denying the fact that interpretation of myths, proverbs, wise sayings, symbols, and other cultural carriers of meaning have something philosophical about it. The way these are handled goes to define one's understanding of philosophy. It is in this point that ethno-philosophers show their true colours. Here Hengelbrock has an important point to make. However, he appears to be overexploiting this point in that he uses it to dismiss all the works of African philosophers as lacking in philosophical merit. On his part, Kimmerle has equally an important point to make. This is the case, when he equally dares to expose what he has come to perceive as Hengelbrock's "hypocrisy". This is when Hengelbrock gives the impression that those African scholars who delve into themes other than those belonging to their realm of myths, symbols, wise sayings etc. are doing nothing other than copying or imitating European style of philosophising. What Kimmerle is telling us is that going by Hengelbrock's position what has come to be characterised as modern African philosophy is nothing other than comments on European philosophy. In this case, there is no African philosophy as such but philosophy of the type of his "Westfalian country". The implication is that, contemporary African philosophers are a special breed of amorphous philosophers. He captures this fact by observing: "Böhme's partners in Lagos and Hengelbrock's partners and friends in Abidjan will be deeply disappointed when they are told that their philosophical work is not about African philosophy, but just European or Western philosophy performed by them as Africans." In plain language, the African philosophers in Lagos, Abidjan and elsewhere are *stealing* European and Western ideas. We are dealing here, once again, with another case of serious accusation about "stolen legacy", but this time the thieves are Africans and not Westerners. Relating to African philosophy or to philosophy in general with such a mindset is typical of a milieu that is hostile to the complementary character of ideas in its genesis and further development. In other words, these two philosophers hardly believe in mutual complementary genesis of ideas. For them, philosophy originated in the West and all others are copiers or imitators of Western philosophy. To distinguish this type of philosophy from the philosophy of "Stolen Legacy" proper, let us call it the "Copycat Philosophy". However, both brands of "appropriator philosophy" have one thing in common, they are instances of the negation of mutual complementary genesis of ideas. To be a philosopher and creative, we do not need to recoil to what we imagine are our pristine intellectual ghettos and operate from there. Such do not exist, since all ideas in their excogitation remain mutually complementary. In view of some of the obvious serious consequences of this type of protectionist reasoning, Janz admonishes, "To require African philosophy to come up with a new and unique method in order to be called philosophy is an unfair requirement" (234). I would even say the same in all human affairs, where our creativity can never be thought of as fruits of our individual efforts alone, either as individuals or as groups. As understandable as our primitive passion for self-preservation instigates us to be exclusivist and to seek those thing that make us special, I think that the legitimacy of any work that seeks to be philosophical and rational is rooted in its capacity to be articulated within the framework of the whole. To overcome banalities inherent in all modes of exclusivist reasoning, much work of noetic emancipation needs to be done. It is in the process of such emancipation that those philosophers who have lost the freedom of uninhibited inquiry resulting from unintended ethnocentric commitment or *ibuarụ*, can be rehabilitated. Such mindset that is always suspicious, lest someone takes away what it imagines belongs to it by right of progeny, is definitely dangerous. It is only when people come to understand that human heritages originate on account of mutual complementary dependence of all actors and factor that they have chances of sleeping in peace. This is also the moment they have the chances of ridding themselves of all undue burdens.

This form of accusation and counter accusation and suspicion about double-dealing etc ensues the moment the mind has not freed itself fully from ethnocentric excesses most especially of the elitist Aristotelian type. This is that mindset that seeks to see itself as the origin of all good things. It is within this context that one can understand how Afrocentrism is a reaction to Eurocentrism as those exclusivist tendencies for units to define themselves outside of the legitimacy provided by the totality of reality. However, this exclusivist egoistic tendency appears to be more pronounced in the Western mind as the fruit of long years of wrong pedagogy, socialisation and indoctrination. We see this tendency quite widespread in the way most Western philosophers relate to other cultures and ideas. In most cases, they often look out for connections and such that shows that they are the originators of everything. Thus in his comments in the preface he wrote for Sophie Oluwole work's work (Oluwole xiv), Kimmerle hardly resists the temptation of pointing to the fact that the issues being raised by Oluwole have already been raised in European philosophy. In other words, he appears to be claiming that there is practically nothing new in Oluwole's contribution. This is when Kimmerle enlightens us immediately "As it is well known in the context of Western philosophy, Martin Heidegger has also worked on a philosophical reading and explanation of literary works, especially the late poems of Hölderlin, in order to find a new way of thinking. This is not mentioned here to point at a Western forerunner or to give a justification of what Oluwole is doing". Kimmerle's idiosyncratic predilection is almost repeated by Stegmüller, who referring to the "Main Currents in Contemporary German, British and American Philosophy", claims that, "There are few philosophies today that are not characterized, among other things, by some particular judgment to which they have come regarding the philosophy of Kant. This does not mean that the greater part of today's philosophical literature can be taken as a positive continuation of Kant's conceptions" (Stegmüller 2). Within the context of this statement, one sees how Stegmüller seeks to project and protect what he identifies as the excellence of Kant's philosophy, which others seek to imitate. In other words, we are dealing in these two quotations with typical examples of "copycat philosophy", even within the rank and file of the West. This protectionist type of reasoning is a remnant of our natural instinct of self-preservation in the course of which we seek to be considered as special types of human beings, along with our cultural heritages. Hardly would this tendency have attracted any attention were it not that it can mislead inquirers to make bogus claims about the world. Again, such tendencies can easily lead to those fallacies that could have very serious implications for coexistence of peoples.

We can then understand why, on account of unintended ethnocentric commitment, Kimmerle and Hengelbrock are inclined to see African philosophy mostly from the optics of "African thinking" or "African thought" and African philosophers as native "Westfalian country" thinker; "Originell" or eccentrics. One easily gets the impression that for them "African thought" has a special connotation and one that has to do more with the thinking of provincial philosophers in native Bavarian attire. Doing philosophy with ethnocentric mindset merely succeeds in reducing it to mere rhetoric, knowledge to myths, science to ideology and gossip. It is important to remark in this connection that whenever we make recourse to collective categorisations like, "African thought", "European Thought" in view of doing philosophy, they are not always to the best interest of scientific objectivity. This is all the more the case when such collective categorisations are used pejoratively in view of showing differences or similarities that can be generalised as to apply to all categories of individuals within a given location. Even if certain thinkers can be rightly identified as representing the idea of certain localities, recourse to such categorisations is a matter of convenience, as this helps us to adjust to the ordinary or common sense ways through which human beings grasp reality in the process of apperception. We do not through the use of such categories capture reality as to be informed that all individuals at a certain given location think alike. All Germans are not Hegel, and to equate "German thought system" with Hegel's philosophy is a big mistake. The impression that one easily gets from the statements of these two philosophers - something that is almost a general practice - is that African philosophy, even in the contemporary epoch, has hardly undergone any changes, and can hardly go beyond reports of Ethnologists. Worse still is the tendency to reduce the works of all African philosophers to preoccupation with myths, magic, sorcery and ancestral spirits.

In view of the above issues, and in consideration of the fact that Hengelbrock and Kimmerle think of African philosophy almost always within this bracket of reductionism, there is every reason to believe that they probably have the inclinations to see African philosophy as something different from a certain standardised type of philosophising, which they have in mind. In this case, it may not be very wrong nor impudent should one ask what exactly their conception of African philosophy is and whose cause they appear to be championing vigorously? As this matter relates to Kimmerle, I shall show further in this book some of the most grievous implications of his approach. This is specifically where he identifies the ideas of Achebe and Oluwole with "the thought system" of specific African peoples. This way of viewing African philosophy achieves one thing, namely, it gives misleading information with regard to the enormous progress that is taking place in African philosophy. Its focus is very backward looking and anachronistic, as it seeks to see philosophy only from the perspective of traditional African philosophy oblivious of the fact that philosophy in Africa is now progressing in leaps and bounds. Besides, many African philosophers in our contemporary epoch have other paradigms of reflection beyond myths and folklore. Even then, when they preoccupy themselves with myths and folklore, this does not make them less philosophers. Human existence at all moments is enshrouded in myths; if it is not the myth of the supremacy of technology, it is the myth that only those Ayatollahs with long beards have the prerogative of instilling fear into all of us. Besides, their ways of viewing philosophy fail to recognise that contemporary Africans, with all their training and exposure, cannot, without further modifications, be safely categorised as "traditional", in a certain archaic Bavarian or Westfalian country sense. Again, their mode of thinking creates the impression that the origin of our ideas is not inherently complementary, but something that ensues between distinct discrete quantities, and where accidents are distinct from their essences. In this case, the optimal imaginable form of co-existence among units is that of a non-relational paradoxical parallel mode of co-existence between distinct essences or monads within any given framework.

Generally, one can say that the advocacy of these two thinkers concerning African philosophy is marked by elements of disdain and parsimony, as is characteristic of most so-called Western thinkers in their relationship to matters concerning other cultures. This is a mindset that hardly comprehends that philosophy has its origin and started its tedious, ill-fated journey neither in Egypt nor in Greece, since the origin of all human ideas, achievements and civilisation can be thought of only within the context of mutually complementing units, outside of which nothing can be thought of. It is an intransigent, benevolent type of mindset, with a deep sense of mission, destined to rescue the world from darkness and backwardness just as the wise knows the causes and is as such destined to lead the unwise. This is that obdurate attitude that hardly changes and listens. If it listens at all, it does so from the inner recess of its most cherished dogmas, as is characteristic of all who are deeply engrossed in this type of *fanatical religion*. The mixed feeling this type of mindset brings to bear on matters has much to do with what the phenomenon of unintended ethnocentric commitment is all about, as it shares deeply with the ambivalence of all human existential situations. It is for this reason that it can grossly hamper the way the thinking subject perceives reality and the way human beings relate to each other. Hence, it can be seen as one of the greatest challenges facing what goes on today under various names as *intercultural philosophy*. This is precisely why it is a heavy burden – *ibuarụ*.

This type of unintended ethnocentric mindset can have very grievous consequences for one's overall personal attitude and approach to the world. Bearing this in mind, one easily understands why what should be an intellectual "encounter" between these two eminent philosophers degenerates to a mock intellectual battle designed to reclaim Hegel's inglorious legacies in matters dealing with Africa . It is amazing that both discussants waste their time haranguing, in mutual suspicion and accusations, as to who should eventually be declared the proud unhappy heir to Hegel's infamous legacies. This is how in reply to Hengelbrock's accusations, Kimmerle claims: "If Jürgen Hengelbrock tells us that there is no African philosophy, but something different, which he calls wisdom, it is he who has not freed himself from Hegel. He says the same as Hegel about this part of the world". In other words, each believes that the mantel of Hegel's legacies fits the other, its big size notwithstanding. This unfortunate contest in infamy is quite uncalled for, bearing in mind Kimmerle's and Hengelbrock's invaluable contributions, not only to intercultural philosophy, but more so to African philosophy in general. Yet, such derailments are quite unavoidable, if one considers the fact that unintended ethnocentric commitment, as *ibuarụ*, can invalidate all good intentions.

Theirs is not different, and cannot be different, since all human actions are dictated by the most primitive of all drives that of the instinct of self-preservation. This is that instinct that tells us and instigates us to find differences, to try a little bit harder in showing where the differences lie. In ambition, petty jealousies, spitefulness, unfounded fears, unbridled passion to excel and to put final little touches and finesses, this passion surfaces very intensively. It magnifies differences and similarities unduly in view of securing and protecting our petty advantages and interests. It instigates the mind to use subtle means in the application of wisdom, since it is probably wiser than others are. This is the moment when *uche/obi akọlọ* (hegemonic mindset or negative wisdom) is easily mistaken for wisdom. Hence, its primary target is to make us appear wiser and better than others in our bid to secure our interest first and in those matters that would enhance our prestige both singly and collectively, even to the point of sounding absurd. Unless we rise boldly and challenge its impositions, it is likely to draw us into the abyss of its primitivism, no matter what we profess and no matter how highly we rate our achievements, ourselves and our ideas. When we engage in open contests of this nature, as is characteristic of most things that go under scientific dialogue, this can easily weaken our research efforts and give our cultural inquiry, as intercultural philosophers, the outlook of traveller's tales designed to gratify some curiosities and those of our contact givers. This is why, in most situations, what is designed as dialogue easily reverts to a gladiatorial contest with motives that can be interpreted along line the unnecessary heat being generated by "Black Athena".

ii) The character of unintended ethnocentric commitment as *ibuarụ* and some historical considerations

By *unintended ethnocentrism or unintended ethnocentric commitment, as this concerns research,* I refer to that tendency for philosophers or scientists to go about their subject matter with ethnocentric frame of mind but *unintentionally*. Here, inquirers allow the basic assumptions of their inquiry to be controlled by the dictates of what I call their *raw primary cognitive ambience*. It is an attempt to project and protect the legacies of one's cultural affiliation, at the risk of being exclusivist, though unintentionally. By so doing, scientists *unintentionally* cling to and defend those ideas, ideals and values they cherish most in an exclusivist non-relational manner. The consequences of this problem supersede those connected with the classical debate about "value-free" science. The primary target of unintended ethnocentric commitment is ideological oversimplification and misuse. Thus, it has untold consequences beyond science, as to determine the way human beings relate to each other globally. This is just like a bad habit which when once formed, dies hard and can militate against scientific objectivity and interpersonal relationship, the good intentions of the person concerned notwithstanding. It can also be seen as an infection of the mind arising from long years of socialisation, education and indoctrination within given cultural contexts. This is why one of the primary functions of philosophy in multiethnic contexts is the enlightenment or liberation of the mind from difficulties of this kind. Herein is rooted the noetic task of any inquiry. As this matter relates to philosophy as a science, it can rightly be designated as unintended *ethnophilosophic commitment, to underscore the moment of unintended ethnocentric commitment in philosophical inquiries.*

Ethno-philosophy proper is that variant of ethnocentric inspired method of inquiry that is easily identifiable. It is that variant of philosophical methodology which considers collecting, describing and informing over the general worldview of a people the target of philosophical investigation. It thereby underestimates the role which personal critical reflection plays in inquiry.

Where this type of inquiry is done specifically from the point of view of ethnic considerations, it has another dimension . In such cases, it is an attempt to build research on ethnic biases. Although human actions are driven by motives of various kinds, ethnocentric motives enter almost always into the way we view the world. This must not be a disadvantage. It becomes a disadvantage the moment it becomes a reason to do science in a way that disengages it from its practical objective among which is to build closer relationship among peoples. Such ethnocentric considerations that are divisive, polarising and exclusivist can hardly be of use to scientific progress since human beings need each other to progress. This is why unintended ethnophilosophy presents itself as a problem directed against scientific progress. This is unfortunately a phenomenon that is today widespread but one which is hardly acknowledged as a problem. This is why, even many critics of ethno-philosophy proper are often caught in the web of the same difficulties and mistakes, which they are criticising without realising this.

Whenever this phenomenon is prevalent, it is a clear indication that the subject is succumbing to the demands of our fundamental instinct of self-preservation. In such situations, inquirers seek mainly the advantages of the ego in an exclusivist non-relational way. The challenges arising from this drive shows that we are beings in dire need of emancipation from some of the primitive ways we relate to the world. It is in the efforts we invest in overcoming the excesses arising from this primitive drive that we can show our commitment to more advanced and refined ways of doing everything in science, technology, society, religion, interpersonal relationship, resolution of conflicts and indeed in all those things that define us as human beings quite removed from the lower creatures. Attaining a high level of awareness concerning the challenges of this drive is also a clear testimony that we wish to rid ourselves of the impositions arising from circumstances.

In the case of African philosophy, unintended ethno-philosophic commitment has much to do with ultra-nationalist sentiments of a radical fundamentalist type. And these again have their roots in the overall human drive to excel, to be different, to conserve their interests and do these within the framework of those nearest to them in the evident insight that *the nearer the better and the safer*. This issue is very crucial today in a fast globalising world, with divergent claims about the nature of reality. One of the most difficult tasks today is how to harmonise the expectations arising from divergent ethnic and cultural differences in view of unavoidable dialogue and encounter between diverse peoples as this is necessitated by globalisation.. Here, the impact, which such variables as unconscious passionate adherence to one's cultural heritages can have in inquiry, cannot be underestimated. It is in this connection that the issue of ethno-philosophy gains in actuality, most especially, for African philosophy, which has of late come to be deeply associated with this type of philosophy.

As a global matter, one of the main factors that favour unintended commitment is the issue of past historical experiences and misfortunes. On the one hand, are those who feel that the dominance of western ideas in philosophical debate has been most unjust and as such this has to be counterbalanced, and if possible corrected by a more liberal and tolerant type of philosophising, where every worldview should get the opportunity to be presented, represented and heard. In this way, philosophical methodology turns to a form of compensatory therapy aimed at addressing perceived unjust superimposition of alien thought categories as these relate to those nations and peoples that have been the unfortunate victims of colonialism and conquest. On the other hand, are those who feel that they are the very victims of unjust external domination, manipulation, exploitation and oppression. Here, philosophical methodology is easily perceived as a tool needed to address, and if possible recoup those things one feels is one's own, and which other have always denied him due to historical factors. Due to these constraints and impositions, philosophy in many quarters today, is vigorously being pursued with the mindset of restoration of lost cultural heritages, values and prestige. From both angles, the feeling is that of the need to make some sort of restitution or amend. However, there are doubts about the effectiveness of this type of philosophical approach, which has almost devolved to both a propitiatory and defensive type of ethnocentrism.

Within the ambit of African philosophical circle, this form of ethnocentrism has turned out to be a choice rallying point for unrepentant representatives of diverse ideological camps who converge against a common enemy. These are immigrants from the ultra-conservative camps of African socio-political theorist who are bent on propagating a vile form cultural intolerance packaged in the glorification of differences, which they misunderstand as measures needed towards erecting impermeable barrier against neo-colonialism and neo-imperialist types of external intervention and manipulation. The emotional undertone of this matter is so charged that there is a mutual migration, from among diverse camps, for ideological reinforcement. This is how there is now mutual infiltration from the philosophical camp to the political camp and from the political camp to the religious-cultural camp and vice versa, due to their obsession with a common enemy in the person of agents of external manipulation. In this case, champions of such idea as Ujamaa, Ubuntu, communalism, trade-unionists, diehard Afro neo-Marxists, unapologetic traditionalists, admirers of Afro-American Afrocentrists and various brands of Afro-leftwing hard liners, team up with proponents of ethno-philosophy to form a formidable alliance of ideological inbreeding, which threatens even their own existence. Unfortunately, they fail to realise that the overall rate of development and progress in Africa is very much dependent on what Africans undertake to integrate positive elements into their conceptual schemes, even if this comes from the outside. Here, one can justifiably say that limit of my world is the limit of my complementary capability and vice versa.

iii) Some major drawbacks of unintended ethnophilosophic commitment as *ibuarụ*

With regard to African philosophy, and doing science in Africa generally, their growth and dynamism can be dependent on the measures their practitioners adopt to counter this manner of inbreeding and reclusive exclusivist tendencies arising from our primitive instinct of self-preservation to remain ourselves and shield ourselves from external interference. Where this instinct remains negatively active in inquiry, this is one of the clearest indications of the intrusion of unintended ethnocentric commitment. One of the greatest dangers in matters of this nature is that relating to the loss of perspective for philosophy as a scientific discipline and this loss of perspective has characterised most works in African philosophy for a long time now. Due to over sensitivity about issues of ethnic undertone, the main subject matter of philosophy as a science gets lost. What has been said about African philosophers is valid for all philosophers who see philosophy as a means of conserving their cultural heritages. Hence, there is dire need for philosophy to be restored to its primary and exalted task of investigating reality devoid of ethnic biases. Wherever this issue of a clearly stated focus with regard to the subject matter of philosophy is overlooked, the critical function of philosophy as that meta-science that investigates ultimate realities from the preceding conditions of their interrelatedness is put into serious jeopardy. The same thing is applicable to that character of philosophy to lay the foundation even for the progress of science itself and society in general. This issue, as a global matter, has become worrisome, because there is every indication that philosophy, with special accent on culture, is being misunderstood as an arena for the exchange of ideas without a clear-cut legitimising focus. Definitely, philosophy is more than the arena for cultural display and mutual exchange of ideas. Where philosophy devolves to an arena for ethnic contest, ethnocentric interests easily take the upper hand and thereby erode the subject matter of philosophy itself. Even as a culture-bound enterprise, philosophy as a science can never be disengaged from its main subject matter.

In African philosophy, which has until now been dominated by restricted culture-relevant themes, this form of commitment can threaten even the more promising methods of philosophical investigation. This is the case with hermeneutics of culture, which Azenabor describes as, "a reaction to the identity crisis due to the presence of a foreign and dominating tradition and the necessity for self-affirmation in the construction of an authentic culture and tradition" (Schools of Thought, 26). Going by this description of hermeneutics of culture, which is not very wrong, one understands all the more why it is very much endangered. This is mostly due to its close connection with the issue of definition of one's identity. This threat arising from over-sensitivity concerning one's identity permeates African philosophy. Some of the dangers this poses are at root of Oguejiofor's reflections in the work "Philosophy and African Predicament". Since his concern has to deal with motives, we see how it can be subsumed into the paradigm of self-preservation as that ultimate motive driving all human actions and conditions. In this way, he captures a problem that is relevant, not only for African philosophy, but one that can be articulated within a wider universal context. This concerns the way we do philosophy by getting it entangled in some of the worst forms of predicament to which belongs that of forgetfulness of the very subject matter of philosophy. I would say that this is one of the heaviest burdens of philosophy.

With regard to hermeneutics of culture, which rightly sees African culture as the starting point of reflection, it is deeply entangled in this predicament as it *can* miss the main focus of philosophical investigation. This it does, the moment the ethnic undertone takes the upper hand. This point becomes most evident in some of the works of Theophilus Okere, a passionate culture-philosopher and who never tires of extolling the merits and excellences of his Igbo culture and Tsaney Serequeberhan who takes Okere's position some steps further as he seeks to merge hermeneutics with Marxism as veritable weapons for the total emancipation of Africa from the clutches of colonial domination (Serequeberhan, Tsenay, Colonialism and the Colonized: Violence and Counter Violence). In view of the critical function of philosophy, I quite agree with the conclusion of Janz that "both Okere and Serequeberhan have recognized the significance of mediating between lived conditions and theory, but that both have not gone far enough to make African philosophy truly self-critical and self-understanding" (233). This self-critical task can hardly be accomplished, when unintended ethnocentric commitment is adopted as a methodological principle as is consistent with what is paraded as hermeneutical approach in African philosophy.

The counter-productive result of this form of unintended ethnocentric inspired method of philosophising is there to be seen. Thus, Okere's thoroughgoing unintended ethnocentric commitment almost resulted in self-contradiction. This has earned him, of late, most severe criticisms as is fully documented in the work "African Philosophy and the Hermeneutics of Culture" edited by Oguejiofor and Onah. For Agbakoba, for example, Okere's approach is nothing other than "patriotic romanticism" that has nothing in mind other than extolling African culture and most especially his Igbo culture (Agbakoba, An Evaluation of Okere's Conception of the Place of African Values, 230-238). In line with Agbakoba's observations, the overall verdict of most of the contributors in this volume is succinctly captured by Osuagwu when he avers, "One might very well doubt that Okere succeeded, in the long run, in escaping the ethnological or ethnophilosophical pitfall that he, with good reasons, criticized so vehemently" (Philosophy of Non-philosophy 59). Njoku takes this criticism further when he avers, "His [Okere's] position and those of ethnophilosophers he set out to criticise become a matter of scratching at the same place at different times. ...Philosophy seems to lose its enduring universal structure in Okere – the greatest master of the African hermeneutic school of philosophy" (Njoku, The Originality of African Philosophy 101). These severe criticisms notwithstanding, the overall positive merits of Okere's pioneer work in African philosophy remain undisputed. Unfortunately, he has not guarded himself well against unintended ethnocentric commitment.

The form of self-immolation arising from unintended ethnocentric commitment can be avoided, if we seek to capture culture within a comprehensive, universal complementary future oriented perspective and not necessarily relative to one's own circumscribed location only. It is for this reason that hermeneutics of culture must be complementary in orientation to be complete, and should it attain the noble objective it has set for itself. In this sense, culture within the ambit of complementary reflection can be grasped adequately within the context of all the actors and factors that determine the ideas of a thinker and of those individuals and communities under consideration. Here, we are exposed to a wide variety of choices, in an interconnected world of today. Therefore, any attempt to grasp at one's culture as unique artefacts or worldviews would always remain unsatisfactory, as this can easily end in a debacle. It suffices now to take a more detailed look at some of the main features of both ethno-philosophy proper and unintended ethno-philosophic commitment as it concerns African philosophy.

2. On the similarities between ethno-philosophy and unintended ethnophilosophic commitment

Ethno-philosophy proper is that way of doing philosophy that has attracted most severe forms of criticism within the last thirty years, or more, in African philosophy. In many African universities and institutions of higher learning, philosophy, as a culture related enterprise, is still taught with an ethnocentric or tribal mindset. This is still the case contrary to what most of its practitioners think. Here, philosophy is hardly different from ethnology or even archaeology with the attendant fieldwork aimed at the documentation of the general worldview of a people with the intent to inform or describe. Whereas ethno-philosophy proper in its approach is triumphal, supremacist, conservative and dogmatic about African cultural heritages, which it seeks to document, describe and inform about, unintended ethno-philosophy is equally conservative, triumphal, supremacist, but somewhat critical. In other words, both approach their subject matter in a subtly different manner, but they are exposed to the same danger. This is the danger of ethnocentric commitment and disregard of the main target of philosophical investigation. Wherever the supremacist, conservative and triumphal dimensions take the upper hand, the target of philosophical investigation, as the universal science of ultimate reality or the science of being as being insofar being can be grasped within a complementary framework is grossly jeopardised.

Generally, one can then say that both ethno-philosophy proper and unintended ethno-philosophy share the common weakness of the danger of forgetting or missing the target of philosophical inquiry. In this, they easily restrict the philosophical perspective grossly to localised interests without making very serious efforts to bring these to full relationship to all modes of existence, in a universal comprehensive manner. It is for this reason that they have the capacity to retard the growth of knowledge and stifle creative thinking due to the conservative type of inbreeding that consistently threatens their approaches. Whereas the weaknesses and excesses of ethno-philosophy proper, as a form of empirical ethnological study, are very glaring, those of unintended ethno-philosophic commitment are not always evident. Thus, it is a concealed type of active danger that is capable of invalidating the good intentions of those caught in the web of its debilitation effect. Generally, unintended ethno-philosophic commitment is a habit of the mind of a compulsive neurotic type, which always seeks to see things from an ethnocentric perspective. This is why, it is defensively triumphal and conservatively unchanging. Having illustrated what is meant by unintended ethnocentric or unintended ethno-philosophic commitment, from the perspective of two Western philosophers, it may be interesting to see how widespread this phenomenon is also in African philosophy.

Here, the book edited by Momoh serves as a good point of departure for this illustration. Going by somewhat curious title of the book, and the list of contributors in the work, one easily has the impression that the work is what it claims to be, namely "The Substance of African philosophy". Evidently, most topics handled in this book are recurrent themes in African philosophy. However, one is yet to understand in what sense the book claims to be offering "the substance of African philosophy". Sixteen years after the publication of the first edition of this work, Oladipo comes out with a more befitting title for works of this kind. Here, he talks of "Core Issues in African Philosophy". Even then, most contributions in this band hardly transcended the constraining unintended ethnocentric and ethnophilosophic undertone characteristic of Momoh's collection.

In the book edited by Momoh, he classifies himself as belonging to what he calls "The Purist School of Thought" within African philosophy. Besides himself, he reckons to this purist school of thought such thinkers as Sophie Oluwole, Claude Sumnea, W. E. Abraham, Barry Hallen, J. O. Sodipo, Akin Makinde, K. C. Anyanwu, I. C. Onyewuenyi, Jim Unah and Enyeribe and Godwin Azenabor" (Nature, Issues 18). Commenting on the focus of the purist school of thought, Godwin Azenabor, a supposed member and insider, avers that for them: "Authentic African philosophy… is pure and unadulterated, i.e. free from foreign influence and culture. …Authentic African philosophy…should break away from western paradigms, conditionings and conceptual schemes. It should be oriented towards African environment, basic assumptions, culture and goal" (Azenabor, Schools of Thought 29). In keeping with the manifesto of this purist school of thought, a researcher, according to Momoh "can focus on the 'Hausa concept of Beauty: an Essay in African Aesthetics'. In metaphysics, we can focus on, say 'Yoruba Cosmology' or Cosmogony or Ontology" (Nature, Issues 19). In other words, this purist school of thought pursues a research methodology that focuses on worldviews congenial to given ethnic groups and tribes.

To start with, it is good to note that for Momoh "there is no universally accepted definition of philosophy"; a conviction that, of recent, many practitioners of African philosophy never tire to emphasise (Momoh, The Nature, Issues Edited by Jim I. Unah 315). This warrants charting an understanding of philosophy according to one's taste and sentiments. Thus focusing on the above themes, as outlined by Momoh, entails doing philosophy as one defines and steers the subject matter. This stance to philosophy has its prize, most especially with regard to the intrusion of ethnocentric sentiment into inquiry. The result is that of a situation where people imaging that because philosophy has no universally accepted definition, then everything and every approach is justified and acceptable provided this satisfies the philosophical project one has in mind. This position is pursued in utter disregard of a clearly stated subject matter of authentic philosophising. Armed therefore with this conviction of lack of commitment to any fixed definition, Momoh sets out to do a philosophy that is in harmony with his ethnic bias, even if he hardly believes that this is the case. It is in tune with this mindset that he imagines that his research-outline, resting on the explication given by Azenabor, satisfies the minimum requirements expected of anything that has to do with the philosophical subject matter.

Even if one can do philosophy according to one's mode of definition and understanding, this does not make the necessity of philosophy following a guide, in the sense of a clearly stated subject matter, superfluous. Philosophy can never dispense with a clearly stated unified subject matter and remain scientific. Like all sciences, this guide gives it its definite character. This guide imposes itself on all manners of inquiry irrespective of the pretensions of the inquirer that it can be substituted with other interests of ideological and cultural nature. This guide is all the more very essential when philosophy is understood as a culture-bound inquiry. It is due to the presence of this guide that all statement regarding any particular culture, in multicultural, trans-cultural or intercultural contexts can be fully validated. Here, we are thinking of the authentication of the truth claims of such statements, which might be at variance with each other on account of unavoidable differences arising from diverse ways of seeing the world. Here, one can say that the very criterion that guides all modes of philosophical inquiry and determines their subject matters ultimately is the search for truth, certainty and authenticity. This criterion is applicable to all sciences, but falls more to the province of philosophy, as it investigates the ultimate nature of reality, including the way this ultimacy can be perceived and represented even outside of the philosophical framework. It is in this sense that philosophy is a critique of science, society and ideology. This very guide sets the standard of inquiry and seeks to tear down completely all the artificial barriers and boundaries imposed by definitions in view of getting at what is actually intended.

3. On unintended ethnocentric commitment and the nature of a philosophical question

Due to the very crucial nature of this matter, as it relates to the growth of African philosophy, it is important to dwell on it for a while in view of providing insights on the character of a philosophical question. This is important since many seem not to be very clear on this point and this is why they easily mistake philosophy for other disciplines. Here, Momoh's research-outline provides again a good starting point in view of understanding better what a philosophical question or preoccupation might look like. To begin with, there is basically nothing wrong for someone to study worldviews as they occur in given cultural contexts and as they build points of departure for further reflection. This is appropriate if we remember that reflection has to be consummated within an ambience; but it should not stop there. If stops there, as is likely to occur if one were to adopt Momoh's proposal faithfully, this would invariably lead to those ethnophilosophic excesses that render the philosophical subject matter obscure, if not completely imperceptible. These are some of those unfortunate and lamentable deficiencies we see in most research projects that have ethnocentric undertone. Thus, according to Amaku "one stumbles over a book interestingly entitled 'African philosophy', but a glance at it exposes one to mere descriptions of marriages, new yam festivals, initiations rites, wrestling matches, burial ceremonies, folklores and so on" (Amaku 68). What Amaku is describing must be extreme cases, but it is not unusual. The problem arises when we substitute description of "marriages, new yam festivals" etc, for example, with description of words, concepts and ideas; a practice that is very prevalent in what many today misunderstand as doing African philosophy. This is when instead of "marriages, new yam festivals among the Yoruba", we have "'Yoruba Cosmology' or Cosmogony or Ontology"

Coming to concrete examples, it is not enough to embark on a research on "the phenomenon of Witchcraft among the Ibibios", for example, in view of giving us a descriptive details or analysis of what Ibibios believe or do not believe about a phenomenon of this kind. It is again not enough to try to recoup the original meanings of these concepts in their "pure and unadulterated" form, "free from foreign influence", as Azenabor tells us is the main target of "The Purist School of Thought" in their approach; an approach that of late has come to characterise the procedure most students adopt in their research projects in our institutions of higher learning. To avoid unintended ethnocentric excesses that might arise were we to follow this route, there is need for inquiries to aim at a critical determination of, for example, the epistemological truth claims of the phenomenon under investigation. In this case, the primary target of such research efforts should never be rooted only in seeking to inform or describe the phenomenon chosen for study. Hence, it is one thing to inform the reader, and describe witchcraft among the Ibibios, and the mechanisms and tools involved, either as an outsider or an insider. It is another thing to inquire about the epistemological, ethical, ideological or ontological status of what obtains in such practices. Here, the philosopher is expected to take *a critical personal stand*, even if this entails holding a view that is contrary to popular views and practices among his own people. He is not there merely to give official stamp of approval concerning known practices. The aim of philosophy is to help us understand reality clearer, separate appearance from reality, and this must not be context bound, even if it cannot be articulated outside the context. Where a researcher sees the world in a differently, as to disagree with current practices and opinions, he must give reasons and produce evidence to demonstrate what is being contended or recommended. In matters of this nature, it is not enough to show that the issue at stake is in harmony with the prevalent worldview. Where there is disagreement, it is also not enough to say that what obtains in such practices as Witchcraft cannot be reconciled with sound reasoning. It is again not enough to state dogmatically, without giving good reasons, that such practices can or cannot be recommended. Our claims and recommendations should have enough evidence as to appeal to anyone who might be interested in the matter under discussion. In this case, some of the questions that might interest a philosopher are questions concerning what meaning such phenomena make within a universal complementary cognitive ambience. This is that horizon shared by all actors as their interests are complementarily interwoven with each other.

At this level of articulation, certain questions become relevant. Thus, we might be interested in knowing what it entails to be a witchdoctor; whether such assumption can be inter-subjectively verified or justified and on what basis. Are there reasons why such phenomena should be given a special status while investigating them and who sets the standard for such? Again, what is the epistemological, logical, ethical, ideological and ontological status of such phenomena and what information do they wish to communicate? Can claims based on such phenomena be categorised as true or false and how do we verify them? In what ways do such statements differ from those obtainable in other areas of human cognitive experience? Do such phenomena appear in other cultural areas and what measures are devised to address them at these locations? How do these measures compare to each other? Are there areas where conflict resolution strategies overlap? If not, how do we bridge the differences? Have we made enough efforts to match our investigative standards with more refined ways of determining causes? Are we open to new ideas or are we blind adherents to tradition? Are there reasons to ascribe special meanings to what a witchdoctor does and why? Still in concrete terms: What does it imply, for example, that a witchdoctor can transform the essence of a human person to other lower beings? To what extent are such claims, both physically and metaphysically tenable, and what are the laws guiding them? To what extent are such laws subject to the demands of principles of sound reasoning as these are anchored on the first principles and principle of non-contradiction? What is the character of power distribution in these matters in terms of free access to vital pieces of information among stakeholders? These and many more questions can be asked within such contexts. Some of these questions are second order conceptual questions that go beyond obtaining or supplying mere information and describing given phenomena. If analysis and description become inevitable, they must be subjected to higher philosophical principles in view of their legitimisation beyond localised interests. This is why fundamental to all these questions is the question: Are there interests other than those of scientific integrity, objectivity and truth underlying our inquiry? These are questions that can interest and guide any human being who may tend to see thing differently from the way these phenomena occur in given localities. In other words, delving into such questions in a philosophical way is definitely quite different from stating or informing that this is "'Yoruba Cosmology' or Cosmogony or Ontology". It is again quite different from pursuing our subject matter from the misleading perspective of focusing on "'Hausa concept of Beauty: an Essay in African Aesthetics'". If we pursue the subject matter in these misleading way, we may end up committing all the errors associated with unintended ethnocentric commitment.

Hence, it is definitely not enough to state that in our villages there are people who do such things that are known as witchcraft, magic and sorcery, fortunetelling etc, and are engaged in professions or acts that are widely known by other people in particular ways. It does not matter if such professions are fascinating, awe-inspiring and mystifying to onlookers. Where they do occur, it is our philosophical task to understand the principles underlying them, bearing in mind such questions as outlined earlier. Answering questions in the manner that has just been outlined, naturally places the inquirer above the object studied, even if the inquirer shares the same context with the object. This is the philosopher's critical distancing from the event, which the inquirer brings to bear on matters of inquiry before accepting or rejecting them. In dealing with these questions, we do not need to restrict ourselves only to what our villages, old people and ancestors have to say or offer us about these phenomena. If we do, dangers are that we lose the philosophical perspective, which transcends our raw primary cognitive ambience. We respect the opinions of our elders and the general worldview in vogue, but we have to bear in mind always the transformation and evolution to which concepts and traditions are exposed due to the mutual complementary dependence between all missing links. These changes and transformations are reasons for caution and critique. In relating to the world in this critical manner, we are dependent on the totality of all possible relations that might be adjudged useful towards providing credible answers. These relations are all the actors and factors that condition the inquirers as his universal complementary cognitive ambient world. Besides, this wider comprehensive framework shows that philosophical questions have an ontological character as being seeks expression in all missing links. In other words, the philosopher, though a creation of his ambience, is not enslaved to it. He or she is not only a gestalt but more so a reformer of his ambience. It is in this sense that we can say that the philosopher belongs to an overarching universal ambience that conditions his reflection.

In all cases, the inquirer has the right to coexist and be coextensive with the world of all missing links, which he or she shares by those rights conferred on account of all beings sharing the same horizon of being and meaning. To these fundamental rights belongs the right of the inquirer to know the truth. The same is applicable to his obligation to accept the truth when it becomes evident. This cannot happen when the event remains hidden and shrouded in mysteries. Hence, we do not consider the matters closed the moment we have shown that this is the way things are, and as such, nothing can be added and nothing subtracted. We are dealing here with questions about questions and with matters that can be elucidated by recourse to the tools of philosophy in the critical analysis of what is given. In this case, the mind operates in consideration of the applicability of those rules guiding sound reasoning, as this involves people who may be operating from different backgrounds. Here, stakeholders, as mere mortals, should never pretend that they have some privileges conveyed by recourse to some sort of hidden knowledge or wisdom because of which they have special advantages of insight over others. Where such advantages do exist, for example through special types of training, this has to be shown through evidence. Where this does not happen, viable communication can hardly take place due to enforced modes of cognitive asymmetry. This is where asking questions and seeking answers that might be termed philosophical end. In such cases, we are entering a completely new domain that may need a special type of initiation. This is the domain of encrypted phenomena.

In other words, should we be in a position to answer philosophical questions adequately, an enabling atmosphere for free inquiry has to be crated in view of probing the character of given phenomena. In those confounding cases dealing with issues of extraordinary significances like, witchcraft, sorcery, magic, divination, etc, we try to reconstruct the character of the phenomena, as much as possible, when vital pieces of information are not available. Here, we collect the requisite pieces of information, while maintaining our critical philosophical distance to the event or phenomena. It would be a mistake to imagine that the work of the philosopher ends with the collection of data concerning requisite objects of study. Fortunately, there is a division of labour in matters of this kind. Here, the ethnological, archaeological and other empirical sciences are there to complement what the philosophical science stands for. This is the advantage of interdisciplinarity, which is often ignored. No discipline makes the other superfluous. It is in this mode of interdisciplinary inquiry that the complementary structure of reality starts to emerge and in this case, the type of mindset needed to comprehend reality in its most ideal mode of expression. Where the inquirer has these raw data, as provided by these other empirical sciences, they are merely the very conditions or substratum from which authentic philosophising arises. At every moment, we must bear in mind that the raw data, as we have them in our diverse cultural milieus, are, not only in need of exposition but more so, in dire need of validation. This is still the case even if such patrimonies have been handed down to us by our ancestors no matter how highly we hold them in esteem and regard their views.

Thus, the philosophical perspective turns out to be one that knows no respect for age or stature as it seeks to establish the truth and authenticity of statements and ideas enshrined in worldviews. This is what makes philosophy wisdom, since the wise seeks to grasp the truth and possess it. As wisdom, philosophy is not disrespectful, but abhors all that impinge on the truth. Those who engage themselves in this type of preoccupation do so in full awareness that reality evinces itself complementarily comprehensive and in full consideration of all possible relation. Here, the philosopher's task might be quite different from those of the natural scientist who might be interested in single occurrences, without bothering to articulate this within a more universal framework. In this case, the main target of philosophical inquiry is not merely to describe, to reclaim, to inform or conserve in the patriotic way, but to explore, reclaim and conserve in the spirit of truth and authenticity binding on all stakeholders in a universal framework. We are dealing here with truth and authenticity as it can be made evident to anyone who has eyes to see and ears to hear.

Unfortunately, what one encounters in most works that are concerned with what many tag as variants of "African philosophy" is a spirited effort to describe and reclaim cultural patrimonies. These are those alleged treasures tagged "specific African phenomena". In the case of some of these so-called specific African phenomena, a critical observer, who has even little knowledge of other people's cultures, other than those of his Africa ambience, would be inclined to ask: Since when have issues dealing with witchcraft, spirits, fortunetelling, ghosts, reincarnation, mermaid, *ogbanje, ogwu,* charms, wise sayings, proverbs, sorcery, magic, and various forms of extra sensory perception (ESP) become unique African experiences? It is important for students and practitioners of African philosophy to get the fact burnt into their minds that these experiences are not uniquely African; as such, it would be very deceptive to dwell on them and dogmatise on them as if others are ignorant of these phenomena who happen not to be Africans. Not quite long ago, I encountered some indigenous native Austrians, having to travel from Austria to Germany in desperate need of consultation with necromancers, because of a beloved dead relative. Such experiences reveal how similar human beings can be when they face very difficult challenges. Where we do not bear this type of similarity in mind, that is when we would be interested to demonstrate that between Zulu and Ibibio witches there are very fundamental differences. Where an inquirer, is merely interested in describing and informing us about the tribal or cultural uniqueness of given phenomena, such an inquirer is exposed to all the dangers associated with unintended ethnophilosophic commitment. Where these experiences occur in many cultures, philosophy is definitely more than the arena to display different brews of witchcraft, for example.

In doing philosophy as a culture-relevant undertaking, we have another case where many have been misled into doing ethnology under the guise of philosophy. This is why we have to take particular notice of it. This is the case when we formulate our questions in this form: What does it mean to do epistemology, metaphysics, ethics, political science, etc within the African frame of reference? Even if we are dealing here with a conceptual philosophical question, the answer that one gets can very easily take a descriptive informative character. This can easily lead to giving an answer that has the outlook of uncritical history of African philosophy. In some cases such answers often take the form of a philosophical ethnological outline or descriptions of events. Again, it can take the form of what might still be called an ethnological philosophical description or outline. In both cases, we are dealing with those approaches that lack in sophistication, criticality, depth and rigour. It is for this reason that much caution is needed when reading Kai Kresse's recommendation of an "anthropology of philosophies" (Towards an Anthropology of Philosophies). This is all the more the case, when he makes such a recommendation with specific reference to African philosophy. Admittedly, works of investigation based on this type of suggestion, can serve as an attempt at chronicling the history of ideas of given cultures and the attendant commentaries attached to them. This is precisely what is often being practised by many who undertake the description, analysis and further interpretation of the contents of rituals, myths, symbols, and ideas etc., enshrined in traditional African conceptual systems. If this is well done, a critical philosophical engagement may result. Here one admires what such people like Copleston (History of Philosophy of Western Philosophy in many volumes) and Stegmüller (Stegmüller, Main Currents; Copleston, A History of Philosophy) are doing in the cases of documenting carefully the currents of thought, as they occur and the way they do it. It is within the context of the approaches of these two great historians of European and American philosophies that one can perhaps understand Nwala when he submits: "ethnographic studies, works on traditional religion, art, symbols, idioms, myths, proverbs, etc, provide the raw materials from which scholars have tried to give systematic accounts of such traditional philosophy" (The Concept of Traditional African Philosophy 21). The only difference, in the case of African philosophy, is that such scholars often give their commentaries and accounts without reference to concrete philosophical currents and historical personalities. All ethnographic-inspired works have to be directed by concrete thought systems, ideas or personalities that can help give them some philosophical guide. Since philosophical reflections, even when they are based on the interpretation of arts, symbols, idioms, myths, proverbs etc. span human existential living, whether traditional or contemporary, interpretation of these carriers of meaning can still form the foundation of reflection of individuals in view of giving their own private philosophical opinions about reality in general. The misconception that many have is that they must dwell on the interpretation of these carriers of meaning as things that have to deal with dead ancestors in the collective. Here, we forget that these carriers of meaning are dynamic and continue to gather momentum as history progresses. To pretend that we are giving unadulterated fixed meanings is illusory. Due to unintended ethnocentric commitment, there is often the tendency to steer philosophical reflection only backwards in a fixed mode. This must not be the case.

In answering the question, for example, what does it mean to do ethics, metaphysics, political science etc within the African frame of reference, there is no point trying to say what our ancestors did sometime in the past only. Where this must be done, care should be taken to give names and currents of thought in the past also, in the form of history of ideas. Since this question relates to African philosophy in general, we have to approach it with an open mind and give it the comprehensive touch that it deserves. By so doing, we realise that there are philosophers whose works also deserve attention and who have expressed opinions on such issues. This is when we start thinking of such philosophers as William Amo, Chukwudum B. Okolo, Odera Oruka, P.O. Bodunrin, C.S. Momoh. The same is applicable, when we start thinking of currents of thought within African philosophy, beyond general worldviews e.g. complementary reflection, where such themes have been handled. In other words, in answering such questions, all answers that tend to handle them within the confines of general worldviews are under the influence of unintended ethnocentric or ethnophilosophic commitment.

To break the apparent insurmountable difficulties presented by the challenges of unintended ethnocentric commitment, it is important always to bear in mind that we are dealing with the history of ideas of a given people or cultural area. When the word "worldview" is used, it often lacks much in philosophical sophistication. We have to remember again, that dealing with such history of ideas is more than chronicling the ideas of individual philosophers, both known and unknown. It entails also an attempt at capturing currents of thought within given historical contexts.

In the case of traditional African philosophy, we should not assume that there were no identifiable historical personalities as to warrant wild speculations over ideas and currents of thought. There is every indication that we have such identifiable historical personalities and currents of thought. To start with, this was a milieu where people consciously chose to store information in human memory and other carriers of meaning, as outlined above by Nwala, most philosophers of this milieu remained anonymous in keeping with the practice in vogue during their time. This is the practice whereby most matters of information were stored in memory or entrusted to such community human-data storage devices like community historians. These often served as the community libraries. They were receptacle for the storage of community intellectual heritage. The same purpose was achieved by the use of other physical data storage facilities like works of arts, proverbs, symbols etc. By recourse to these intellectual facilities, those I call anonymous traditional African philosophers excelled in their works. These are those philosophers whose biographies may not be know to us, but whose ideas sustain worldviews and give them, in some cases, definite systematic character. This is the case with anonymous African philosophers of the complementary system of thought.

To answer the question about what it means to do ethics or metaphysics within the African frame of reference, one must not single out proverbs, symbols and wise sayings and interpret these in void. Bearing the history of ideas as it relates to African philosophy, an inquirer can anchor his or her reflection around those of identifiable currents of thought in traditional African societies. I came to this conclusion due to my own personal experiences in seminars. Here, students are often asked to compare Plato's idea of education for example with African idea of education. What is striking in such a presumptuous precarious undertaking is that a researcher has to compare the idea of one man with that of a wide variety of peoples and cultures. This is why my approach in matters of this nature is definitely different from Momoh's and his "Purists" where they talk of "'Hausa concept of Beauty: an Essay in African Aesthetics'. If we start searching for currents of thought in Hausa philosophy, we would definitely find many. The same is applicable to historical personalities. Where we have such, we can then compare such currents of thought with the current of thought underlying Plato's idea. Among the Igbos, for example, there are many currents of thought. This is brought to the fore when we say *uche bu akpa onye ọbula nya nke ya* (intelligence is like a bag and each person carries his own). It is based on this observation that I contest what Kimmerle says with regard to Achebe that Igbo worldview can be designated as relative without qualification. Where one thinks this way, one is definitely under the influence of unintended ethnocentric commitment and this can have untold consequences for inquiry.

It is in consideration of this general tendency for human beings to see reality differently, even in the same locations, that philosophy is a critique of worldviews and cannot be equated with the documentation of worldviews or an attempt to inform over it. If an inquirer must be interested in "'Hausa concept of Beauty: an Essay in African Aesthetics', this person must do this as his or her own personal critical reflection. Again, this person can do so as commentary on available worldviews in the sense of commenting on the history of ideas of known or unknown thinkers. In this case, we can talk of "An Essay on the Idea of Beauty of anonymous traditional Igbo philosophers of the complementary system of thought". This saves us the embarrassment of having to describe something homogeneous about all Igbos. When we try to articulate our thoughts guided by the history of ideas, we seek to anchor our reflection on the ideas of those men, women and groups amongst us, both known and anonymous, who have articulated their ideas in full consciousness of the incommensurability of being as it seeks expression through missing links of reality. These are those philosophers, who representing diverse regions as they uphold their creativity and quasi-autonomy of reflection, can match any ideas anywhere both in quantity and quality. The existence of such philosophers in African societies, both traditional and otherwise, is no longer a matter of dispute. Definitely, carrying on our philosophical works in void and in an ethnophilosophic mindset would no longer suffice. However, where a person articulates his or her thought around a given system within any given culture, the person has the task of giving sufficient evidence that such actually exist and are worth the troubles.

4. On patchwork philosophical approaches and unintended ethnocentric commitment

One can make a distinction, in African philosophy, between two unintended ethnocentric methodological approaches. The first are those inquirers who seek to comment on the worldview of their people with the intent of describing and informing about their content only. To the second group belong those who, beyond mere attempt to describe and inform, subject such worldviews to critical review and interpretation. The latter are more committed to a philosophical task and their approach can rightfully be characterised as "patchwork philosophical approach" bearing in mind the dimension of critical personal insight underlying their work. This level of philosophical sagacity or sophistication is still far removed from serious attempts to articulate philosophical ideas in a universal systematic methodological sense due to the restrictions imposed on it by unintended ethnocentric commitment. To this patchwork philosophical approach belong the works of such thinkers as Tempels, Kagame, Mbiti, and most contemporary researchers who keep telling us something about the worldviews of their people. If one has understanding for the time Tempels and Kagame wrote, this can hardly be said of today, were researchers are supposed to own up their ideas and not pretend that these can be subsumed into general worldviews. When a person does not say what he or she wants to say, but prefers to hide behind generalisations to do so, we can hardly give the person full credit for his ideas, due to its patchwork character. Being hesitant or unable to hold any private opinion about matters, the researcher keeps others at a loss as to what he actually wants to contribute to knowledge. In some cases, other researchers are tempted to say for this person what he or she actually wants to say. This is the problem with Tempels idea of "vital force" which many assume is the idea of the Bantu. The danger with patchwork philosophical approach is its restrictive character ensuing from the underlying unintended ethnocentric commitment. Due to the restrictions this commitment imposes on the way we express ourselves, it can end up making us less of philosophers and more of commentators. The question is, why not hold fast to one's ideas, and develop them around given themes within specific cultural milieus? Where we do this, there is the likelihood that such ideas develop with time and around our individual ways of seeing the world. Thus, one of the greatest challenges most patchwork philosophical approaches pose to the way philosophy is done in Africa is that of carrying philosophical reflection beyond unintended ethnocentric constraints. In this case, such approaches are hardly interested in articulating philosophy in a way that reflects a systematic methodological confrontation with reality. On the contrary, it delimits itself to comments and observations from the background of ethnocentric reduction and impositions. When this happens, it is not always very clear what an inquirer wishes to communicate *personally* and how his ideas differ from those of his ancestors, his background and the general world view of his reference. For African philosophy to progress, more works of more broad-based systematic methodological type need to be done. Philosophy has never grown in any region by patchwork hit and run approach, it is the fruit of sustained systematic methodological reflection.

When carefully considered, what I characterise as patchwork

philosophical approach appears to capture what many practice today in African philosophy under the guise of hermeneutical method. Thus, when now Oguejiofor sees elements of personal critical reflection in those instances of doing philosophy with a historical analytic touch of an informative descriptive type, as they obtain in most works tagged African philosophy, he is not completely mistaken. Oguejiofor's enthusiasm for a philosophy built on isolated critical comments is understandable when his position is viewed within the context of his apologia for the African predicament and his zeal to mend Okere's flaws (Oguejiofor, Ethnophilosophy and Hermeneutics 81-84). Evidently, there are promising patchwork philosophical essay that have prospects of wider systematisation as the one written recently by Olusegun Oladipo over "Rethinking Yoruba World-View and Ideals of Life". This type of patchwork philosophy has to be commended because it shows how one can use elements of one's culture as basis for further philosophical reflection of far-reaching global consequences.

In the absence of this patchwork philosophical approach, the common practice within African philosophy today, that is very disturbing, is one of uncritical depiction of worldviews with the intent to inform and regain the status quo ante often as "original thoughts" and common African patrimonies. This is nothing other than what has come to be characterised as ethnophilosophy proper. Where this is done in the spirit of patchwork philosophy, we are dealing with cases of unintended ethnophilosophy and nothing more. Therefore, it would be highly interesting to probe how many works done in African philosophy today are actually done with the intent of subjecting these worldviews to critical scrutiny and in view of probing their truth claims and content within a more universal setting. In other words, there are only a few who can rightly be designated as patchwork philosophers. For this reason, I would read Oguejiofor's remark, to the effect that there are elements of personal critical insight in such approaches, as a much-needed recommendation and not as an attempt to depict accurately what is obtainable today in African philosophy. Even then, doing philosophy in a patchwork mode is exposed to all the dangers of unintended ethnocentric commitment.

In most cases, and due to forgetfulness of the challenges of unintended ethnocentrism, the researcher ends up dogmatising on what he or she has identified as "original thoughts" belonging to the African or Africans of his description. This is precisely when one misses those answers directed towards the challenges, which reality brings towards the inquirer. Generally, it may no longer be enough to hide behind such statements as "African idea of this or that", "Hausa conception of this or that" "Zulu conception of this or that", "Western idea of this or the African idea of that" as a way of doing philosophy. To avoid this manner of reductionism, it may be proper for philosophers, from time to time, to state in clear and unequivocal terms, what they think about the issues at stake bearing in mind the challenges posed by reality in its most sublime and comprehensive constitution.

In other words, the ideas enshrined in worldviews should constitute the raw material for further dynamic personal critical philosophical reflection of the non-static conservative type. It is in this way that philosophy becomes that second order discipline that it is. It is for this reason also that one can say that philosophical ideas and systems are deeply enshrined in wise sayings and religious symbols of all peoples and at all times. These can be considered the much-needed materials of history of ideas, which need to be made explicit in the process of personal critical reflection. This is valid, not only for African philosophy, but also, for all peoples who equally have their own symbols, wise sayings, proverbs, witches, fortune-tellers, wizards, sorcerers, lands of the living dead, medicine men and women and all those phenomena that many have come to regard as typically African experiences. The world of symbols is not the world of myths in the debased sense of the word, as many suppose. The world of symbols is the world in which we live, since symbols and myths continue to evolve and determine our perception of the world. If we had the symbol of tortoise yesterday and yesteryears to represent wisdom in Igboland, we have today other symbols to represent the same like our acquisition of university degrees and other visible signs. If it was the myth of Sisyphus of yesteryears, it can be the myth of the absolute character of technological digital militarism of today. Philosophy probes what these symbols and myths represent in any given age. This is what most people who search for myths and symbols in Africa and some distant cultural patrimonies tend to forget.

The incapacity for philosophers to transcend relative fragmentary cultural impositions would ever remain the bane of any philosophy that has not learnt to free itself from the attractions of its cultural background in view of universal applicability of all modes of meaning. This is one of the greatest difficulties which hermeneutics of culture as a philosophical methodology has to contend with, as it seeks to dogmatise on fixed meanings attached to words, names, symbols, wise sayings; more often than not, by reference to some distant ages past. As long as philosophy does not fully free itself from ethnocentric excesses of this kind, it would continue to solving fake puzzles, battle with self-imposed restrictions and even with self-contradiction. Besides, philosophers would hardly be free individuals, since they would be professing one thing and be doing another thing as "one finds elements of Western thought firmly rooted in Okot p'Bitek's works, even as he viciously critiques the impositions of Western categories on African thought system" (Masolo, The Conceptions of the Person 85). There is nothing basically wrong for one to aspire towards the revival of one's cultural patrimony and with pride also. However, this has to be done correctly, if philosophy must be seen as one of the most important tools for the invigoration, revival and purification of culture. In this case, it must perform its functions well, as the critique even of one's own culture. It needs not be a raw presenter of one's culture, since the philosophical attempt at grasping being as being, in a second order fashion, is definitely different from the work of a poet, an essayist, a dramatist, a novelist, an anthropologist, an ethnologist, a sociologist, a historian or a theologian.

Having stated the above, we can now say: Where philosophical questions are not clearly formulated as to depict unambiguously their subject matter, they can be misleading. Even if interdisciplinarity is commended among the sciences, on account of the necessary mutual complementary structure of reality, this does not vitiate disciplinary independence in any way. This is why philosophy may have an anthropological, an archaeological or an ethnological undertone or interest since it concerns itself with the study of being. However, its main trust remains ontological as the science of being as being in its complementary interrelatedness. Here, philosophy is not purely a descriptive, value-neutral, informative discipline, it is more a critical prescriptive normative undertaking beyond the insinuations of unintended ethnocentric commitment.

5. On how complementary reflection relates to other philosophies of culture

In his critical comments about complementary reflection, Oguejiofor avers that it, with its method, reduces the "inherent hermeneutical tension between philosophy's tendency towards universalism and the inevitable demands of contextualism." (Preface to Method and Principles). What is striking in this assessment is his bringing the method of complementary reflection into close relationship to the hermeneutical method. Even if both methods share certain things in common, it suffices to specify the nuances between them and other methods of prevalent in philosophy of culture. Between ethno-philosophy proper, hermeneutics of culture, patchwork philosophy, intercultural philosophy and that variant of philosophy of culture understood as dialogue of cultures, complementary reflection understands itself as a transcendent systematic ambient reflection about reality with a comprehensive future related outreach. As this relates to cultural inquiry, it thus turns out to be a methodological critical inquiry into claims, phenomena and statements based on culture-specific insights with the intent of determining their ultimate validity within a comprehensive complementary future oriented perspective. To achieve this, it has the ideas of anonymous traditional Igbo philosophers of the complementary system of thought as the ambience of its articulation. This is how its ontology turns out to be an attempt at mediation between the ontologies of Aristotle and the ideas of traditional African philosophers of complementary system of thought. Thus, unlike patchwork philosophical approaches that dwell on critical comments about aspects of reality, complementary reflection carries its inquiry based on a distinctive method in a systematic manner. In this way, its conclusions are carried on systematically as to be applicable to diverse aspects of reality, based on a method it calls its own. Its recourse to African culture is, therefore, due to its understanding of philosophy as an ambient reflection that takes into account all the actors and factors that enter into the determination of our ideas.

If now I make recourse to my African ambience in this reflection, as Kimmerle, in his critical reaction, rightly points out that I did, I did this only indirectly insofar as I cannot consummate my reflection except within some ambience, which takes into account *all the possible relations* that determine my thinking. This approach has always characterised philosophy in its self-understanding as wisdom. In this case, culture, within a complementary framework connotes more than African culture as to include all the missing links that enter into the ideas of a thinker. It is by way of this approach that I wish to show how philosophy can today be a cultural inquiry within the domain of any given culture. This notwithstanding, it can still be articulated in a systematic methodological way without losing much in attraction. Complementary reflection pursues this objective by way of its mediating role as a philosophy of integration and social progress. In this way, I wish to demonstrate beyond reasonable doubt, that philosophy of culture can be an instrument of liberation from ethnocentric reduction and impositions being now understood as an inquiry that has a wider universal transcendent vocation. This objective cannot be achieved unless the mind is open to see reality through the optic of complementing units destined to attain full authentication in the act of mutual interdependence in complementarity. To achieve this, entails doing philosophy with a mindset that has a place for all possible relations as the very ingredients of authentic philosophising. We can then understand when within the context of complementary reflection a noetic propaedeutic takes precedence over all forms of discourse. This that type of propaedeutic in the process of which thinking subjects come to realise the type of intrinsic mutual bond existing between all missing links of reality. This is why I insist that all modes of culture-related philosophising must be carried and sustained by that transcendent faculty designated as *obi/mmụọ eziokwu* (complementary totalising mind) in view of yielding *obiọha* (comprehensive or philosophical mindset). From this *obiọha* ensues that type of transcendent experience that is indispensable for culture related acts, as this is enshrined in the experience of transcendent complementary unity of consciousness *(onye aghala nwanne ya)*, among the practitioners of philosophy.

This complementary transcendent approach does not in any way wish to be understood as a substitute for other contending methodological approaches. On the contrary, it sees itself as an embodiment of what is needed to reflect the driving force underlying them as it insists on the mutual complementation of units within any given framework of action or interaction. For this reason, the question how a philosophy of culture can be possible has to be understood as a transcendent complementary comprehensive ambient inquiry into the basic assumptions of the philosophy concerned as to determine how the methods of such a philosophy makes mutual coexistence of units within any given framework possible. It furthermore connotes the question about the conditions needed for harmony of differences, bearing in mind the character of being, as that on account of which anything that exists serves a missing link of reality. In this way, complementary reflection merely seeks to explore a way through which interacting units can legitimise themselves beyond bounds imposed by unintended ethnocentric constraints. Thus, complementary reflection aims at freeing philosophy from all kinds of exclusivist tendencies of the capricious, defensive type masquerading as localised rationality which create the impression that the idea of being is culturally divisible as to make such a comprehensive complementary outreach superfluous or impossible. Within a complementary framework, reality as a whole, including human history, as we know it today, is the result of mutual complementary relationship of all the actors and factors that enter into its genesis. It is for this reason, that a philosopher is nothing other than a being of many colours, as he or she seeks to serve as an *ogwe* or a bridge between all missing links as they seek complementary mutual interaction in service.

Complementary reflection in contradistinction to all forms of restrictive ethnocentric methodologies strives towards digging out or excavating being from the perspective of its dynamic essentiality devoid of ambivalences. This, it does from the perspective of the mutual complementary relationship of all thinkable and imaginable realities as missing links and as these can be conceptualised as staying a relationship of positive service to each other. It is in a commitment of this kind that all the missing links come to appreciate the character of what is needed to uphold their individual existences within a complementary comprehensive future related framework. This approach to the philosophy of being lays emphasis on the intrinsic relational character of being, which makes recourse to an abstract, non-relational ideal form of ontologism, not only unattractive, but more so, impossible. Even if being appears within this framework as the ultimate foundation of all existent realities, this ultimacy must first be ex-cogitated, articulated, regained and expressed within the framework of fragmentation of all existent realities, as missing links in their mutual complementary essentiality and service. It is in this sense, that this method can be seen as something useful for discussing concrete issues that touch diverse cultures, as they seek full expression today. What this means, is that, complementary reflection understands itself merely as one among the many alternative methods devoted to the same task of finding lasting solutions on how diverse units can coexist. It does not understand itself as an absolute alternative, since for it anything that exists serves a missing link of reality. It is as missing links that are in mutual complementary relationship that all methods of inquiry can be accessed with regard to their validity and usefulness. Any method that proves exclusivist and undertakes anything that impinges on the complementary comprehensive structure of reality makes itself suspect in its intentions. Such methods show their hegemonic ambition and this can hardly be in harmony with the noble objective driving all philosophical inquiries, as they seek to penetrate reality in a comprehensive universal way. Most especially in the face of globalisation today, it is difficult for a thinker to set the point of demarcation between different cultural heritages that enter into his reflection and in the determination of the content of his conclusion. It is then understandable that any philosophy that seeks to be faithful to the demands of philosophical subject matter has to conceptualise its method in a way that spans and permeates the whole of reality, as this offers the common framework of legitimisation of statements and claims arising from such a context.

Hence, if we now "know more about Igbo-philosophy by Asouzu", as Kimmerle reminds us, through complementary reflection, we should bear in mind that the focus is not on Igbos philosophy, Nigerian philosophy, African philosophy, German philosophy, "Westphalian country" wisdom as such. Were we to think this way, this would probably mislead us to make assumptions that have unintended motivations. Perhaps, what we can say is that complementary reflection is a philosophy of being that is complementary in constitution and one undertaken by an Igbo Philosopher as to be tagged Igbo Philosophy, just as Aquinas' philosophy can be tagged European philosophy without losing its universal significance. In this sense, it is a philosophy in keeping with the ontology of anonymous traditional African philosophers of the complementary system of thought, as it seeks to grasp into the structural elements of being in its essential dynamism but based on a systematic methodology that it calls its own.

The hallmark of authentic philosophising reveals itself mostly in its ambient attempt at grasping reality from the preceding conditions of universal complementary determination. All forms of unintended ethno-philosophy delimited our horizon, constrain our views and restrict our efforts. Where this type of unintended exclusivist ethnocentrism is prevalent, the dangers of undue comparison and competition would always fire the passion for the perpetuation of differences under the guise of dialogue and at the cost of harmony of differences. Complementary reflection, as a movement within contemporary African philosophy, aims at exposing those hidden agenda and other unintended mechanisms that can grossly impede authentic philosophical reflection. By so doing, it seeks to break with the vicious circle endemic to all methodologies plagues by inherent forms of unintended ethnocentric commitment. It does this in view of restoring philosophy to its exalted status, as the critique of localised conceptual schemes. In this way, it seeks to rid human reason of the impositions of ethnocentric exclusivism and to sensitise the mind about the phenomenon of concealment (*ihe mkpuchi anya*) as this is capable of leading the mind astray, into error and holding it perpetually in bondage. Its target is to redefine philosophy within the ambit of the totality of reality, bearing in mind that being in its most dynamic essential constitution can be thought of and be articulated creditably in a complementary comprehensive future perspective. This is valid not only for African philosophy but for human experience of the world in general. With this, the conditions are given towards overcoming the difficulties raised by the challenges of ethnocentric reduction and impositions.

6. On intellectual protectionism and the heavy philosophical burden (*ibuarụ*) of non-interference

As a philosophical approach that understands its task to be comprehensive and universal, complementary reflection does not exclude a priori any conceptual scheme in the process of articulation of being and meaning. On the contrary, it operates with an open mindset that sees all missing links as constituting the focus of its attention. In this case, complementary reflection, without hesitation, is very sensitive to any approaches that seek to interpret *non-interference* in a one-dimensional, non-differentiate fashion. Where we have cases of non-differentiation, the principle of *non-interference* is automatically interpreted to mean *no-interference at all or aloofness.* These are those stifling and oppressive cases of pseudo-liberalism. Most especially in the political arena, there is often the tendency to misunderstand the doctrine of non-interference in a hypocritical manner, where this is unequivocally equated with no-interference. In this case, non-interference is interpreted in the sense of respect for sovereignty and self-determination; an understanding that has often led to tragedy. This apparently liberal understanding of the concept can be misleading at times, as to suggest that the term "non-interference" is a neutral concept. When carefully considered, we notice that the expression "non-interference" is one that is shrouded in ambivalence. For this reason, it has to be handled within this ambivalent context to attain full expression.

This is why, for complementary reflection all matters dealing with policies of non-interference have to be approached with caution and encountered in the paradox that underlies them. To avoid misuses arising from misunderstanding of this concept,, complementary ontology reaffirms without equivocation the fact of the dynamic intrinsic mutual relationship existing between essence and accidents, by reason of which judicious intervention is always an allowable option. Were we to insist on separating substance from accidents on arbitrarily grounds, insurmountable difficulties are bound to ensure. This is when the idea of non-interference is understood in a very straightforward manner of no-interference. If we remember that there is an intrinsic mutual relationship between all missing links, even in their otherness, we would have reasons to interfere, when this becomes inevitable, since all missing links always share the same horizon of being. Over and above all, all missing have the obligation of mutual penetrability in a dynamic essential mode. One can say that in all cases, complementary reflection seeks to understand the conditions for judicious interference and non-interference and seeks to interfere when this must be, bearing in mind the type of linkage that connects all missing links of reality.

We have to bear these facts and initial observations in mind when reading Kimmerle's critical comment about my work that "it is a remarkable contribution to the history and the specific problems of philosophy in the Western world that "complementary reflection leads to a possibility of 'overcoming the subject-object dichotomy'". The fact that Kimmerle considers this fact remarkable is what makes his statement indeed remarkable. This is a full pointer to the fact that in many quarters today, many researchers carry on their work with a mindset of non-interference, in the sense of no-interference in those matters they think concern their intellectual sovereignty and intellectual territorial integrity. This is a typical case of the importation of the banalities of folk's political ideology into inquiry; a clear indication of unintended ethnocentric commitment or *ibuarụ*. Where this type of attitude is dominant, actors approach their subject matter under the assumption that certain themes are specific to their region, such that it surprises them when such issues are raised outside of their cultural intellectual context. In other words, we are dealing with a situation where many expand precious energies, unintentionally, dealing with issues they imagine are specific only to their localities.

This is that type of mindset that hardly believes that reality, in its ultimate ontological constitution, can be penetrated and grasped in an intrinsic form of mutual relationship that makes meaning accessible to all stakeholders, irrespective of their specific geographical localisations. Again, these are those who do not believe that such themes as "subject-object dichotomy" are no monopoly of any intellectual region, since such themes have to deal with the ontological character of being and has nothing to do with spatio-temporal localisations. On the contrary, these are some of those matters that arise because of ambivalence to which human consciousness is subjected, irrespective of localisation. Where we are committed to this latter insight, we would come to realise all the more that all human problems ensue the moment the historical conditions that necessitate them are given. Hence, in their genesis, nature and intensity human beings have similar, if not identical problems, and it should never surprise anyone if what we think are our peculiar problems surface elsewhere. Where we are not committed to a universal framework of meaning and to the validity of a universal complementary ontological horizon, we would think that certain issues are reserved to certain sets of human beings only and because of certain unchangeable rules or conditions to which they are subject. The disadvantage of this mode of reasoning is that, alienated from the mode of operation of the human consciousness and the character of the world in its complexity, we are ill prepared to face the same problems when they confront us suddenly in our localities. Hence, complementary ontology is committed to the universal structure of the human consciousness in view of forestalling most serious problems that have universal relevance and in view of tapping fully into the reserve of the immensity and multidimensionality of reality. This would not be possible were we to be committed to a protectionist type of reasoning that sees the major issues of our humanity as things specific to some localities.

Where and when the mind imposes boundaries on certain themes and considers these special or location-bound, there is also the temptation for thinkers to employ all means adjudged necessary to secure these as localised intellectual properties and patrimonies. This is when such thinkers also start to imagine that such themes belong exclusively to their acclaimed *specific intellectual terrain.* This is the moment also when the thinking subject starts to see the world in such categories as "specific West", "specific South", "specific European", "specific Asian" problems. Where this type of boundary reasoning, as is echoed in Kimmerle's observation, is carried too far, it can easily crystallise to an exclusivist policy of non-interference of the worst form and to some of the worst consequences associated with this. The assumption underlying such exclusivist policies is that no one should interfere in those matters or themes that are not specific to one's acclaimed specific areas. This is where each person minds his business even if the neighbour's house is burning. In international relationship, this translates to each region having its specific terrain to protect and cares less if the world goes ablaze. This tendency to clench to specific areas and to those things we assume make us specific and special stems from our natural instinct of self-preservation, as it instigates us and fires our passion that there are things specific about us, about our ways of reasoning, about the way we do things; things that mark us out when compared with others. It is precisely because of the fundamental role which this primitive drive plays in a matter of this kind that utmost caution has to be invoked when dealing with certain matters and declaring them as areas of non-interference. This is important, should we be true to our responsibilities as fully mature human beings. When we make such distinctions as to declare certain areas specific, we do so merely on arbitrary grounds and this is an artificial arrangement designed by the mind to defend its interests.

Even if certain matters, as such, do not concern us directly, there is hardly any reason(s) to justify non-interference when there is dire need for one to interfere actually. This is mostly the case with matters that have to do purely with our humanity. This is the character of those themes underlying philosophical investigation. These are fundamental matters, which should be open to debate and discussion in view of enriching a common human patrimony, beyond specific intellectual terrains. Such is the character of the question surrounding "subject-object dichotomy", and many other coinages devised to capture specific human problems. Artificially imposed boundary reasoning in such themes easily kills resourcefulness. Beside, when researchers approach their themes with such restricted and restricting mindset, they can easily constitute themselves to undue obstacles and problems in research. This is when they can easily believe that because certain themes are congenial to their localities, they, also, are those most qualified to handle them. In this case, they are induced to think that they have a monopoly of insight with regard to such matters by reason of some special capabilities bestowed by their specific cultural affiliation and intellectual traditions. This they do in total disregard of the mutual complementary relationship existing between all missing links, as these have a common foundation in being and share the same horizon of meaning. It is specifically from the background of this over sensitivity about what belongs to whom that Beck, for example, espouses a philosophy of geographical and biological determinism. In this case, he sees philosophy as a regional enterprise where specific cultures have definite assignments based on the type of biological pre-dispositions peculiar to them (Beck, Europe-Africa-Asia.) That such a geographical biological determinism is hardly tenable ensues from the complementary character of reality.

Alluding specifically to intercultural philosophy and in view of the obvious consequences of this type of anachronistic intellectual protectionism and boundary reasoning, Marco Massoni has this to say, "The reciprocal relationship of our time with regards to cultures, philosophies, religions and political worldviews have another quality compared to those of the past, as we are living a de facto existing hermeneutical situation and, for example, it is not the case that Europe seems to be surprised of the fact of being interpreted itself by non Europeans" (Mutato nominee, de nobis historia narratur? 269). This tendency to be surprised when one is interpreted by others or when we, per chance, notice that others are engaged in discussions that we consider peculiar to our intellectual tradition, is definitely an indication of ethnocentric mindset. Such a mindset is alarmed that its intellectual boundaries are being trespassed. As is often the case in such matters, those who imagine that theirs is a special type of inquiry also devise very subtle mechanism to reclaiming and safeguard those things they have identified as belonging to their precious intellectual domains and wish to be known and associated with such and with such only. This is often some of the strong motives driving such coinages as "Western thought system - Arab thought system", "Japanese truth - Red Indian truth", "African logic", "Hindu logic", "Western Civilisation", "Modern Civilisation" etc. Admittedly, and as is to be expected, some advantages accrue from a person being conscious and proud of his or her heritages and achievements. However, these get full validation within the context of all the actors and factors that make them possible. Besides, one cannot overlook some of the more severe consequences that might arise were we to pursue our positions from an ethnocentric induced reasoning. This is precisely that mindset that fires those Eurocentric and diverse brands of Afrocentric movements in their claims of special types of heritages akin to their races; a phenomenon that has made it somewhat precarious doing philosophy today. This is that situation where one is in perpetual danger of being branded a thief or plagiariser of ideas, which in some cases are even obsolete. I feel that these gossips are occasioned, at times, by want of more reasonable preoccupations or they are the indulgence of many who have run out of new ideas. In this case, they wallow in the prestige bestowed by the achievements of their dead ancestors. This matter is relevant and becomes very significant in the face of diverse forms of ethnocentric inspired method of philosophising. This is all the more the case with regard to regions with long established philosophical traditions and where certain themes have come to be guarded jealously as to be elevated to their "specific" or special types of problems and themes. This is that type of thinking that goes about gossiping about who copies from whom. That a person writes about something in a book does not mean that this person has a monopoly of the origin of such experiences. There are themes that cut across all human traditions, due to the mutual complementary structure of ideas in their genesis, such that no one should be surprised if they find parallels in other cultures. This is all the more the case when we come to think of it that humans share a certain common horizon bestowed by some fundamental experiences that characterise their being. The differences in articulation of meaning may differ due to certain minor accentuations arising from localisations. Fundamentally, the meaning sought and pursued remains the same. Hence, the tendency to suspect each other of theft, plagiarism etc. does not arise, strictly taken, if one realises that all human inventions and achievements can be thought of, in their genesis and development, only within the framework of mutual complementarity. It is within this mutual complementary framework, and not outside of it, that knowledge grows and can be sustained. Within this context, inventing the wheel remains a metaphor, since all inventions ensue by reason of complementarity of the efforts of all the actors and factors that enter into their genesis and further development.

This notwithstanding, when people start being creative and their ideas inspiring in specific senses, no one is left in doubt. This is why the issues of "Stolen legacy" and "Copycat Philosophy" would ever remain some of the greatest "scientific" pastimes; this for those who have such time, because as Igbos say, it is he who has money in excess that starts thinking of purchasing a cat for a pet (*onye ego fọdụrụ na azụ nwamba*). One of the most adverse effects of unintended ethnocentric commitment is that it induces the mind to lay claims to specific intellectual terrains congenial to our ethnic biases. Its most pronounced effect in African philosophy is the sustained efforts by African philosophers, just like Kimmerle, to believe that there are specific intellectual terrains congenial to all Africans. To these belongs the idea of "vital force" as propounded by Placid Tempels.

7. On the "Tempelsian damage" as the special ibuarụ of African philosophy

Since Placid Tempels announced in his epoch making book "Bantu Philosophy" that for the Bantu being is force and dynamic, there has been a noticeable concerted effort to perpetuate the idea that for all Africans reality is "force" and "dynamic" in the sense of Placid Tempels. Two very important points have to be borne in mind when considering Tempels' use of the word "vital force" or "dynamic" as he uses these to capture the central moment of Bantu ontology.

1) Due to wrong a situation analysis, Tempels sets up a false thesis and goes about investigating and proving it. The thesis is

rooted in the statement: "We [the West] can conceive the transcendental notion of 'being' by separating it from its attribute, 'Force', but the Bantu cannot" (Tempels, Bantu Philosophy 50).

2) Tempels in his analysis of the Bantu ontology was faced with the general problem of the ambivalent tension common to human existential experience or reality. He could hardly address this issue adequately and grossly misunderstood this phenomenon as it applies to the Bantu. It was on this wrong situation analysis that he built his thesis. This phenomenon with its world immanent predeterminism is not common to the Bantu. It is a phenomenon that is fundamental to human experience of reality.

Issues revolving around these two points constitute the "Tempelsian damage". With regard to the first point, one can say that Tempels is presenting us with an idea that sees African conception of the world from the perspective of a peculiar type of non-transcendent, world-immanent pre-deterministic ontology. Thus, in its reductionism, his "vital force" theory leaves us with an ontology that has nothing elevating, except magic and superstition (Bantu Philosophy 58-60). All other talks about Bantu notion of God, as propounded by Tempels, when weighed against this background lose their merit. By recourse to the theory of "vital force", he remains committed to a bifurcating elitist Aristotelian metaphysics that uses the idea of "vital force" as a smoke screen to capture a special type of debased rationality that he senses in the Bantu. This is a form of rationality that in its inherent world immanent pre-determinism can hardly grasp being in the abstractness of its transcendent otherness but only in the dynamism of its world immanent expression. This matter deserves a very elaborate exposition and I have done this in the book *"Ibuanyidanda* – New Complementary Ontology". It is really unfortunate that Tempels' compromised notions of "vital force" and "dynamism" have found their ways into philosophical vocabulary, as to capture the way all Africans see the world. This is precisely what is being paraded in many quarters today as the very essence of African ontology and experience of reality. The sooner this repugnant idea is repudiated and expunged, the better for the growth of philosophy in Africa and the mental health of many.

Unfortunately, Tempels' ghost appears too ferocious that it resists all forms of exorcism and his invention too attractive to many to resist and denounce. One can say that many have found in Tempels' theory of "vital force" an irresistible intellectual fortification for what they consider a worthy cause in reclaiming a unique African intellectual heritage. In other words, when carefully considered, one can say that his influence in this regard is sustained more by ideological consideration than by the philosophical merits of this ideas. The sooner the full epistemological and ontological implications of "Tempels' magic" become evident, the better for African philosophy. From the ideological perspective, many appear to be easily carried away by the romantic idea of having found an African ontology that is dynamic and which they can easily contrasted with a Western ontology, which they consider static. Many African researchers who submit themselves to this type of ideological oversimplification end up also misrepresenting the world in keeping with a wrong paradigm, which they have imposed on their thinking. This is when such researchers convince themselves about the otherness of the African mode of representing reality, which as a matter of fact is non-conformist. Thus, induced by such ideological oversimplification about the otherness of the African Nwigwe claims "a would be critic schooled in Western European philosophy would dismiss as fetish and occult a theoretical frame work involving gods, ghost and all forms of telekinesis" (Nwigwe B. E, "Causality in Selected Igbo Cultural Novels 3). Why does one need to be schooled in the West to be sensitive to incoherence and contradictions? One does not need to be schooled in the West in order to be critical and sceptical concerning prevalent belief systems and their implications. Those who are under the spell of Tempels often end up dividing the world between a Western ontology that is rational and an African ontology that is occult, fetish and semi rational. Generally, human beings have their reservations about aspects of the world around them. They do not normally need outsiders to remind them of anomalies and inconsistencies around them. Even in traditional African societies, with its heavy metaphysical orientation to reality and widespread belief in spirits of all kinds, not all were committed to belief in the reality of such spirits. Here, we do not need to assume that such individuals and groups who remained sceptical and held their critical distances to these beliefs needed to be schooled in the West. What we can say is that such individuals and groups remained critical and sceptical because they, as human beings, can sense inconsistencies. This is at least one of the major lessons we learn about *"egwugwu"*, those alleged "spirits of the ancestors" that had absolute power of adjudication (Things Fall Apart 62-66). Contrary to generally held belief about *egwugwu* as "spirits of the ancestors", we are reminded that there were some sceptics who thought otherwise. "But if they thought these things they kept them within themselves" (Things Fall Apart 64). *Ibinukpabia* is recognised as the most influential oracle in Igbo land and many believed in the physical reality of the spiritual forces underlying this oracle. This notwithstanding, "there is a saying by the Aros that *Nwa Aro adighi asi ibe ya Ibinukpabia ajuola* gi – Aro does not intimidate his fellow Aro man by telling him Ibinukpabi asked of you" (Nwala 91). In other words, most owners of the oracle, i.e. most Aros knew that behind the "spiritual veil" stood human inventive capacity even to play spirits and gods. It is a similar critical attitude that stays at the sceptical Fanti insight that 'Nananom npow nyimpa na woyeé (The mysteries surrounding the grove of the dead fathers were created by men) (Oguah, African and Western Philosophy 219). In other words, rational and sceptical thinking is a universal fundamental attribute of the human person such that in traditional African societies many remain critical and sceptical about common held beliefs and practices. They do not need to be schooled in the West to acquire these qualities as Nwigwe makes us assume.

Due to blind accession to Tempels ontology, many end up presenting us an African conception of the world that defies the basic rules of common sense. Most of these theories share much with Tempels' bifurcating mindset. It is a mindset that uses the idea of "vital force" in the most debasing manner as to capture a special type of rationality that is peculiar to the Bantu; a rationality that in its inherent world immanent pre-determinism, is so uncritical that it can hardly grasp being in the abstractness of its transcendent otherness. It is this extreme bifurcating mindset that many carry with them into matters relating to African philosophy. This is that moment when many see a Western ontology that is static and an African ontology that is dynamic; two philosophical paradigms that exist at parallel axes without any form of mediation and without any hope of meeting in their extreme otherness. It hardly occurs to proponents of this form of extreme ontology that human reason hardly operates at such extreme frequencies. Whenever it tries to do so, it does this due to some internal constraints or external imposition. Such a rationality that bifurcates and polarises, since it is not free, is in dire need of overhaul. Hence, a purely dynamic African reason and a purely static Western reason, where such exist, are in dire need of overhaul. For the avoidance of doubt, human reason is caught in the tension generated by the ambivalence of all human existential situations and such that creates an apparent division in human consciousness which gives us the impression that reality can be grasped in the dual basic dynamic and static modes without any form of mediation and devoid of mutual complementary relationship.

What is most unfortunate is in pursuing an African ontology many identify as dynamic, and which they seek to contrast with what they identify as Western static ontology, they commit most of the fallacies inherent in Tempels' "vital force theory" without realising this. Worst still is that unlike Tempels, who unintentionally dogmatises and prescribes a form of thoroughgoing world immanent predeterminism for African experience of the world, his most ardent admirers celebrate this thoroughgoing world immanent predeterminism as a positive dogma of African existential experience. All attempts to grasp reality in a static-dynamic bifurcating bracket, outside of the legitimacy provided by the mutual complementary interrelatedness of all missing links, will always present difficulties and worst still end up distorting our picture of reality. If there is any form of dynamic ontology, this must be defined within a complementary bracket bearing in mind the transcendent future referential dimension of human consciousness, be this as traditional African, as contemporary African, be this for a Bantu or for a Flemish. This is why what many refer to as dynamic African ontology, in its Tempelsian world immanent non-transcendent form, would ever remain deficient, if it fails to recognise also that reality has an inherent static dimension.

A cursory look at extant literature easily shows how prevalent Tempels theory of "vital force" has become and how very little attempt is made to rectify some of the dangers it presents. Thus, Anyanwu claims "Because everything is a vital-force or share in this force, the African feels and thinks that all things are similar, share the same qualities and nature...The unity of the self and the world, mind and matter, is something magical because it defies any rational understanding" (The African World-View and Theory of Knowledge 91). Echoing Tempels' theory of "vital force", Obi goes on to discover that "In the absence of "ike" [power], Being cannot be thought of or even discussed because "ike" is the dynamic principle that makes an entity achieve its purpose or proper end". ...For traditional Igbos, the essence of divinity is power or better still being powerful (idi ike) (Senses of Being in Igbo Metaphysics 6-7). Here, we sense deeply the contamination of Obi's thinking by Tempels' exclusivist vital force theory. What Obi says of "ike" (power) can equally be said of some of the attributes of "Das Heilige" (the sacred or the holy) in Rudolf Otto's coinage, this is that phenomenon that is characterised by "superiority of power", as Eliade succinctly summarises its nature (Eliade, The Sacred and the Profane 9). The difference, as our African colleague makes us understand, is that the African dynamic principle defies the rules, as these are applicable to such phenomena in other cultures. It is the same theory of "vital force", with its underlying questionable anthropology and ontological irrational reduction, and whose main target is to deny the Bantu the capacity of abstract reasoning, that many respectable thinkers, quite unrefined and uncommented, have made the very foundation of their interpretation of African experience. A typical example is Jim Unah whose idea of a dynamic African ontology builds heavily on Tempels' erroneous idea. In keeping with Tempels' understanding, Unah comes to the conclusion that "It is this dynamic conception of reality that essentially characterizes African metaphysics" (352). Interestingly, he brings his analysis of the idea of dynamic metaphysics close to what he sees as Heidegger's understanding of the notion of being. This is where for him, Heidegger's idea of being is equally dynamic. By so doing, he seems to assume that Heidegger's authority stands to rectify some of the major weaknesses inherent in Tempels' vital force theory. This is that theory that consigns African experience of the world to a notion of dynamism that is not only debased but also repugnant. Here, Unah fails to recognise that Heidegger's fundamental ontology, irrespective of its disdain for classical idea of being, is hardly free from the exclusivist bifurcating mindset that is characteristic of Aristotle's metaphysic itself – an idea that is basic to Tempels' hypothesis. Evidently, Tempels would subscribe to Heidegger's dynamic understanding of being while denying the Bantu the same. The idea of "Dasein (the being there) or the human person, Heidegger's invention, shows all the traces of a bifurcating metaphysics that considers substance and accidents as belonging to diverse regions of being – an idea fundamental to Tempels' reasoning. Both for Tempels and Heidegger, the idea of being, even in its dynamism, can hardly be grasped within the type of dynamism provided by mutual complementary genesis of ideas - a mode of thinking very typical of most ontologies hatched and nurtured within an exclusivist Western intellectual milieu. An understanding of Heidegger's idea of "Dasein", its dynamic pretensions notwithstanding, can never be complete unless one takes into account what has come to be regarded as Heidegger's "Nazi Connection" or would one say, his "Nazi sympathy" (The Nature of African Metaphysics 337-352). This is that mindset that helps to drive home to us what "Dasein" fully connotes.

As if irrationalism is a constitutive element of African existential experience, as this derives from Tempels conclusions, Onyewuenyi endeavours to erect his interpretation of the phenomenon of "reincarnation" on Tempels' "vital force" theory. What is indeed very striking about Onyewuenyi's conclusion is that, he seems to assume that the rules guiding the principle of non-contradiction are not applicable to African reasoning. This can hardly surprise anyone, if one remembers that Tempels indirectly denied such of the Bantu. In a matter of such crucial importance, we see how Onyewuenyi is misled by his fidelity to Tempels' insinuations concerning a thoroughgoing world immanent pre-deterministic non-transcendent African rationality. Thus, in seeking to resolve the inconsistency he finds in what he sees as African notion of reincarnation, he sees this as having a bearing with an African logical reasoning. This is that reasoning that he compares to modes of reasoning prevalent at other places. Here, he claims, "One can see the logic in the Pythagorean theory of reincarnation in that when the soul of a deceased person informs another body or animal or tree, it does not exist any longer in the spirit world. This is also true of Jewish and Hindu positions. They uphold the principle of contradiction which state that a thing cannot be and not be at the same time in the same manner" (African Belief in Reincarnation 27). With this type of comparison, that is common in African philosophy, one merely succeeds lending credence to Tempels' erroneous claim that "We [the West] can conceive the transcendental notion of 'being' by separating it from its attribute, 'Force', but the Bantu cannot" (Tempels, Bantu Philosophy 50). In this connection, and in view of resolving some inconsistencies in some traditional African reasoning, Oguejiofor claims that "the traditional Igboman did not bother himself about how logical or consistent these beliefs are" (Oguejiofor J. Obi quoted in Ekwunife Meaning and Function of "INỌ ỤWA" 30). Neither Onyewuenyi's stand, which is anchored directly on Tempels' "vital force" theory, nor Oguejiofor's position is explanatory in a matter of this kind. Going their way is equivalent to adopting irrationality as a methodological principle of traditional African existential experience; a thesis consistent with Tempels insinuations. I would say that traditional Africans, and traditional Igboman for that matter, just like all rational beings bothered themselves much how critically, consistent and rationally their beliefs are. They bothered to resolve rationally most daunting and fundamental problems of existence and this in keeping with the intellectual climate of their milieu. It is another question how far reaching such critical attitudes are. To answer such a question, one has to put into consideration many factors peculiar to human existential situations. In the case of the traditional African, one has to put into consideration some of the peculiarities of this intellectual climate. Most importantly, to get at the root of the apparent paradoxes prevalent in this climate of thought entails a critical analysis of human reason itself in view of determining the cause of the tension inherent in it. Here, we notice that generally a thinking subject always seeks its autonomy outside of the foundation of its unity. This is one of the greatest potentials for weird ideas, apparent paradoxes, preoccupation with fake puzzles and error. Traditional Africans are no exceptions to this problem, their situation even helped to compound this problem.

To start with, hardly is there any human being, who in spite of the basic logic of explanation inherent in human consciousness is immune from error and irrationality of some kinds. The apparent contradiction inherent in idea of reincarnation and most other phenomena, as we find these in most African societies, is not something unusual and cannot be attributed to incapacity to think logically or lack of interest for coherence and consistency in logic. Such paradoxes ensue the moment the logic of human interest and ontological logic run into conflict with each other, as is occasioned by the ambivalent tension of all existential situations. Such is not typical of traditional African experience of the world. This can happen to any human being and any human society. In other words, in matters of this kind, it is always important to bear in mind the relationship between the modes of operation of the two fundamental logics inherent in human consciousness as these concern the logic of human interest and the ontological logic guiding human interest. Both logical planes must cohere to give us a true picture of the world. Where both do not stay in mutual complementary harmony, the thinking submits itself immediately to diverse forms of stress. This is likely to lead to errors of unknown proportions. Where this happens, the subject can easily project its errors to the outside as eternal truths. Thus, the difficulties we encounter in such matters as are presented in the phenomenon of reincarnation, are existential type of errors, induced by the conflict of the two basic logics controlling human affairs. The problem arising from this conflict is not restricted to traditional African experience of reality. It is rather a general human problem. To understand the character of existential errors of this kind entails understanding the phenomenon that has the capacity to distort human consciousness as to put it on its head. Understanding and interpreting this phenomenon insightfully and correctly is one of the greatest difficulties Tempels had in his work on the Bantu. Many who base their interpretation of African existential experience on Tempels' theory, invariably inherit

Tempels difficulties and problems. As I pointed out in the book *"Ibuanyidanda"*, Tempels had great difficulty understanding the phenomenon of human ambivalent experience, as this has the capacity to give us a false picture of the world and the human person. With this wrong situation analysis, Tempels proposed his theory of "vital force", with all its ugly implications for anthropology, ontology, epistemology, ethics, logic etc. To appreciate Tempels errors, one has to be acquainted with the character of the phenomenon he misunderstood. This is a phenomenon that can complicate human interpersonal relationship in its tension-ladenness. It is a tension that has the capacity to distort all forms of logical reasoning, but does not abnegate the fundamental formal logical constitution of the human mind. All forms of logic are exposed to the challenge of this ambivalence, which can render them infective, even as to suggest that they are non-existent. This is a universal existential challenge that cuts across all cultures whose intensity can be heightened due to specific historical factors. As a human problem that cuts across cultures, it does not warrant in any way a denial of the formal logical structure on which human reasoning is fundamentally erected.

Traditional African existential experience with its predominantly world immanent pre-determinism, did not lack the dimension of transcendence. This dimension was enshrouded in this ambivalence, such that the dimension of world immanent pre-determinism took the upper hand. This is that situation, where, in spite of human commitment to monotheism, other brands of ultimate commitments remained attractive, and were indeed actually pursued, like, polytheism, animism, magic, etc. In this world immanent pre-determinism, in the midst of this existential tension, such phenomena like "reincarnation" present those apparent irreconcilable paradoxes ensuing from the conflict between the logic of human interest and the ontological logic. This is precisely the phenomenon that Tempels had difficulty understanding such that he constructed a straightforward theory based on the idea of "vital force" in its thoroughgoing world immanent pre-determinism and hung this around the neck of the Bantu. It is based on the same assailable theory that many seek to capture the very essence of what they assume is the experience of reality of all Africans.

In other words, it is this ambivalent tension that needs to be addressed. This is precisely the very phenomenon that Onyewuenyi mistakes for lack of commitment to the principle of non-contradiction and Oguejiofor for intellectual nonchalance. In the face of this tumultuous and tension laden ambivalent experience, the mind is so challenged that it can lose control. Even then, the thinking subject does not shed, in any way, those elements that give its constitutive character as an active rational being. This is why, we said that to be, in the true sense of the word, is being-in-control (*ima-onwe-onye*) of our tension-laden existential situations. Where this mode of being-in-control is lacking, even if the subject tries to exercise its intellect to the utmost, it is bound to remain blind to its errors. We can hardly resolve the paradoxes inherent in human thinking successfully, be this African, Asian, American, Western, by recourse to the idea of "vital force", in the Tempelsian sense. Beyond this pre-deterministic world immanency, human existence has a dimension that is comprehensively transcendent in its future relatedness. This is that dimension that Tempels' idea of "vital force", in its thoroughgoing world-immanent pre-determinism, forgot completely.

In other words, the type of picture that Tempels presents us with in his Bantu ontology of "vital force", which he assumes is peculiar to the Bantu, is incomplete. It would be erroneous to reclaim this type of ontology for all Africans and call it their own. We are dealing here with an ontology that gives us a picture of the human person that is overhaul worthy. The non-transcendent reason inherent in this type of ontology has to be transcended should it be worthy of the predicates "force" and "dynamic" ascribed to it. Generally, human reason, as a faculty, is far from being perfect and has to be addressed in its tension-ladennes. It is a faculty whose underlying operations are firmly erected on the applicability of the principle of non-contradiction, but one whose operations can be limited, if not rendered completely ineffective, by the tension to which it is subjected. This is that faculty, which though imbued with the transcendent categories of unity of consciousness (*akara obi*), can still misrepresent reality in the most embarrassing ways. At those moments and places where the subject is not being-in-control *(ọmagi-onwe-ya)* of its ambivalent situation, we see this principle of non-contradiction virtually put on its head. We can then say that the manner and level of response of the subject to this ambivalence by far determines the level to which its actions can be described as human both theoretically and practically. One can say that the concept "vital force", in the way Tempels uses it, is a part of the problem of non-transcendent reasoning that must be addressed and transcended. It is not automatically the ideal category of being that has to be reclaimed immediately for the Bantu, talk less for all Africans.

Hence, Tempels uses the idea of vital force to capture what should be rejected as an inherent attribute of being as this is applicable to the Bantu and as many, by extension, have done for all Africans. Here, Tempels fails to build on the fact that the world immanent pre-determinism found in the Bantu ontology has also a dimension of it that is transcendent and future related, all at the same time. Even if this transcendent future related dimension of the Bantu experience of reality is grossly hampered in its applicability, due to the ambivalence to which the Bantu had great difficulty mastering, the Bantu remains a being that is fundamentally transcendent in constitution. Hence, an ontology that is inherently non-transcendent in its pre-determinism can never be ascribed to the Bantu as fundamentally constitutive of their nature and generalised for all Africans. The attributes of "vital force" and "dynamism", in the Tempelsian sense, can only make sense as a deficient existential mode of representation that is universally applicable, not restricted to the Bantu. In this case, it refers to those moments the human mind is challenged by the ambivalence of its situation subject to being fully transcended. This act of transcendence can happen, for example, in the process of transcendent complementary existential conversion or being-in-control *(ima-onwe-onye)*, which is open to all human subjects. This is the transcendent operation of the mind in the process of which the subject seeks to transcend all acts that have bifurcating character, including those driven by "vital force" in the dynamism of its world immanent pre-determinism. In other words, the capacity to misrepresent reality as "vital force" in the Tempelsian sense is a universal human experience that is not peculiar to the Bantu or to the African.

Were we to adopt the idea of "vital force" in its raw Tempelsian form, as inherently representative of the Bantu or African notion of being, we do so at a great risk. Here, I quite agree with Echekwube that even if the concept "force or energy" has an important role to play in interpreting African worldviews, "they are deficient to some extent in demonstrating the full dynamism of African philosophy" (5). Even if Echekwube's main bone of contention wishes to point out that the use of the term "vital force" in relation to African ontology does not always bring to the fore "the subjugation of all powers to the Supreme Being, God and man's superiority to the lower creatures" (6), he nevertheless senses deficiencies in the use of this concept, as it relates to its thoroughgoing world immanent predeterminism. Okere, radicalised this point through his conclusion that "Tempels' work shows every evidence that his theory of forces is no more than this now discredited theory of primitive magic, put in other words. …In short La Philosophie Bantoue is the theory of magic promoted to ontological status" (African Philosophy 4-5).

Bearing these limitations in mind, we see how difficult it is to uphold the opinion, as is very widespread today, that "Tempels rightly points out that in African conception the world is controlled by a FORCE VITALE (vital force)" (Onyeocha, Africa's Idea About the Nature of Reality 10). I would rather say that Tempels ***inaccurately*** points out that in African conception the world is controlled by a FORCE VITALE (vital force), without further qualification. Tempels' coinage is not only inadequate due to its overgeneralisations about African experience of the world but also more so misleading due to its inherent world-immanent reduction, unintended ethnocentrism and Aristotelian elitist bifurcating hardliner approach. Granted there is an inherent moment of dynamism in the ideas of some traditional African philosophers, it can hardly be interpreted adequately in the Tempelsian sense of "vital force". It suffices to state that there is an ontology prevalent in the systems of some African philosophers that can be designated safely as dynamic. This is still the case in the so-called traditional African setting. It is not dynamic in the Tempelsian senses, but dynamic in a transcendent complementary future referential way. This is the case with the dynamic ontology of the traditional Igbo philosophers of the complementary system of thought, whose more refined variant has been fully articulated in the method and principles of complementary reflection with the relevant ontology.

8. On radicalisation of the "Tempelsian damage" in the rediscovery of encrypted phenomena and ideas of science in Africa

The Tempelsian damage takes a radical turn in African philosophy when some African philosophers assume that African philosophy has to deal exclusively with what I call encrypted phenomena. This is the moment such inquirers set out creating the means for investigating such phenomena. To encrypted phenomena belong most things that have spiritual supernatural foundations and such that lay claims to some special types of preconditions for knowing them. Some of the major constituents of those means devised to control and penetrate these encrypted phenomena include, encrypted languages, encrypted mentality, encrypted individuals and all resources adjudged necessary to obscure the character of such phenomena against outside intrusion. Thus, in keeping with Tempels' view that African experience of the world is "vital force and dynamic" many set out to declare these encrypted phenomena and the means needed to investigating them as the special domain of African philosophy. It is still striking that they do this in keeping with Kimmerle's mindset that there are "specific problems of philosophy in the Western world". In other words, if the West has her specific philosophical problems, so do Africans. What we can learn from this is that most things we call scientific statements share in the dimension of encrypted phenomena. They thus have an implicit ideological dimension that cannot be ignored. These are those moments when researchers seek to segment scientific subject matters and the means needed to investigate them along ethnic lines and in view of protecting private interests. In all cases, it belongs to the duty of science, and with it philosophy, to rid scientific methodologies of all moments of bifurcation and unintended ethnocentric commitment should they be in the position to salvage the truly scientific image.

As this matter concerns African philosophy, many appear to assume that where there is no phenomenon, that is obscure, abstruse and encrypted, there is no point also talking of African philosophy and authentic African experience of reality. Since these phenomena belong to the exclusive domain of Africans themselves, to be entitled to investigate such phenomena, one needs to have a typical African mentality and one in keeping with some of the major demands of Tempels' findings. We can distinguish two major types of this approach that are theoretical and practical. The basic assumption of the theoretical is that phenomenon is spiritual. Its practical variant holds that no task can be accomplished without reference to spiritual supernatural forces. What is striking about this approach, is its implicit claim that the validation of any scientific statement has to proceed from insiders who are Africans. For this reason, these insiders have the prerogative of fixing the subject matter and determining the method for investigating such phenomena. In this case, whatever is assumed as true, receives its validation by help of mere conjectural imputations arising from the inside. Both the theoretical and practical variants combine to capture the overall foundation of this radicalisation.

To start with, we are dealing here with a typical case of intellectual protectionism comparable to the type of claims we meet in all those cases where people give the impression that there is something congenial to their type of thinking, their type of science and the means needed to investigate them. In the case of Africa, this form of intellectual protectionism surfaces in diverse forms. These rang from those who give the impression that Africans are by nature very religious, very spiritual and morally very sensitive, humanly unrivalled, have peculiar ways of relating to the world and solving their problems, to those who say that Africans follows a logic that can even make the basic stipulations of the principle of non-contradiction superfluous. In effect, they are saying that in African science and experience of the world, everything appears to be different and the rules change. Over and above all, almost everything is allowable within this context. Since everything is encrypted, all matters dealing with African experience of reality, and what they identify as African science are shrouded in mystery. It is important to emphasise that going by this view, nothing is humanly achievable without recourse to some external supernatural powers as this concerns African experience of reality. This is nothing other than trying to introduce investigative elements into inquiry, that many consider fitting for what is identified as African conception of the world; a conception that incidentally carries with it all of Tempels' stigma.

Remarkably, this mode of relating to what many identify as specific African experience, continues to yield peculiar types of dividend. It is an approach that seems to determine most matters dealing with choice of problem, the technique adjudged fitting for resolving them, attitude to science, research and development, management of resources, both human and material; in the areas of medicine, religion, commerce, sports, politics. Hence, the overall impression is that almost everything is allowable provided it can be subsumed into what many identify as typical African idiosyncrasies and African mentality. Here, there is a visible push to make spiritual supernatural forces the foundation of authentic African experience of the world just as Tempels has decreed and this, in a world immanent pre-deterministic non-transcendent mode.

In the area of philosophy, it should not surprise any one when with such a mindset Momoh announces proudly that, "any work that claims to be on African philosophy, be it by an indigenous or non-African philosopher, is not on African philosophy if it is actually not in harmony and congruence with the spirit of African philosophy" which for him is rooted in the fact that "reality is primarily spiritual" (Nature, Issues18). Along line Momoh's thinking, Dukor affirms, "In the African universe, the reality is spiritual. In other words for the African the super-structure underlying the gravitational field in GRT and the wave particles in QFT is spirit energy" (16). Within the context of radicalisation of Tempels' vital force theory, the utterances of these two eminent scholars are comparable to those of ringleaders who stimulate and embolden others to action. This is why their positions deserve some measure of attention. To start with, one keeps wondering how these spirit enthusiasts or "spiritists" came to their conclusions in the face of numerous hardcore materialists in Africa today for whom reality is primarily material. Should we banish the works of such individuals from the corpus of African philosophy reflection just because they happen to see reality differently? We know that complementary system of thought is one of the major currents of thought in African philosophy and here, the main focus is the mutual complementary relationship between diverse aspects of reality.

Where we encounter claims of this exclusivist nature, as being propounded by Momoh and Dukor and their ilk, there is reason to assume that they are remnants of traditional African world immanent pre-deterministic mentality, which Tempels failed to identify correctly. This is that mindset, that he, without further differentiations, has given an official scientific stamp and approval. Many, seeing this as something pre-given eternal dogma, have now endeavoured to incorporate it into the way they do science without further comments. The result is that there is a massive inversion of the scientific arena today by the widespread superstitious practices prevalent in contemporary African societies. Here, both the scientific and the vulgar merge in mutual reinforce. This is why, it may not surprise anyone to find scientists who invoke spirits and deities, at the private sphere, and who carry occult mentality into their research workshops. One of the major lessons we can learn from this, is that scientists are human and have to be seen as such. This is applicable not only to African but to scientists the world over. This is why when approaching their works, we do not do this as if this is a closed world. In the case of Africa, it is therefore always important to bear in mind the varied ways in which scientists understand their profession and carry along with their works.

Even if many claim that for Africa reality is spiritual and go ahead doing science in a way that suggests that science in Africa is nothing other than preoccupation with encrypted phenomena, there is always need to bear in mind that there are varied conceptions of science and varied shades of scientists in Africa today. Hence, we cannot reduce the way science is done in Africa today to a common denominator called spirit-inspired of "the *egwugwu* type". What this means is that we can hardly discuss the way science is done in contemporary African societies without taking into account the diverse shades and colours of its composition. As professionals in Africa today, these are mixed bundles of intellectuals and practitioners, some hardcore materialists, who would definitely disagree with Momoh's exclusivist claims, and view this as gross misrepresentation. Most universities whose core areas are the natural and applied sciences, are populated with teams of searchers who do their work beyond the insinuation of Dukor. They have no reasons wasting public fund at the laboratories invoking spirits. Except there is reason for such, which is often difficult to come by, scientists are expected to attune their works to some minimum expectations. Hence, I do not see any reason(s) to see those African scientists whose methodologies happen not to be in tune with the spiritual supernatural predetermination as lost African minds, who must be brought back to the fold and to order and into a peculiar type of African science. It is this penchant to paint and project African scholars and scientists in such an exotic light that the scientific efforts of most Africans can easily be misconstrued and discountenanced as some strange sort of occult science following its own peculiar types of laws. Why must some of the basic rules applicable to Research and Development take a radical turn when it comes to Africa? It is understandable that people making scientific propositions do so with some sort of contextual biases. However, science grows richer from positive biases aimed at augmenting its gains and not from what might be characterised as negative isolationist biases. When one has something to contribute to learning and scholarship, this person does so, his or her personal reservations notwithstanding. It is for the generality to assess this contribution to see to what extent it helps in advancing learning itself. The moment our reservations turn to exclusiveness, that is the moment we stifle the spirit of scientific mutual enrichment. This approach is applicable even in primitive societies, where the basic rules of learning, which are rooted in imitation and association has always been applicable. It is therefore hardly to the interest of anyone to restrict scientific methodology to only super-naturalistic techniques that resist penetration. A part cannot make the whole, neither can the whole be conceived without its parts. Hence, research into spirits constitutes only an aspect of scientific subject matter, the same is applicable to those methodologies that have the spiritual-supernatural at their foundation. These cannot be applied in isolation of the comprehensive character of human consciousness, which beyond its transcendental intentional dimension has a world immanent naturalistic moment.

An African engaged in questions of the pure and applied sciences, in mathematics, physics, biology, chemistry etc. has to do so with an open and free mind. This person should always be aware that all questions raised within science, their presuppositions and conceptual formation have a history. It is within this history that we have to define ourselves and not outside of it. To pretend that one has to re-invent the wheel just because one belongs to another culture is not being realistic enough. In all cases, the question would be how to ornament the wheel to the admiration of others starting with what one has. In doing science, there is hardly anyway our presuppositions, arguments, questions, object of inquiry, content of conclusion can be based on pristine African ideas, conceptual schemes and experiences of the world. It is not even recommended, neither is it practicable, unless we wish to kill reflection and research all together. The same is applicable to any scientist anywhere in the world. Thus, the question about an African science, an African philosophy of science, African logic, African mathematics, African chemistry, with bold African stamp, appears to be grossly gratuitous and anachronistic. Whoever poses such questions has a premonition into the character of the answer and what is intended. This is the hermeneutical circle, which makes the question superfluous, since in posing such questions, we define a priori the context of the answer, the character of explanation and the methods of investigation. All these can be obtained within the history of science itself, which has a form that embraces all. Hence, I find it more rewarding to go about our research efforts as free global individuals whose existences are possible due to the mutual complementary interdependence between units within any given framework. When we have contributions to make in any matters, and have ideas, as they occur to us within any given context, it is our natural rights, as beings who share a certain framework that is complementary, to articulate these freely. In all our engagements, we are dependent on the enormous human resources at our disposal and these belong to us by right of mutual dependence of all missing links. Were we to approach this matter otherwise, we would see ourselves negating the mutual complementary comprehensive mode of seeking solution to problems in a transcendent future related way. By so doing, we would even be under developing our own conceptual schemes and frameworks due to under exploitation and under exploration of the potentialities at our disposal.

In other words, it is not sufficient trying to inform anyone that there is African mathematics, African logic, African chemistry, African physics etc. All these arts follow from the character of our being. Here, we are fundamentally mathematical, logical, chemical, physical, political, religious beings etc. Even if the way we go about these matters may differ, it would be absurd to imagine that the differences are irreconcilable. As this matter relates specifically to technology, Heidegger's view is instructive. For him, technology, in the real sense of the word, is deeply embedded in being, such that its very essence is the digging out of being and truth (Die Technik und die Kehre 12). In other words, the capacity to be defined technologically follows from our fundamental capacity to exist or to be. Since to be is not to be alone (*ka sọ mụ adina*), it is by being conscious that the basic nodes of our beings are in mutual complementary linkage within a wide network of relations that we seek to make our contributions towards the general advancement of knowing and wellbeing of all. We do this, not with the mindset always of reinventing the wheel but of keeping it in progress for the joy of being. It is when a human person or society does not have the capacity to conceptualise being or to dig it out, that is to say, when it has no transcendent notion of being, that we start suspecting that the capacity for these aforementioned mutual complementary acts are not given. Per definitionem, all humans have the capacity to dig out being. It is another question, how and to what extent? Here, full access to the nature of being, and by implication to those acts that make us human, can only be had by way of mutual complementary dependence between all missing links. We say this bearing human relative condition in mind. It is only within the context of Tempels' predilection that such proposition as special types of African science, logic and the rest of them can be posed. We know that Tempels' case is one of misrepresentation and for this reason, the questions ensuing from his insight are wrongly posed. It makes more sense to identify conceptual nodes within any given cultural context, no matter how imperfect, and bearing in mind the a priori character of these nodes, and articulate them within a wider universal framework. This is how such essays as "Uncovering Logic in Igbo language and Thought" (Nze 126-144) can have more impact beyond showing that Igbos also have logic. Where one operates with the mindset of proving that Igbos have logic, one by implication falls into Tempels' traps. It is gratifying to note that many are breaking with this Tempelsian straight jacket such that they go about their scientific preoccupations quite undeterred by the insinuations of these "spiritists". This is that situation, where major scientific works and research efforts going on in Africa today are pursued in the spirit of accepted international standards.

Taking Nigeria as an example, most scientific works going on in our institutions of higher learning, in our universities, polytechnics, colleges of education etc, are not primarily inquiries and investigations into the nature of spirits as these "spiritists" seem to suggest they are, most especially Dukor. In most cases, these research works follow internationally laid down rules, procedures and recognised standards guiding scientific inquiry, which give spirit related matters their rightful places. This is the case, mostly with the natural and applied sciences, where most researchers go about their business having as their points of focus and subject matters the study of general theoretical entities and concrete material object beyond speculations on some special types of spiritual supernatural entities. Naturally, where the study of such encrypted phenomena must be studied, they follow laid down standards and procedure akin to psychic and Para-psychological presuppositions. It would be a big mistake to reduce science to psychic phenomena or to brands of pseudo-religious and super-sensible phenomena. Not even religion as a science is reducible to preoccupation with spirits of the *egwugwu* type.

Therefore, as things human, and as is to be expected in a complex matter of this nature, we cannot rule out that there are inquirers whose scientific methodologies have hardly transcended those of traditional African witchdoctors. All professions are subject to transformation and to think that the methods of traditional African witchdoctors are sufficient, just because they are Africans, is to make a terrible mistake. Those who think this way are those who think that because they are Africans nothing changes. To be is to be in mutual complementary relationship and here reality is dynamic but not in a world immanent pre-deterministic fashion only. Our complementary cognitive ambience gives us the framework to become human and it is within this framework that being becomes dynamic. It is gratifying to note that in the area of medicine alone, what is hitherto known as traditional medicine is taking a completely new face and is been streamlined to some internationally accepted standards as to be admitted into the courses of study at the university level. The capacity to retain what is genuine, true and authentic belongs to the essence of science as science. It is also a moment of being in action, as it keeps unfolding and evolving dynamically. This has nothing to do with traditional- classical, African-Western dichotomy, since being in its fundamental dynamic essentiality is indivisible and beyond contradiction.

What should remain objectionable are those works tagged African science or African philosophy which are tainted by such insinuations deriving from Tempels' ontological reduction. This is when researchers lay exclusivist claims to the objects of their inquiry, which remain encrypted, obscure and shrouded in supernaturalistic mysterious fantasies. It is interesting that most who lay exclusivist claims to these spiritual supernatural domains, do so with the mindset of zealots. This is when once they have identified these entities and phenomena, they go on to describe, document and regain them with a scientific methodology they assume is peculiar to African science. As is peculiar to this form of ethnocentric indoctrination, most of these methods of investigation approach their subject matter with unrealistic mindsets very difficult to substantiate. This is how, along line Momoh's protectionist way of thinking, many African philosophers proceed from the assumption that there are specific themes congenial to African philosophy to which such phenomena as occult practices, superstitious practices, magic, sorcery, divination, witchcraft, telepathic conjectures, extra sensory perception (ESP), spirits, fortunetelling, medicine man and woman, ancestral worship etc. belong specifically and necessarily. It is with this type of mindset that Dukor further claims, "In African thought much is given to esoterism or transcendence and the space time travel is very common without the use of machine. The point here is that they are removed from common experience and experimental regulation into an esoteric and metaphysical plane, a fourth dimensional explanation distinct from experiment, observation and physical causation" (17). Not even within the traditional African context did experimentation, observation and the idea of physical causation not always play major roles in the way human beings relate to their world. What more today where one of the basic prerequisites for government to approve junior colleges is presence of laboratories of some sort. Many who do philosophy often give us the impression that they have lost touch with realities and are describing an Africa of their fantasy, and not the one we know very well. It is with this exotic idyllic mindset that they target the objects of their inquiry and give us a picture of reality that is quite removed from the facts on the ground. The advances in science and technology are not the prerogatives of any sets of human beings or any nations, these arose and are held in place due to the mutual complementary interrelatedness between all actors and factors that hold them in place. Since no one has monopoly of anything, no one should give apology for sourcing from the common human pool that is at the disposal of humanity. To isolate one's self from this common source of human resourcefulness can be very damaging.

The impression these exclusivists often create is that most of these phenomena they describe belong necessarily and exclusively to the character of African experience of the world. It has to be stated that the dominance of these phenomena in the lives of Africans at one time or the other has much to do with some historical factors that are not permanent. To these can be reckoned socio-political factors, economic, educational, criminal, psychological and psychiatric factors that cannot be ignored. Since these factors are historically determined, they can be reversed when the necessary conditions are given. For now, some of those experiences many assume belong exclusively to the African, are those overbearing impositions that humanity has always fought hard to eradicate. To give them official stamp of approval as typical African experiences is being unduly anachronistic. By stating that the African experience of reality cannot be characterised as spirit-based, without further qualifications, is not to make any value judgement concerning such spiritual supernatural phenomena. Beyond our value preferences, our likes and dislike, there is need to understand things, first, the way they are historically. Here, the fact is that the African experience of reality is subject to changes in the process of historical transformations.

For this reason, what is disturbing and objectionable in some of these philosophical approaches that concentrate on these themes is that those concerned do this often with some value bias and as such, not with the intention of scrutinising such practices critically in view of understanding the nature of their causes and establishing their truth content. On the contrary, they seek to endorse them as specifically African phenomenon and experiences, not minding the fact that such matters and phenomena are characteristic of the way human beings relate to the world generally in most cultures. What is still more disturbing is that the inquirer, in his overconfidence as a specialist and an insider, imagines that he or she is the one most qualified to speak authoritatively about certain matters. In other words, in their blind exclusivist zeal to reclaim some matters for their perceived intellectual heritages, they fail to see the deep resemblance, and at times identity, existing between issues and phenomena, which are equally prevalent within diverse cultural milieus. In such cases, they also almost consider it an affront should an "outsider" dare delve into such areas. Over and above all, it hardly occurs to these know-all types of philosophers that there is something called interdisciplinarity in inquiry. This is when one tends to monopolise the right of insight and all areas of learning just because one happens to be an indigenous researcher and a philosopher.

This bifurcating tendency in African philosophy is what Iwuchukwu criticises as dominance of a "unitive formula" of "psychosomatism"; a phenomenon he attributes to the influence of Descartes dualism on the way philosophy is done in African (69-84). Iwuchukwu's observation is insofar significant as he alludes to what I have identified as the influence of Aristotle's bifurcating Metaphysics on African philosophy. It is very important that while referring to the dualism of Descartes, one has to bear in mind always its

Aristotelian fidelity. This is insofar very important to enable us understand the fundamental significance of this scourge that is very prevalent in Western philosophy, as it has filtered into African ontology through Placid Tempels. The trademark of this approach is its insistence on the separation of substance from accidents as it treats them as discrete quantities or monads lying side by side each other, without due regard for the intrinsic mutual complementary relationship that sustains them.

The ideological undertone of this approach, which can easily compromise the scientific quality of research works, is not often very evident. It is a form of ideology that can even impinge on one's own self-perception, since it has the capacity to create an artificial world of differences. Where this mode of thinking is operational, the mind is easily deluded, such that it tends to see reality in irreconcilable contraries. We encounter this inflexibility when it comes to determining exactly what the truth content of some of these acclaimed special phenomena of our specific world are. The impression that is often given is that in all cases, they have something epistemologically genuine to communicate as to constitute authentic philosophical themes. I would say that not in all cases involving phenomena of aforementioned type do we have clear instances of philosophical themes worth our attention. Some are cases better reserved to other areas of investigation and most especially to such disciplines as criminology and psychiatry. Where we insist on treating all cases involving these matters as serious philosophical matters, we can easily mistake misdemeanour for authentic human action and sickness with accepted codes of conduct. This issue becomes very important in the increasing number of cases involving experiences, which many tend to endorse as typically African, but which, as a matter of fact, are aberrations eating deep into the very fabrics of society.Within the Nigerian frame of reference, for example, this is that situation where rituals and witchcraft have become almost an obsession such that there are now some people who are capable of identifying witches by their scents and outlook. Thus the "Vanguard" reports "Akwa Ibom State Police Command has reacted to the numerous cases of killing of old men and women suspected to be practicing witchcraft warning that the command will not hesitate to deal with persons that take the law into their hands" (Vanguard, Monday, January 15. 2007). More often than not, issues involving witchcraft and phenomena of this kind are easily endorsed by many Africans as typical African experience, such that they easily subscribe to them and readily condone such extreme solutions and remedies as reported above. What is baffling in these cases is that the high sense of the sacred and those humanistic values often said to be the hallmark of African experience of reality remain to be seen in matters of this kind. Most pathetic are those cases where prejudices easily overcome reason, such that innocent victims have to suffer unduly. What is interesting is that some typical cases involving claims of supernatural causes, upon closer examination have been proven as false and criminal cases. This relates not only to matters that have to deal with witchcraft, as reported above, but also to claims concerning alleged extraordinary phenomena in the name of which people are confused, exploited and duped. Thus, there are growing cases of crimes and fraud committed in the name of religion and supernatural forces. Thus reporting of a typical case, something that is nowadays common place, we read that "A 32 year old self-acclaimed Evangelist Ezekiel Uzoechi, along with another member of his church, Ifeoma Okoro, has been arraigned before an Ikeja Magistrate Court 1 on a five count charge of defrauding a woman of N1,000,000" (Vanguard, Sunday January 28, 2007).The same pertains to matters dealing with diverse forms of juju, charms, *igwọ ọgwụ, ikọ ọgwụ,* oracle consultation, divination, diabolical possession, tele-conjuring of money, miracle healing, harvesting of vital human organs for the purpose of generation of wealth, killings to generate wealth, causing human genitals to disappear suddenly, transforming human beings to other lower creatures for nefarious purposes, diverse forms of extrasensory conjectures and occult practices. Innumerable cases that have been exposed to be hoaxes and criminal go to show that these phenomena have more to them than is normally claimed. Here, more is involved than is spiritual supernatural as to be branded typical African experiences. The interesting thing is that, we have very similar cases outside Africa since human beings in asymmetrical situations of power imbalance tend towards the dictates of the primitive instinct of self-preservation. Here, the powerful and the crafty always devise means to survive at the cost of those they identify as weak and foolish, most especially in asymmetrical situations..

While contesting their specificity as African experiences, there is need for caution in over generalising about them as lacking in philosophical merit. Even if cases of false claims and misuse abound, these do not serve as sufficient reasons to hold the reality of such experiences as absolutely refuted. There is dire need to approach these issues that have become choice themes and obsessions of everyday life, with a critical mindset beyond the type that makes us assume that they are typically African. In other words, the constancy and frequency with which these phenomena occur in African communities are not sufficient evidence to consider them typical African experiences. One of the many important conclusions that may be validly drawn from these is that the many aberrations, allied misuses of these supernatural phenomena and type of endemic corruption prevalent in Africa do not advert for the claim that Africans have a monopoly of morality, spirituality and humane dispositions as most purists make us believe. Thus, the evidence on the ground is a critical challenge to the type of self-image, which many African have of themselves. This contradictory self-image, where it occurs, is in need of investigation. Therefore, it would hardly be proper to generalise in sensitive matters of this kind about all Africans. This makes it imperative to narrow down the scope of our claims.

Hence, due to the many criminal cases involved in matters of these supernatural phenomena and the questionable means devised to determine causes, doubts abound if such can be considered typical African ways of doing things. Those who insist in viewing the matter this way, run the risk of endorsing absurdities and criminalities as typical African ways of resolving conflicts. Even if these modes of determination of causes are prevalent in traditional African societies, one has to see them context bound and in view of some of those historical factors that sustain them. With changed and improved means of determination of causes and resolution of conflicts, it would be improper to rely on means of conflict resolution that portend more dangers than the better solutions desired. Human societies grow, and so do human knowledge and those mechanisms needed to resolve conflicts. Here, the mechanisms most adapted to handle complex situations should keep pace with the growth and complexity of societies and human organisations. To pretend that techniques of conflict resolution that were valid in traditional African societies should be most adaptable for the resolution of conflicts today would be a terrible mistake. With this, we are not saying that all means of conflict resolution in traditional African communities have become obsolete. Utmost care has to be employed lest in our bid to remain Africans we sound absurd and irrational. One thing stands out clearly, within a context of conflict resolution and determination of causes, as we have it in most matters relating to supernatural forces, hasty conclusions and decisions can always be catastrophic. In these matters, due to undue obsession with the spiritual and supernatural forces, in a way that defies clearly worked out criteria for the determination of causes and mapping out of strategies for viable social action, more harm can be caused than the good intended, if one were to submit to their being uniquely African experiences.

9. On the restricting character of two major forms of reduction

All forms of extreme tendencies are overburdened by moments of oversimplification and complication, and the attendant mythological mindset with which actors embrace reality. The worst form of superstition is rooted in having a mythological mindset, which sees the world in a divided mood. This is why, supernaturalism turns to superstition the moment it takes on an extreme character. In this form, it is quite objectionable. These are those moments when bogus propositions seeking scientific significances are clad in special types of encrypted languages sustained by some special types of encrypted phenomena. Where this occurs, the assumption is that investigation into the nature of such special types of objects has to follow some special types of laws reserved only for initiates. This is an approach that evidently divides, discriminates, conceals unduly, creates cognitive barriers and most importantly creates special types of laws and conditions needed to penetrate its claims. This is one of the major dimensions injected into African philosophy by recourse to Tempels' theory of vital force as a methodological option. This is when some practitioners of African philosophy behave as if theirs is a special type of preoccupation bestowed by a special type of subject matter, which requires some special types of capabilities to investigate and master. Wherever this type of approach is to be encountered, it has to be seen as a frontal challenge to the open-ended character of scientific investigation. It would be a terrible mistake to think that this matter relates only to African philosophy or to the way Africans do science. On the contrary, it has been one of the biggest challenges with which science has to deal with from time immemorial, as it seeks to weed out fakes from the mainstream practitioners. We encounter this danger in all those situations where people give the impression that there are impermeable regions of investigation reserved to them alone due to some special kinds of empowerment. We can then say that, any philosophy or scientific methodology that has the tendency to declare certain areas its specific domain, shares much in this weakness. Hence, all forms of superstition start the moment actors approach reality with divided mythological mindset as to suggest that there is an internal division within being itself. This is why, it is important to bear in mind one other type of reduction, besides that variant of supernaturalism prevalent in African philosophy, as this is occasioned by Tempels' vital force theory. This other type of reduction is *scientism*, whose dominant classical modes of expression are *rationalism* and *empiricism*. We find these variants also in African philosophy, most especially within the rank and file of African neo-positivists. We can then understand, Aghamelu, when he observes that "There is no doubt that extreme scientism constitutes a new orientation in African philosophy" (African Development 91). He makes this point while discussion the new scientific orientation for Africa as proposed by Wiredu.

One can say that, supernaturalism and scientism, in their diverse variants, constitute the core of the two major types of reduction borne by mythological mindset of a superstitious exclusivist type. Both are overburdened with the tendency towards extremism. The same is their penchant to introduce an artificial divide in our dealing with phenomena. They thereby negate the complementary nature of all missing links in their mutual interrelatedness. In the case of supernaturalistic reduction or supernaturalism, we are dealing with that situation where the mind submits to the existence of supernatural forces and believes that the explanation of all complex situations can be reduced only to ideas drawn from these forces and allied phenomena. It is that mindset that can make the need for the application of human reason and resourcefulness superfluous. In the case of scientism, we are dealing with that mindset that makes human person the ultimate arbiter in all matters of inquiry, and which can always be called in to intervene at very critical moments in the form of deus ex machina.

Since by following these approaches, a straight jacked has been imposed on the mind, the thinking subject hardly admits of any form of mediation in its extremism. This is why within those contexts of explanation that are borne by the mindset that supernatural forces can explain everything, other scientific theories and paradigms have hardly any chances of being heard. Hence, all alternative theories must be weeded out in favour of those forces, which though incomprehensible, are assumed to hold sway. The same thing can be said in those contexts of explanation where only insights based on pure reason or on some testable data of experience are seen as the only admissible credible foundation for valid knowledge. Such approaches hardly also admit of alternative ways of seeing the world. In this case, what cannot be explained rationally or by reference to some testable data, remains perpetually irrationality and non-existent.

What is disturbing in such extreme forms of reduction is the pessimism and scorn, which they bring towards alternative ways of seeing the world, beyond those limitations imposed by the mind of the thinking subject. All these forms of reduction have an inherent dimension of imposition, which forecloses the future referential dimension of all historical processes, based on which human relativity gets fuller meaning. Where on account of the limitations of resources and insight human reason capitulates to forces unknown to it or where it unduly dismisses those regions of reality not immediately accessible to it as irrational, the mind finds itself in a form of self-imposed delimitation, which can make true explanation of reality impossible. In such situations, the mind is restricted only to known causes, such that explanation does not attain that level of refinement arising from comprehensiveness akin to the nature of reality. These two forms of reductions show unmistakable commitment to a picture of the human person that is fragmented and predetermined. They are attempts at putting to question the historical and cultural modes of predetermination which are the very contexts of self-definition of the subject. Hence, supernaturalism and scientism, as culture-relevant methodologies have an implicit moment of world immanent predetermination that can grossly impinge on advancement of knowledge. We can then say that all forms of reduction have inherent restrictive and divisive moments.

Unlike these two forms of reduction, complementary reflection recognises the fact that human consciousness is not predetermined based on some sets of immutable laws. For complementary reflection, all missing links are windows to reality, as aspects of the dynamic processes inherent in nature in its transcendent future related character. Hence, historical changes are admissible and these can be of spiritual, supernatural or natural origin, due to the mutual complementary character of all missing links. Wherever this type of historical determinism is in place, the mind is free to the extent that it undertakes conscious measures to define itself as a missing link among others and understands other missing links in their relationship to others without any form of arbitrary impositions.

Hence, in the use of the term "superstition" we are not thinking specifically with reference to such clichés as belief in charms, jujus, witches, magic, sorcery and other forms of strange beliefs usually associated with this concept. Under superstition we mean, a mindset that is under the influence of unintended ethnocentric commitment as to indulge in extreme forms of acts contrary to common sense. This is why, there are diverse forms of superstition that are context bound, and in keeping with that tendency of the mind to misrepresent reality according to the promptings of its fantasies. A superstitious mindset is always exposed to the risk of harnessing only those conditions deemed fitting for its interest even at the risk of sounding absurd. Thus, contrary to the impression created by these two forms of reduction that anything is explainable based on some special types of insight and laws arising from our cultural affiliation, complementary reflection avers that in all modes of explanation, there is always something left unexplained and unattended to. This is that region where the human mind builds on the conditions needed to excavate the future more fully and authentically. One can say that extreme forms of mythological mindset become fixed focused modes of determination that contradict what they intend. All forms of paradigm that foreclose the importance of chance and human insufficiency are not only scientifically unviable but can be humanly destructive. In such cases, the mind can always run out of control, as to enthrone itself as the sole arbiter in all matter of true knowledge. This danger is real, not only in African philosophy, but also at all those places where certain issues are declared "specific problems" of certain cultural areas.

10. On the principle of judicious interference and some of its challenges

Although philosophy is a discipline whose range of consideration stretches to all areas of reality, this does not in any way imply that the philosopher has a monopoly of insight into all branches of knowledge. The question would always remain on how to understand "specific problems" in their relationship to the universal character of the philosophical enterprise. In doing philosophy, as a science that has the whole of reality as its primary focus, the temptation is always given that the philosopher seeks to meddle into all affairs. All branches of knowledge enjoy a certain autonomy bestowed by the specificity of the subject matter thereby pursued. This notwithstanding, they depend on each other mutually to achieve their desired goals, even as autonomous disciplines. It is from this mode of mutual complementary relationship that the principle of judicious interference, or what is called in the scientific community "interdisciplinarity", derives its meaning. One of the greatest threats to interdisciplinarity is a divisive absolutistic mindset. We encounter this in philosophy and it can take diverse forms. We do not encounter it only when the inquirer gives the impression that the totality of reality falls to the domain of the philosopher's concern. We find the same mindset given in more subtle ways. This is the case at all those moments where practitioners of philosophy give the impression that because certain areas are their special domains, they alone also have special capabilities to give insightful answers to all the problems that can ever be raised in these alleged special domains. This becomes a problem when due to unintended ethnocentric challenges, philosophers seek to show what makes them special and strive to show how they can give comprehensive answers to reality based on some special types of endowments. Quite unknown to us, these factors that have much to do with subjective motives and considerations can easily be mistaken for genuine concern for the philosopher's quest for objectivity and universality of his subject matter, which stretches, to the totality of reality. This is when such a mindset can very easily complicate matters for the philosopher in his or her dealing with other human beings.

This danger is very acute today in African philosophy for two main reasons. First, the African philosopher faces the challenge that his vocation has very wide-ranging scope. Second, he has the impression also that there are certain domains that should fall to him by reason of his belonging to a specific cultural affiliation. In this case, since others have those domains that they consider as things specific to them, why not the African also. We find this mindset most dominant in all those situations where some African philosophers insist on declaring matters relating to spirits and supernatural forces and all allied phenomena to these as their specific intellectual domain. What is still worst is when they give the impression that they have the key to all that is needed to be explained in these areas, because they are masters in their area. They do this often without due regard to the demands of interdisciplinarity.

Where researchers are under such obsessive pressure to explain all and have a misconceived idea of their discipline, they easily become an obstacle to inquiry. One of the main reasons for this is that they would almost always seek to interfere even in those areas where they are not competent. It is for this reason that I insist that even if philosophy cannot be scaled down to one type of definition, it does not mean that philosophy has no guide that directs it. In all matters of this kind, the very guide that directs philosophical inquiry is that which unifies it with all scientific endeavours, as affairs that have to deal with truth and authenticity. Here, their results should aim at complementing themselves in view of a comprehensive and unified understanding of reality. In all cases, all branches of learning seek to grasp reality truly and authentically and not to distort it. They can achieve this when, in spite of the specificity of their subject matters, they always remember the overbearing need to adhere to the demands of truth and authenticity. It is because of this overarching objective that one can say that all genuine scientific quests are matters that can be carried on in openness and humility and in the readiness to concede to our relativity. Where the spirit of all-knowingness takes possession of the researcher, he or she easily loses control.

In the case of African philosophy where some make us believe that this has to deal specifically with matters relating to the spiritual supernatural, it is doubtful if this entitles philosophers to be experts in all matters that have the outlook of the spiritual supernatural. In other words, it is doubtful if within this domain philosophers can handle adequately matters that are better handled by psychiatrists, criminologists, preachers, medical doctors, psychologists, seers, diviners, or even illusionists etc. There is no doubt that philosophers can give much needed clues with regard to understanding such phenomena, but to imagine that the philosopher makes these professions superfluous is begging the question. The philosopher gives these clues by questioning the foundation on which they rest. The philosopher does this with a view to providing the framework around which the issues arising from them can be creditably handled. Here, the philosopher has as one of his primary duties that of exploring ways for the harmonisation of types of logic sustaining them.

In some cases, the way some African philosophers go about their subject matter today seems to suggest that they consider themselves adequate substitutes for some of these other professionals. They are not totally to blame because within the consciousness of most Africans anything that has to deal with spirits has also to deal with the totality of the human person as such. In this case, the human person is seen as a factor of the spiritual supernatural and which cannot be understood unless it is seen as a pure spiritual entity. This is the fallacy of supernaturalism. Where this understanding is prevalent, the impression one gets is that, the philosopher is a diviner or a witchdoctor who is in command of the secrets of this type of profession. This form of misrepresentation is even more pronounced, when many see the philosopher as a metaphysician, in a certain sense, who is very skilled in matters relating to extrasensory perceptions. This lack of clear distinction is often carried into the way some professional philosophers perceive themselves.

The position represented by Momoh, and many, that in African philosophy "reality is spiritual" gives us a clear picture of what the mood of the moment is in African philosophy. One of the greatest dangers to which inquirers are exposed in such circumstances is that of importing and incorporating uncritically into inquiry some of those superstitious ways of relating to the world that are prevalent in their milieu. As a rule of thumb, it may be useful, within the African frame of reference, and as this concerns practitioners of African philosophy, to ask oneself seriously, when confronted with certain phenomena if these are not better handled by criminologists, psychiatrists, and psychologists. Furthermore, it may be necessary to ask oneself always if it is not better to leave some matters to healers and exorcists and devote one's self to the task of providing the philosophical context of the articulation of these other engagements. It is not always beneficial for the philosopher to engage in reclaiming these phenomena as specific African experiences, the philosopher is rather obliged to explore the conditions of their possibility as human experiences, bearing in mind their universal relevance and implications. All phenomena and experiences have the special character that their relevance is not restricted to their immediate localities but touch on a wider network of relations beyond their areas of articulation.

In matters of this kind, therefore, the principle of judicious interference or inter-disciplinarity is binding since by so doing a scholar shows his or her commitment to responsible and mature scholarship. I say this bearing in mind the fact that all modes of inquiry get their true worth within a complementary comprehensive horizon since meaning is accessible within such a wider framework. Due to the character of its subject matter, which is and remains reality in all its ramifications, philosophy, as a discipline, always faces an enormous challenge and the tension arising from this. In doing philosophy, its practitioners, unlike in other disciplines, are always placed before the difficulty of harmonising their commitments to the totality of reality with some of the restrictions arising from the freedom of judicious interference. Here, the philosopher is confronted with the complex question arising from interdisciplinarity in its full depth and breadth. Generally, adherence to the demands of the principle of judicious interference has some major advantages. However, over commitment to this principle can be counter productive. This is when it gives the inquirer the false picture of his vocation and makes him assume that he is Jack of all trades. In all cases, what is needed is how to strike a balance between extreme tendencies. Whenever inquirers are obsessed with providing much needed insight into matters without any outside help whatsoever, and because of what they consider the wide-ranging scope of their subject matter, they risk stifling the growth of knowledge. This danger is most acute in philosophy and most especially in that mode of philosophising which regards philosophy as an inquiry without very definite boundaries and in this case, one subject to the type of definition an inquirer gives to philosophy. If philosophy must be that second order inquiry that it is, conceptualising it as *an enterprise without a guide* would hardly suffice.

The enduring challenge would always be how to harmonise the philosopher's determination to comprehensiveness with the demands of the moment. Here, the inquirer shares in the tension to which the human mind is subject in all ambivalent situations. This is that tendency of the human mind to strive towards absoluteness and exclusiveness within its relative historical setting. How a subject grapples with this challenge can go a long way in determining the quality of his research efforts, his procedure, and the type of solutions he is capable of offering and the nature of the overall results he is capable of producing. Here, all involved in research can scale through this challenge when they are aware of their limited resources and endeavour to work together in full recognition of certain restrictions imposed by their training and the need to recognise the talents of others.

In this way, philosophy is deeply committed to interdisciplinarity, while not pretending that reality can be segmented in a way that entitles each person to make claims bestowed by special types of mysterious insight. Hence, a genuine type of philosophy has to be complementary in its bid to create room for harmony of differences.

Where we seek to do philosophy in a way that restricts our inquiry only to certain segments of phenomena that we declare our special provinces, we do this at the great risk of being victims of worst forms of ethnocentric reduction and imposition. Wherever this approach is dominant, it can easily inhibit honest devotion to the philosophers vocation to excogitate being from the preceding conditions of its dynamic essential relationality and as missing links seeking full expression. As an inquiry into the nature of being, in this form, philosophy enables us formulate our ideas and seek answers beyond specific ethnic boundaries, beyond the restrictions imposed by our special preferences and beyond those matters we consider belonging to our specific intellectual natural habitats. It is at this universal level of articulation of being that some of those issues we consider specific to our intellectual terrains may eventually turn out to become universal issues that concern all stakeholders seeking full actualisation and authenticity beyond given contexts.

As this matter relates to those, like Kimmerle, who make reference to "specific problems of philosophy in the Western world" they have to bear in mind that where others are discouraged from meddling into these matters, because they do not belong, this has obviously grievous consequences for inquiry. One of such consequences is that it deprives inquiry of the much needed dynamism and intellectual vitalisation because of unavoidable inbreeding. The same is applicable to those who give the impression that there are specific problems of African philosophy that is spirit-based. Conjectures arising from some of these spirit-based phenomena are gradually turning to some of the unquestioned dogmas of the worst type in all branches of philosophy as the cases of Momoh, Unah, Onyewuenyi, Dukor and Onyeocha clearly show. This is precisely why this trend deserves serious attention lest they corrupt the way we view the African experience of the world totally. Generally, one can say that it would always remain illusory to imagine that a philosophical answer and solution can be given to a psychiatric or criminal question while upholding its legitimacy. Philosophy can help us illuminate the character of the problem towards handling them successfully. In doing this, the philosopher has always to bear in mind the line of demarcation imposed by the subject matters of other areas of knowledge while at the same time, also being committed to interdisciplinarity.

11. On the raw primary and complementary cognitive ambiences

One of the greatest difficulties, which most inquirers have to contend with, is how to relate to those experiences that touch on their lives personally. This matter is very relevant in African philosophy where some of its practitioners assume that because some phenomena are so personal to them, there is need to give such phenomena special consideration, beyond what is obtainable in other areas of inquiry. This is when they go ahead creating some special conditions and rules in view of relating to such phenomena. In other words, we are dealing with those cases where one has the impression that those rules that are generally applicable in scientific inquiries cease to be relevant because of the special status of the object of inquiry. The question is, to what extent does scientific methodology allow such conditions that assume special status? Admittedly, as philosophers, we do not speculate in void concerning those phenomena that touch our lives personally. We carry on our research efforts based on the data available to us, starting with the world around us. This data is not as unbiased and uncorrupted as we assume. We speculate from the background known to us and this is that background we inherit and often the one to which we are born into, with all its romantics and appeals. In most cases, we are born into that ambience, to which we have special an often very personal emotional ties. This is the ambience of our cultures, tradition, childhood dreams etc. The way we relate to this background and the overall appeal and impact it has on us, has much to do with the way we do philosophy as an objective critical science. Where philosophers claim that the domain of their investigation is the spiritual supernatural, as this is the case with many African philosophers, we have to remember that those who make these claims do so as scientists. Bearing the influence of our background on the way we do science, it would be most unfair to approach those who make these claims as if they are witchdoctors and sorcerers, knowing fully well the type of prejudice attached to the ambience from which they come.

This notwithstanding, there is often the danger of the researcher operating with the mindset of his ambience and not transcending it. This is an unwritten law, but one that can very easily happen. This is where the problem lies. This type of problem ensues the moment the inquirer has the feeling that certain phenomena that belong to his ambience are too precious to be compromised. For him, they are the very streams from which his being draws its life. These are those phenomena and experiences, which the researcher views as his own, and which he has difficulties handling in the correct scientific spirit. We must make a concession here. Such problems, as intricate as they may appear, ensue from the character of inquiry itself, where the inquirer is also a human being. It is not always a viable option that one renounces one's personal experiences, background, beliefs and customs just because one wishes to become a scientist. These experiences are necessary constituents that enrich science itself. As an integral part of our personality, they are the necessary conditions for doing science profitably. Science becomes viable and interesting, when the totality of the world of the inquirer becomes relevant as the conditions that enable its practitioners find viable solutions. Hence, all experiences that enter into our world have to be taken seriously and fully integrated, such that by so doing, credible answers can emerge. We take this stance bearing in mind that anything that exists serves a missing link of reality. In other words, the background history of the scientist must not be an encumbrance, an unnecessary burden, but enrichment for his or her work. We can therefore say, that it merely depends on how one relates to one's background or ambience of reflection and the type of understanding we have about this background.

However, when one considers the passionate manner with which some inquirers segment reality and lay claim to some areas at the cost of others, one comes to realise that the issue is not as straightforward and simple as it appears. Hence, the main problem would always remain how to make useful statements about those experiences and phenomena we consider very personal to us. In this case, we are thinking of such statements that can be creditably relied upon and upon which useful knowledge can be built. This matter is relevant not only to African philosophy, where many see it as something that has to deal primarily with the spiritual supernatural, but more so in all those cases where some Westerners have the feeling that certain themes are congenial to their type of thinking, as Kimmerle makes us believe. In the face of this particularistic tendency and in the face of the overlapping between the background of the inquirer and the objective character of scientific enterprise, it becomes necessary to shed more light on the character of the ambience of reflection itself.

In all forms of inquiry, two major ambiences have to be borne in mind always. These are the *raw primary cognitive ambience* and *the complementary cognitive ambience*. The raw primary cognitive ambience is that putative ambience into which the inquirer assumes is his own. Thus, it can be rightly be designated as the raw primary cognitive ambience of socialisation, education and indoctrination from which the inquirer draws his vocabulary, inspiration and experience of the world. What actually happens is that we tacitly assume that this ambience gives our world, together with the phenomena we are inquiring into their objective characters. This ambience constitutes for us all what we assume to be the actors and factors that mould and remould our world into cognitive and emotional block. We further assume tacitly that as a putative construct, it is within this ambience that phenomena assume certain fixed characters beyond the value-ladenness and prejudice we ascribe to them later. This is that ambience that can be very true, real and objective to us, such that it is resistant to further changes and indoctrination. Thus, our raw primary cognitive ambience turns out to be that which we assume that we share with others like ourselves based on which we can make predications and assign meaning beyond mere subjectivity. We feel this world and share it with those we call our own. As such, we are a part of their world just as these others are a part of our world. At this cognitive level, phenomena assume certain forms, are communicated in particular ways by individuals and groups of individual, and cannot but be known in a certain way. It is because those who share this world can know phenomena in this personal intimate way that they can make certain dependable predictions based on the structure of this world that is well known to them. This is when we say that the world of this raw primary cognitive ambience is relatively reliable and beyond some brands of biases and value-ladenness. This world can be stubborn and resistant to change in its putative character. Moreover, it is an objective world of some sort that is given and one that can be mutually validated by participants. Without the legitimacy arising from this world, no further statements can ever be formulated concerning reality generally. It is a world on which we fall back to reorganise ourselves in times of crisis. Since we share this world with some individuals and groups, we have the feeling that it has a certain binding and legitimising character that has to be defended against outside intrusion. Over and above all, we have the feeling that it is the fullness of our world. It is not primary to the subject alone but a primary world that is shared by many. It is this sharing that gives it its fundamental character as an objective world beyond the subject alone.

It is very important to emphasise the legitimacy conveyed by our putative raw primary cognitive ambience since overlooking this fact can easily mislead us to many false assumptions. One of the commonest mistakes in this regard is to underestimate its effect on the way we do science and philosophise. To one of the commonest mistakes in this regard belongs the assumption that because we are philosophers and educated, we cannot be prone to the impositions, superstitions and weird ideas arising from our raw primary cognitive ambience. Such derailment ensues the moment we overlook the fact that as real, legitimising and objective as our putative raw primary cognitive ambience may be, it is not the real world. Hence, beyond our putative raw primary cognitive ambience, lies the wider world of mutual complementary relationship between all missing links. It is therefore important to note that we define our real objective pristine world, not in our primary cognitive ambience, but in our complementary cognitive ambience. The hallmark of this complementary cognitive ambience is that it serves as a bulwark against certain types of biases. It does this in the sense that it is resistant to prejudice, since it can be shared with others transsubjectively as it legitimises and bestows their actions with reasonableness beyond mere raw putitiveness. In this case, we are dealing with that world that provides the basis for primary cognitive judgements on account of which we can share our experiences transsubjectively and with some measure of neutrality as we categorise and assign meaning to things. *Thus, the true primary cognitive ambience of any inquirer is his complementary cognitive ambience, which he shares with all missing links of reality.* It is on account of this primacy that inquirers are enabled to relate to the world in a certain way as to be understood by many. We are dealing here with a situation where scientists, including philosophers are creatures of a wider environment in the sense that they cannot change certain things without running the risk of rendering meaning obscure. This is that world that is mutually shared and one that enables actors to mould their ideas in some particular ways, equip themselves with those known means of communicating their ideas such that they can be understood by others in certain predetermined way and most especially by those sharing their world at this complementary cognitive level.

What we can learn from this is that it is possible for a person to be a philosopher and a scientist and at the same time have a weird superstitious mindset. It all depends on how a person relates to his cognitive ambience. Where a person has not learnt to transcend his putative raw primary cognitive ambience, chances are that this person can make himself or herself immune towards acquiring certain forms of judgement bestowed by the wider legitimacy accruing from the complementary primary cognitive ambience. This is the time we can claim that although a person is learned, enlightened and a philosopher, this person can still be primitive in his ways and thinking, and superstitious in belief all at the same time. These are those cases where practitioners of philosophy can be very stubborn in their errors without seeing anything wrong in this. In fact, we can on account of the type of legitimacy bestowed by our putative raw primary cognitive ambience be very resistant to the type of differentiated and critical attitude needed to do objective scientific work. Where this type of resistant mindset is in place, the philosopher concerned hardly sees the need to transcend his superstitious ideas because of the type of legitimacy he senses accruing from his putative raw primary cognitive ambience. If on the other hand, the philosopher understands that reality is complementary in constitution beyond the confines of his raw primary cognitive ambience, chances are that this persons would invariable seek to strive beyond the restrictions arising from this.

What this means is that the issue of truth and authenticity cannot be discussed outside of the known world of a scientist. Again, such matters cannot be discussed within the confines of our raw primary cognitive ambiences alone. All such matters have to be placed within the scientist's world of missing links in the complementarity of their interrelatedness. In other words, our real world of science and authentic existence is that of our complementary cognitive ambience, which is more open and universal. This is even the fullness of our world because it can validate or invalidate those gains arising from our raw putative cognitive ambience. Where researchers go about their business, forgetting this fact they can easily become intolerant. This is when they go on assuming that their raw primary cognitive ambience, which imposes itself on them, is the only real world ever. Here, they may be right, but only partially. However, as long as our world is constituted of all the actors and factors that enter into their genesis, what appears to us as our raw primary cognitive ambience would ever remain deceptive.

In other words, even if our raw primary cognitive ambience is resistant to bias of some kinds and conveys some legitimacy to our judgement on account of its neutrality, at its level of primacy, it cannot be handled as if it is something static and resistant. On the contrary, it is something subject to changes arising from a wider framework of relations beyond our closed worlds. Its reality demonstrates to us that, we are human beings. For this reason, although we are philosophers and scientists who strive towards scientific objectivity and integrity, we are still human beings who have the same worries like other human beings. It is our humanity that spurns us to find solutions relevant to all and not only to those within a circumscribed framework. We are human beings who share in the world of others, especially those outside of our raw primary cognitive ambiences. For this reason, our primary task is to transcend all the impositions arising from our world as we seek viable solutions to our problems, which should be relevant for all missing links of reality. It is in this transcendence that we demonstrate our sincerity to the world around us. To this transcendence belongs our capacity to integrate fully and positively what we have seen and heard, the capacity to borrow and adapt to what other scientists say of the phenomena and the modes of characterisation of the phenomena in view of communicating it. Hence, everything hinges on crossing the divide, from our raw putative cognitive ambience, into our complementary cognitive ambience. Crossing this divide requires some sort of empowerment that ensues through positive education. This is why complementary reflection insists on the primacy of a noetic propaedeutic whose aim is to aid the mind cross this precarious divide. It is the human capacity to convert their restricted raw primary cognitive ambience into a complementary cognitive ambience that makes it possible to relate to those experiences we call our own still better and have them well integrated into our world. This can be achieved in the process of existential conversion, where the subject learns to convert maxims into imperatives. In other words, even if not all meanings may be accessible to all immediately due to certain artificial restrictions arising from some natural conditions, all can have access to the real world more intimately who have the capacity to imbibe the requisite tools needed to acquire the meaning communicated even at the level of our raw primary cognitive. This is possible because all missing links share the harmony arising from the unity of being and consciousness intimately in a mutual complementary fashion.

In other words, the legitimacy to make certain objective apodictic pronouncements about the world ensues the moment we have a fundamental commitment to the complementary character of reality, which secures the universal character of our world. It is based on sharing a complementary primary cognitive ambience that we can make those pronouncements, observations and statements that stay above certain types of biases. Since our complementary primary cognitive ambience is constituted of all the actors and factors that enter into its genesis, its ultimate validity ensues from all missing links that enter into its composition beyond the legitimacy conveyed by localised factors and actors. For this reason, all personal experiences, no matter how dearly we hold and treasure them, get their true worth from this complementary primary cognitive ambience, which is shared by all the actors and factors that enter into their genesis. This wider ambience is the ambience of scientific reasoning. Anyone who seeks to make a scientific claim and has not understood the character of phenomena in this way is likely to encounter insurmountable difficulties. Such difficulties ensue because the inquirer lives in a world created by his or her subjectivity, outside of the legitimacy bestowed by all missing links. One of the greatest mistakes, which most researchers make, is to restrict their knowledge of the world to their raw primary cognitive ambience only, as the world most known to them, a world into which they are born and whose legitimacy they consider impeccable. Where researchers subscribe to the apodictic character of this putative world, they can easily mistake phenomena for what they are not because they are resistant to outside opinions, which necessarily enter into the moulding, even, of their own ideas. This is when superstitious practices, which as a matter of fact, have unchallenged legitimacy in their raw primary cognitive ambience, can easily be mistaken for objective truths. All forms of claims are under consistent threats of misrepresenting reality. These are those claims, which have not taken into consideration this dimension of mutual complementary character of reality. Where the consciousness concerning the character of our cognitive ambiences is not secure, all forms of claims both of the superstitious and scientific character are under the same threat of being pure misrepresentations. Even then, as scientists and inquirers, we cannot wish the raw primary cognitive ambience away just because of its putative character. We must always remember that it is the condition of possibility of all types of further reflection but it is not the answer. The challenge to any inquirer always boils down to striving beyond the legitimacy conveyed by our raw primary cognitive ambience as to seek to grasp phenomena within the ambit of all the actors and factors that enter into their genesis. In this striving, lies the scientific critical function. We find out that in many instances, many prefer the legitimacy bestowed by their raw primary cognitive ambience for very obvious utilitarian and ideological reasons. They thereby run the risk of compromising their scientific vocation. In all cases, the task would always remain how to convert our perception of the world into an enduring complementary cognitive frame such that all the actors and factors that help us mould our ideas actually remain mutually harmonised. In dealing with those matters and phenomena that concern us personally, there is dire need to bear in mind always the character of our world beyond its raw primary value. This makes for a more dispassionate relationship to all those things that concern us most, and for that world we think we have come to know all too well. In all those cases where researchers in the mood of unintended ethnocentric commitment consider some phenomena ensuing from their raw primary cognitive ambiences specific objects of inquiry, the dangers can be telling. By proceeding in this way, an undue and permanent tension and division is injected into inquiry.

12. On encrypted phenomena as pragmatic cognitive postulates

The underlying assumption to the radicalisation of Tempels' vital force theory in African philosophy, both practical and theoretical, is that ultimate realities and metaphysical statements, as aspects of world immanent pre- determination, are mere pragmatic cognitive postulates geared towards utility. Hence, penetrating any of the encrypted phenomena belonging to the province of these experiences, entails outlining some of the major objectives they serve. It is in the realisation these objectives that the reasonableness of these phenomena can be demonstrated beyond shades of doubt. That is to say, we prove the existence of these phenomena by providing the objectives they serve. More pointedly formulated, investigating matters relating to extrasensory experiences is validated the moment we can show the utility underlying such claims. Underlying such utility oriented claims is that encrypted phenomena are typical of African experience of reality and as such, their methods of validation has also to concur with the way Africans relate to the world, which has something to do directly with their brands of practical problems of life. Here, protagonists of this view tend to forget that Africans are not alone in relating to encrypted phenomena in this fashion. The difference is that within some other cultural milieus, effective means that are workable have been put to address some of the problems these phenomena present. Besides, these have been secured through effective legislation and other control mechanisms, which determine how these phenomena can become relevant to life and which objectives can be considered worthy of aspiration. How we handle these phenomena, bearing in mind their impact on the overall welfare of all the actors and factors involved within a wider complementary ambience beyond our raw primary cognitive ambience, goes a long way in determining our sincerity towards resolving some of the major problems they pose. Hence, one can say that all attempts that seek to validate the claims of encrypted phenomena get full meaning when such are articulated within a wider framework of mutual dependence between all missing links, failing which they risk forfeiting such claims, which go beyond known circumscribed values and objectives.

Generally, it seems that statements relating to encrypted phenomena, of the spiritual supernatural mysterious type, have unmistakable wider connotation than the restricted meanings many may be willing to concede or ascribe to them. Here, we cannot overlook the fact that they have the implicit dimension of addressing diverse unexpressed wishes and unknown needs of human beings. If they should be seen as serving as pragmatic cognitive postulates, it is within a wider context and not in view of some restricted motives and objectives. Hence, within any given context, what might interest us about any encrypted phenomenon is to try to find out first the statements or objectives enshrined in them, as these relate to fundamental human needs beyond across cultural boundaries. Generally, one can say that these phenomena serve as explicative indexes driving human quest for meaning in a comprehensive universal sense. They serve most especially as explicative indexes for some known, unknown and unfulfilled wishes, which go beyond the immediacy. What is striking is their serving such wishes in a comprehensive sense such that they can be seen as moments of human striving to ultimate freedom, security and control of one's destiny, even those of others. This is how these encrypted phenomena turn out to enshrine unfulfilled wishes towards absolute possessiveness over one's life, over nature and over fellow human beings. In concrete terms, they are striving towards deliverance from poverty and sickness, pathological fears of the unknown, diverse forms of compulsive and obsessive behaviour. Similarly, they can be seen as moments towards overcoming uncertainties and to have human destiny in firm grips. Besides, they enshrine basic human striving towards enthronement of human vanity, projection of the ego, excessive drive for recognition, desire for scot-free vengeance; unlimited satisfaction of the basic human fascination for adventure and mischievousness etc. Again, these encrypted phenomena enshrine quest for extreme forms of measures needed to address personal or collective security and perceived dangers. This can be with regard to those measures needed to address the shortcomings of inefficient social, political or economic systems. Furthermore, they enshrine measures needed to address distorted perception of one's achievement and capabilities. The same is applicable to effective measures needed to address perceived sense of underachievement and injustice within given social systems that actors identify as dysfunctional, inefficient and corrupt. Furthermore, they give expression to those mechanisms adjudged optimal in view of addressing unfulfilled wishes and expectations generated by social insecurity, excessive poverty and deprivation, diverse forms of oppression, experienced either personally or vicariously felt. The same is applicable to measures needed to address sudden changes in human interpersonal relationship and sustained emotional deprivations. Likewise, they serve in filling optimally the vacuum created by power asymmetry, and the measures needed to address optimally issues arising from sudden changes in human self-perception and self-definition. The same is applicable to their usefulness in addressing changes in value system and other asymmetries arising due to level and type of education, social, economic and financial status etc. In all these cases, the subject naturally seeks relief, readjustment and even redress, which can very readily be found in these encrypted phenomena, which the subject assumes are beyond the province of mere mortals. This is mostly the case, when the challenges prove very stubborn and inexplicable. Here, encrypted phenomena, clad in mysteries, evoking fear and fascination come in readily. In this matter, the human mind and with it the human consciousness, while being assuaged, is at the same time exposed to diverse forms of illusion. These are those illusions that can help distort the image of reality enormously and put the subject further in very precarious conditions in its choices of problem-solving techniques due to the constraints arising from its ambience. Here, no types or levels of education, no types or levels of alleged special achievements, both material and spiritual, are guarantees that a person would not derail due to challenges arising from changed conditions, most especially when these are sudden, unexpected, persistent and enduring. On the contrary, such special credentials may even help to widen and deepen the divide in human consciousness, because of the illusions and false hopes they can generate within the subject.

In other words, belief in such phenomena as witchcraft, spirits, ghosts and other extrasensory phenomena makes sense and, has very strong statements to make. For this reason, we need to dig deeper into some of those objectives driving them for which they serve as pragmatic cognitive postulates, than what is immediately evident. In doing this, it would hardly be proper to focus only on known causes and their effects. As explicative indices geared towards comprehensive explanation of reality, their explicative worth or value gains in importance as they guide us in having an insight into how what is intended can be grasped in a comprehensive universal future related sense. Where this dimension of universal comprehensiveness is underrated, what they intend to express would remain perpetually hidden and defeated. To pretend that African experience of reality can be articulated based on its own parallel axis, outside of this universal framework, and as this relates to human beings within a more comprehensive, universal complementary relationship, is to undermine the explicative value of these phenomena. When this happens, what is encrypted easily becomes more obscure, the codes hardened and more difficult to crack. In other words, those phenomena we assume are typical African experiences have to be measured in their relationship to a complex network of aims establishing them and should not be handled as isolated experiences within the obscure immutable parameters imposed by our particular locations and raw primary cognitive ambiences.

Where causes are determined merely by the types of special

effects we think they are capable of producing and where effects are judged only by the types of known agents needed to produce them, grievous consequences are bound to follow. These are those cases where we are confronted by a predetermined mode of predicting events, beyond the legitimacy provided by all the actors and factors that might be adjudged necessary towards determining the cause of an event. In matters dealing with spiritual supernatural forces, it is often beneficial to see these as incomplete paradigms of explanation that get their partial meaning also within the context of their articulation. Their full meaning ensues when we remember that all meanings get their full worth within a wider complementary context as to reflect the dictum that anything that exists serves a missing link. In the case of traditional African societies, as is typical of most primitive societies, causes are often co-joined to their effects in a world immanent pre-deterministic fashion and in view of forming both sufficient and necessary conditions for the explanation of events. Where this approach is prevalent, they can easily be misused and manipulated in a way that favours those who have the advantage of insight and the requisite power to enforce their ways. This is that instance in traditional African societies where those who had the power and advantage of insight often misused them against the weak and uninformed. This observation is very pertinent to matters dealing with recourse to oracles, diviners, recourse to trial by ordeal, medicine men and women and other legitimising forces whose modus operandi are not always questioned. These are those legitimising forces whose ways of operation often remain shrouded in mysteries, as they serve as paradigms of explanation and causes. Such events and processes can easily be manipulated due to uneven distribution of power arising from cognitive disparity and imbalance within any given explanatory contexts. Due to human insufficiencies and natural fascination for the mysterious, the possibility of manipulation is never ruled out where there are individuals whose powers derive from foundation establishing their authority, such that both what is needed to be explained and the explainer share the same encrypted horizon. As long as this disparity exists, and as long as the explainer is an extension of the same unquestioned world immanent pre-deterministic forces, possibilities of misuse is bound to endure. Here, the powers to manipulate and explain arise from the same unquestioned source that is in dire need of elucidation.

13. On encrypted phenomena and context of understanding

The moment we see encrypted phenomena as issues lying outside of the range of human understanding and management, that is the moment we contribute to the complications surrounding them. This is also the moment we create those conditions conducive for manipulation, both of the subject and the object. Such difficulties are deeply endemic to any bifurcating approach that sets out to segment reality a priori into diverse irreconcilable regions. In other words, matters of this kind are better handled within a wider complementary ambience, bearing in mind the far-reaching consequences of our actions and omissions. The rule of thumb is to proceed from the known to the unknown and to place such phenomena within a historical context of understanding. It is within this context that we can explore all the actors and factors that might be adjudged useful towards their explanation. In order that we are not easily carried away by exaggerated forms of otherness, it is always important to bear in mind the following distinctions when dealing with phenomena whose characters appear mysterious to us.

1) Those things that appear mysterious to us due to paucity of knowledge or due to ignorance. Here, the mysteries disappear the moment the knowledge or information that is lacking is made available. We are dealing here, with cases of mysteries arising from human limitations.

2) Those things that have to do with the character of human consciousness, which is challenged by its ambivalent situations. Here, we are dealing with the human mind in its confluxing role as it seeks to harmonise all missing links as they mutate, form and transform.

3. Those things that remain mysterious to us because of hallucinations arising from impairment. These can be impairments, either of the mind or the body. There are four major kinds of impairment worthy of remembering. These are, nature induced impairment, person impairment, character induced impairment and substance in-

duced impairment. In nature induced impairment, we are dealing with that situation where a person suffers from various kinds of natural ailments that make actors amenable to manipulation. In person induced impairment, we are dealing with the art of mastery of those techniques needed to manipulate fellow human beings to bring them under our control contrary to their wills. In character induced impairment, we are dealing with defect or bad habits in a person's character. This are those cases when human beings due to excessive greediness, for example, can be manipulated easily by others. In substance induced impairment, we are dealing with those circumstances where due to intake of hallucinogens, like cocaine, heroin, opium, morphine, hashish etc a person is prone to illusions. The same is applicable to over consumption of alcoholic beverages, intake of other *unknown* hallucination inducing substances consisting of mineral, animal and plant extracts. I say unknown, bearing in mind the fact that there are such substances which may be known only to a limited circle of individuals. Worst still is when such substances are introduced into the human body through the agency of unsuspecting individuals, through manipulation and illicit means, as to induce desired effects.

4) Those things that remain unknown because they defy compliance to known natural laws as these laws become accessible to us through intuition or learning.

5) Those things that appear to us mysterious, because some individuals have created artificial conditions to make them appear so and to exploit the ignorance of victims for selfish interests. We are dealing here with cases of manipulation of given phenomena by those who have the requisite knowledge to make certain phenomena appear mysterious to the uninitiated. It is also the case, with members of secret societies, sororities and fraternities, who mystify certain phenomena with the intention of upholding some advantages for initiates.

6) Those things that would ever remain mysterious to us because we have been preconditioned through uncritical thinking arising from indoctrination and socialisation to regard them as such.

What is striking about most of these cases is that these are those moments when actors either follow rules crated by themselves alone, or are victims of impositions arising from outside influences. Problems arise when actors seek to interpret these situations without reference to the central position of human subject as a part of the totality. When the thinking subject is ignored, this is when issues of this nature are seen as matters that go beyond human intervention and not within the scope of human capabilities. These are precisely those moments also when some actors seek to carve out niches for themselves in view of exploiting others for their own selfish purposes. It is again those moments where due to paucity of information, actors behave in keeping with projections arising from their own minds.

One of the major characteristics of our raw primary cognitive ambience is that it supplies us with encrypted modes of addressing the world around us and supplies us with those things we assume are special or specific in the process of cognition. By so doing, this ambience evokes within communicators some impeccable feeling of security, which can influence the way they relate to the world generally. It is in view of the character of this ambience that most special epistemological paradigms and postulates can be creditably handled. To these belong those matters we consider special and restricted to outsiders. As phenomena that have special character and can be communicated through encrypted language, this framework makes all thinkable and imaginable phenomena and modes of being possible, provided they are affairs stakeholders identify as belonging to some special realm. They share the common characteristic of being encrypted and exclusivist. Over and above all, we are dealing with a situation where knowledge is brought into direct contact with power, such that, what is known, how we know it, and who knows what, is determined by who has the resources to decrypt encoded cognitive blocks in view of some advantages. Since it is on account of strict adherence to the dictates of our raw primary cognitive ambience that such encryption become relevant, actors endeavour to adhere to the empowerment bestowed by these special phenomena by making recourse to those resources needed to secure them. This is how it turns out that those who happen to master these phenomena, and the strategies needed to communicate them, have undue competitive advantages over others. Since acquaintance with these encrypted modes of communication, and familiarity with those phenomena that enhances their worth, generate within those thus empowered some feeling of security, they actually set out exploring new ways of guarding their advantages. Similarly, they employ all the mechanisms needed to safeguard these through creating artificial barriers and other restrictive devises to hold outsiders in check. Thus, these modes of encrypted phenomena turn out to have the character of cognitive blocks and postulates designed to gain some advantages in given asymmetrical situations. Where the subject has not taken time to be aware of the dangers such cognitive blocks, in their raw form can pose, it always runs the risk of misrepresenting reality massively. Worst still is when some of the major constituents of these cognitive blocks enter into what human beings assume are necessary for them to preserve themselves in the face of challenges. In this case, both the actor and the most depraved constituents of these cognitive blocks can become mutually reinforcing, as to produce a distorted picture of a reality that is mutually complementing. When these forces are negatively complementing, this is precisely the moment when the situation of the subject is complicated; a situation, which the actor considers as normal, but which in actual fact, leaves much to be desired. This is precisely also the moment and why this situation and the disproportionate expectations arising from it can evoke false hopes, extraordinary feelings and induce false pictures of reality that can be difficult to manage, but in the most disharmonious and world immanent pre-deterministic fashion, that can be both odd and dangerous.

14. On encrypted phenomena in their dynamism and pseudo-legitimate transformation strategies

Like most things that have pragmatic existential undertone, encrypted phenomena are best placed within the context of their expressiveness in view of understanding them better. Most matters that have to deal with human interest follow certain laws comparable to the basic laws of economics as this relates to demand and supply play very significant roles. As this relates to encrypted phenomena, we can then understand the character of mutation, evolution and adaptation characteristic of them as situations demand. Thus, under changed circumstances, these phenomena have the capacity of assuming various faces. The same is applicable to the meaning ascribed to them and the role they play in society. One of the greatest mistakes people make is to ascribe the same meaning to seemingly identical phenomena in changed circumstances. Where human consciousness is subjected to this error, it is likely to be entangled in illusions of no mean proportion. This is precisely when encrypted phenomena take deceptive outlooks that are quite removed from certain meanings actors usually attach to them. We see cases of this quite widespread today in diverse areas where people's needs suddenly run into conflict with their expectations and where they seek radical forms of deliverance. It may be deliverance of economic, psychological, religious or even ideological types. Worst still is when these problems are so intractable that they engender other problems to the extent that a victim becomes so entangled as to loose perspective. These are those victims most prone to exploitation. Here, we cannot underestimate the powerful role which religion can play in highly deprived and stressed conditions of near hopelessness. As a phenomenon, one of its major points of focus is the ultimate mysterious and the relief ensuing from therefrom. In this form, it offers itself as a breeding ground for all forms of attractive encryption that have the power to confound and to confuse. This is when in the name of religion encrypted pseudo-legitimate realities of pragmatic cognitive significances are projected in view of addressing certain needs comprehensively (Asouzu, The Impact of Pseudo-legitimate Strategies of Survival on Systems and Institutions). As a phenomenon that can easily be uprooted from some of the genuine ideas underlying it, it is very prone to misuse and manipulation. This is why modes of expression of religious phenomena keep mutating and adapting as situations demand. In the face of demand and supply, variants of similar phenomena easily contest for recognition and acceptance. This is how excessive fear and feeling of desolation have the capacity to create other phenomena, persons and instruments needed as countermeasure. It is in this sense that we can say that in changed situations, new trades, terminologies, problem-solving techniques arise and compete with each other for scarce resources. We can then understand why most phenomena that have a pseudo-legitimate dimension, make recourse to transformation strategies through which they give new meanings and create new actors in view of holding sway. Here, actors in each existential domain have unique ways of evolving terms, symbols and gestures to remain relevant. What is striking in these cases of recourse to transformation strategies is that familiar terms and modes of expression assume new meanings and significances as they help to solidify the encrypt. Hence, to uphold their edge against each other, some of these strategies, vying for position, develop special types of encrypt and solidify already existing ones. Here, they do not defy the basic laws of demand and supply, but help to confirm them. One can say that in matters of this nature, the more and better a strategy is rewarded, the bolder it becomes and the more the pretensions of those who employ them. Likewise, the more their success are rewarded, the more they gain in dynamism in view of mutating and assuming even unrecognisable faces. It is not only in the realm of religion that we encounter such cases, but also in all situations where people's expectations are deeply conflicting with the means needed to address them effectively.

There is no doubt that positive experiences can be won by recourse to encrypted phenomena This is when subjects use their special knowledge deriving from encrypted phenomena for some profitable purposes. In this case, the encrypted phenomena is identified as a means for positive self-actualisation and social transformation. Where this happens the mutual reinforcement between the object and its ambience can be positively reinforcement in view of producing rewarding results. Every human society needs people with extraordinary gifts and special training. Such people are to be found in almost all areas of life, be this in the economic, political or religious arenas. Here, psychologists, parapsychologists, psychiatrists, fortune-tellers, *dibias* or native doctor, who, due to their special type of knowledge and training, can deal creditable with some forms of special conditions. While giving an insight into the modus operandi of professional psychics, and with special reference to Harold McCoy,

Jerry Adler shows how through skill, commonsense, luck and other natural contingencies, these can be very useful in solving difficult puzzles. (Jerry Adler, Unlocking Minds 52). We are not then surprises when the services of people in some of these professions are highly cherished by individuals and complex organisations alike. Thus, consumer psychologists, when this must be, have proved indispensable for the prediction and monitoring of moods, consume pattern, likes and dislikes of consumers. The same thing is applicable to those who rely on the services of fortune-tellers and astrologers to unlock future mysteries. *Ikenga* served traditional Igbos in this capacity of looking into the future.

Admittedly, in the exercise of their functions, practitioners of these professions are expected to uphold modestly some trade secrets relating to their trade. This is normal as it can help them maintain a decent living, boost the ego and appease human vanity. This notwithstanding, their activities are expected to conform to certain rules guiding the affairs of mere mortals. One can say that in matters dealing with encrypted phenomena, the more the human element is pushed to the background, and the more the mythical, mystical extraordinary in the encrypted phenomena are emphasised, the more these phenomena are prone to abuses. Hence, measures taken to underplay the human element at the advantage of extrasensory phenomena are what it takes to solidify the encrypt. People who indulge in certain professions that have to deal with the mental extra sensuous may resemble themselves by their special gifts, but their methods of data collection, analysis and presentation of results may differ. This is where we start to make the distinction between the humans and the human-gods. Whereas, some in upholding their trade secrets, give clients reasons to assume that human ingenuity is at play, others, in upholding the same trade secrets, seek to absolutise the super sensuous mystifying, as the very phenomena that dictate to humans in a one dimensional absolute form. This is when the contractor easily assumes the form of the contract giver. When this happens humans play roles reserved to supernatural phenomena. Thus, the paradox of humans playing God is the foundation of all types of crisis of identity and misrepresentation.

What this means is that a mindset that sees things only in a one-dimensional absolute way always runs the risk of misrepresenting reality for what it is not. This danger is real, not only for those that assume that reality is purely spiritual, and devise all means to solidify the encrypt, but more so, for all who seek to approach reality in a disharmonious non-complementary way. The most pronounced are those who assume that the intellect alone has the capacity to provide us with a complete picture of the world. The same is applicable to those who assume that it is only the material sensuous that deserves human attention. One of the greatest difficulties generated by the introduction of bifurcating tendencies into inquiry is that, it gives us the impression that there is also a rigid distinction between what should qualify as orthodox science and what should be regarded as mere superstition. This is why for some, the spiritual supernatural tendencies seen in African philosophy is immediately tagged superstition. As tempting and justified such a conclusion can be sometimes, due to the type of secrecy inherent in such bifurcating approaches, we distinguish genuine science from all forms of superstition by reason of the approach adopted. All concerted attempts geared at polarising reality, in a one dimensional exclusivist absolute manner, qualify as superstition, due to the inherent illusions on which they are erected.

This is why in matters of this kind, what is known as orthodox science is equally threatened by the danger of excessive intellectualism, for which anything that cannot be explained rationally or empirically has to be rejected. On its part, spirit based supernaturalistic approaches give the impression that all matters dealing with the spiritual realities require special laws to penetrate them, outside of the framework provided by the mutual complementary relationship between all missing links. In all cases of superstitious approaches, the human reserve and pool of knowledge remains underexplored, since exclusiveness is seen as a methodological option. In this case, what is needed to attain full explanation and exploration of reality remains grossly under exploited. It is by placing phenomena within a wider epistemological framework of understanding that they can be creditably decoded and conflict potentials defused.

15. On encrypted phenomena, confluxing role of the subject and basic epistemological problems

Most of what we call special phenomena arise, not due to the singularity of their otherness, but due to the speciality of the conditions of their articulation. These conditions are not object-bound in the sense of being dictated by some special objects of inquiry. These specialities have to deal with the character of our being. For this reason, the answers sought must be geared towards specialities of this kind. We can say that the human person is a special type of being. Were we beings other than humans, then these problems would probably not present themselves in the way and intensity they do. However, since we are humans, we have to reckon with some problems that touch on the special conditions surround our humanity. Here, all humans share in these types of conditions without exception. Whoever thinks otherwise would be playing into Tempels' traps, which seeks to create special types of human beings that generate special types of problems. Hence, a credible approach to these problems would start with an analysis of the subject and the types of problems that are associated with it as a human being. Here, we are dealing with special conditions that are not restricted both in time and localisation. These are rather conditions that define the human person in the interiority of his being wherever we find one.

Therefore, it appears that all attempts at understanding reality, boils down at making serious efforts to understand the human person and the special position and conditions of the human person in world. Here, the human person turns out to be one of the major possessors of the codes needed to decrypt phenomena. What this means is that the human person itself is an intrinsic constituent of what needs to be explained when we are dealing with encrypted phenomena. The human person plays this significant role as *the conflux of all missing links.* Of all the things striking about the human person, some remain more significant than others do. To start with, humans are subjects that remain mysterious and open, accessible and inaccessible, personal and impersonal, all at the same time. Here, we are dealing with the human person, which in every challenging situations would usually prefer encrypted phenomena and languages in view of preserving its interests. This notwithstanding, it is a human person that would like to be serviced and handled like the rest all at the same time. Here, we are dealing with a human being that is not only benevolent and charming, it is also a human being that in its ambivalence, is naturally fascinated by the extraordinary, is adventurous, is curious, jealous, has the sense of fun and can pursue mischievousness in view of satisfying its fundamental instinct for pleasure and self-preservation. Besides, it is a subject that can be fearful, vengeful, provoking, can be compassionate, destructive, suspicious, self-justifying, capricious, can seek scapegoats, as it reflects the intrinsic dynamics of all missing links in their mutual complementary interrelatedness.

These facts as perplexing as they are, are also some of those that are easily forgotten when we are dealing with those phenomena that appear encrypted, inexplicable, incomprehensible, bewildering, mysterious and supernatural to us. What we can learn from this, is that in all matters dealing with a polarised approach to the world, the strategic role, which the human mind plays, cannot be underestimated. The mind as the conflux of the complementary relationship between all missing links is at the same time the place where the tension generated in such situations is most intensively felt. In other words, although the mind is the equilibrating faculty, it does not escape the challenges arising from the tension created by its ambivalent situations. On the contrary, it is drawn into this with greater intensity due to the centrality of its position as the epicentre of this harmony. Hence, in all matters involving extreme forms of bifurcation and division, the mind stands mostly challenged and stressed. This is why the mind in its attempt to represent the world, can misrepresent it to the deepest disillusionment and embarrassment of both the actors and all stakeholders.

Any philosophy that delves into the mysterious, into the unknown and the incomprehensible must reckon with the special character of its inquiry. This special character must not be object-bound but has to proceed from the special character of the human person, as a being of multiple allegiances. Those who view the spiritual supernatural as if these deserve special attention also create the impression that theirs is a special type of philosophy destined for special types of human persons. However, the speciality they are seeking is not one that has to deal with special types of subject matters, since all philosophies have to deal with reality in the immensity of its incomprehensiveness. In this form, all realities have a special character, since they always have those aspects of themselves that remain incomprehensible and unknown. Here, the human person as the conflux of all missing links can help us shed some light into the character of the unknown, if we first embark on a process of critical self-analysis. When this happens, we discover that the thinking subject turns immediately to one of the most encrypted phenomena that remain incomprehensible such that to elucidate or decrypt what is encrypted entails starting from the base. In this sense, the ego, as an extension of the incomprehensible encrypted, shares the primary focus of our attention in all matters dealing with encrypted phenomena. In this matter, philosophy is naturally devoted to the spiritual supernatural and encrypted phenomena, not as things special, but as things that belong intrinsically to its subject matter, due to its concern with all missing links of reality. It is for this reason that the philosopher seeks to understand what is normal in the special, what is natural in the supernatural etc. The moment we lose focus of the complementary character of all philosophical inquiries, that is the moment we seek to segment reality and with it the subject matter of our inquiry. Should this happen, then, we may be tempted to concentrate only on what we assume is the special, and forget the subject matter of philosophy all together. This is the moment we declare the spiritual to be the subject matter of our inquiry and nothing more. Contrary to this approach, the subject matter of philosophy is all embracing, as all missing links cohere to form a mutual complementary whole. In taking this stand, we recognise the position of the subject as the conflux of all missing links in the comprehensiveness of their interrelatedness and complexity of their being.

Since many assume that typical African experiences, have to deal with spiritual supernatural encrypted phenomena only, they immediately also tend to position this outside the range of the subject matter of philosophy, as this deals with all missing links in their mutual complementary interrelatedness. This is when they seek also special types of answers to problems ensuing from the special subject matter they have created for themselves. Thus, if one of the central problems of epistemology can be affixed in the question, to what extent can the mind know without reference to sense impression, a typical epistemological question within what many assume is the context of African existential experience is: How far can the human mind know without the intervention of supernatural forces and other forms of manipulations? For many, the answer, within this African context would definitely be that the mind cannot know without recourse to any external aid and cannot be itself unless it is manipulated. What this means is that the knowing subject always needs some external aid in order to know and attain higher levels of self-actualisation, even if this implies relying on manipulation. This is a very precarious answer. With this answer, we are dealing with a situation where obscurantism and manipulation are easily elevated to explicative methodological principles and accepted pragmatics of social dynamics.

As far-fetched as this may sound, this assumption appears to be at the foundation of the existential pragmatic that determines human action within the African context. This is consequent of a milieu that is deeply committed to an epistemology of bifurcation and embraces concealment as a methodological option. We can then understand why this approach to reality stays in diametrical opposition to a complementary approach, which lays much emphasis on mutual linkage between units in a comprehensive future related way. Through recourse to encrypted phenomena and language, actors create a bulwark around themselves. By so doing, they limit the range of what we know, how we know it, and what happens with what we know. The same thing obtains with regard to what can be explained and how we explain it. In this way, they can easily become an obstacle to creative inquiry, positive social changes and transformation ensuing from the linkage between all the actors and factors in their mutual complementary interrelatedness.

As this matter concerns African experience of the world particularly, there is no gainsaying the fact that phenomena of spiritual supernatural character are prevalent in African societies, both traditional and modern. This prevalence is not something unusual if one considers the fact that human beings seek solutions to their problems in tune with their level of enlightenment and given socio-economic conditions. What is unusual is when the impression is given that this mode of relating to the world should be interminable as it constitutes a typical and special type of African experience. When we think in this way, we seem to imply that the African cannot know beyond enforced codes and manipulation. Generally, humans are beings that seek remedies in tune with given conditions and not outside of this. It is for this reason, that we can understand the prevalence of some codes of conduct when certain conditions are given. We cannot from these draw generalisations that no changes can ever occur under changed conditions and in newer environments. Faced with the complexity of the problem, as it relates to incomplete knowledge of the aims guiding our actions and insufficiency of the means needed to realise them, we cannot pretend that our limited and deficient problem-solving techniques are always adequate to handle some complex matters. Where we think this way, we would also do everything in our power to manipulate the limited means at our disposal, just as we seek to distort the aims to suit our means. Here, common sense shows that some complex problems can be better handled within the context of the enormous potentials and resources accruing from the mutual complementary dependence of all actors and factors. Where one ignores such enormous resources accruing from this mutual complementary linkage, there is reasons to question any strategies devised to achieve certain objectives.

Naturally, an unenlightened, highly constrained and relatively illiterate situation, as we have this in most traditional African societies, is bound to pursue matters with a mindset akin to its conditions. Even here, common sense demands that problem solving techniques have to explore all the viable options thinkable. Unfortunately, due to the character of this social setup, exploring such devises and strategies was not always possible, due to the constraints placed by prevalence of encrypted phenomena themselves. These are problem-solving techniques, which are seen as unquestioned dogmas in traditional African existential living. In changed situations, as we have this today, it would be myopic and grossly irresponsible to assume that the same techniques would be sufficient to address the similar problems in changed circumstances. In changed more sophisticated circumstances, the same phenomena are very likely to assume new forms and address more complex motives than those driving them in their raw primary cognitive ambiences. Hence, to assume that issues relating to encrypted phenomena can be approached with the same techniques as we have these in traditional African societies is to be threading the part of illusion. Phenomena gather momentum, get new meanings and are subject to diverse laws as historical conditions change. This is why most matters that remain mysterious to us have to be adjusted to new conditions and handled within a wider framework of understanding. It is in view of these changes and adaptations that the encrypted languages and codes surrounding them can be better understood and if possible decoded. Hence, the moment we try to give a homogenous account of known phenomena, bundle them into known clichés, that is the moment we solidify the codes in which they are immersed. Hence, to understand encrypted languages and the phenomena that sustain them, we have to expose them to as many keys as possible. This is the advantage of placing them within a wider framework of relations ensuing from the mutual complementary interrelatedness of all missing links.

In handling such complex issues, it is important to note that African experience of the world is in no way unique in being challenged by superstitions arising from the resistance posed by its raw primary cognitive ambience. We find diverse modes of superstitious practices, incredible beliefs and weird ideas quite widespread among diverse peoples of the world due to unbending adherence to the insinuations of one's raw primary cognitive ambience. Where we are successful in aligning our world to its wider complementary ambience, chances are that our relationship to those encrypted languages and phenomena would change massively. Where we ignore those positive factors that have the capacity to transform our raw primary ambience, these encrypted meanings and the forces behind them would remain perpetually immune and resistant to change. To such positive factors include alternative educational methods, openness to alternative paradigms, readiness to learn and accept new ideas, resisting the temptations to be dogmatic about certain creeds etc. This is why we said that our raw primary cognitive is validated by being in mutual complementary dependence with all missing links of reality. Where this mutual complementary dependence is ignored, we can hardly talk of betterment of any sort. We contribute to upholding the status quo when those matters that concern us most assume that overbearing character that renders them unique to the point of absurdity. We can therefore say that problem solving techniques in vogues in any given society and the range of success with regard to breaking sealed codes are in tune with the level of complementary exposure obtainable in such a society. Most matters that have mysterious characters and significances become truly human problems when they are handled within a wider framework of all the actors and factors that constitute the missing links of reality. Remove this type of mutual complementary determination, most issues would remain mysterious and encrypted, since they cannot be grasped fully within the context of their determination. In mutual complementary dependence, human beings deepen their knowledge about all missing links, refine their problem solving techniques, seek better answers and unite in calling evil by name, just as they congregate to reward and celebrate goodness.

Humans are beings that have always grappled with complex problems. More often than not, these problems are so mutually related that to isolate them from each other merely helps to deepen them. This is why spiritual problems cannot be handled in isolation of the economic, psychological, psychiatric, and other dimensions of the same problem, when the requisite means are given. To act as if the subject is a monad enclosed in itself, and for itself alone, is to distort the image of the human person. This can have very grievous consequences as it can help to solidify encrypted languages and phenomena restricting social progress. Hence, in all contentious situations, it pays to discover the human person for what it is in the comprehensiveness of its complementarity determination and not in the fragmentations of its polarisation. This manner of fragmentation ensues the moment we isolate the human being from the complex network of all missing links that enter into its determination and treat its problems as if they are unique in any given location. Where the problems and techniques needed to address them are seen only in the uniqueness of their composition, the tendency is to act as if these problems and the techniques needed to address them are not natural but supernatural ones. The moment we do not identify them as human problems, we run the risk of not tapping fully into known human resources and potentials needed to address them. In other words, we can hardly improve on the human condition if we segment our conceptualisation of reality and thereby segment our approach to such issues. The human condition can be improved upon if we harness all the actors and factors at our disposal bearing in mind the enormous recourses ensuing from the mutual complementary dependence between them.

16. On encrypted phenomena and context of explanation

An important question that remains to be answered is how we can validate the claims connected with these encrypted phenomena. In matters dealing with encrypted phenomena, most researchers give the impression that there is actually an internal division within reality itself such that what is needed to be explained has no intrinsic relationship to all the actors and factors in their complementary mutual interrelatedness. In this case, they assume that what is needed to be explained has only a restricted validity bestowed by prerogative of some special type of knowledge. This is when a necessary intrinsic mode of relationship is established between the explainer and phenomena, between those claimants of superior knowledge, encrypted phenomena and some limited circles of individuals and institution. The moment we divorce what is to be explained from the wider framework of its articulations that is the moment they continue to relapse into obscurity and create more problems. Hence, no phenomena claiming special status can be divorced from the special character of reality itself which can be grasped creditably only within the context of mutual complementary relationship. It is only in this mode that all encrypted phenomena can be seen as things serving pragmatic cognitive postulates geared towards comprehensive explanation. It is when researchers seek to consign these phenomena only to their explicative worth within fixed ambits, as these are dictated by the raw primary cognitive ambience, that most complications arise. Such a fragmented procedure has its own special problems, insofar as it can create phenomena that stay in a disjointed relationship with each other beyond the internal mutual complementary necessary link that gives reality its internal harmony. When encrypted realities such as matters dealing with witches, wizards, magic, *ogwu,* charms, sorcery, oracle, divination, myriad of supernatural forces, are handled only within the dictates of our raw primary cognitive ambience, there is always the danger of superimposing encrypted cognitive categories drawn from the same ambience and such that make understanding and explanation difficult if not impossible. Since these phenomena remain encrypted, the philosopher is interested in the types of claims we seek to make through recourse to them, bearing in mind always the complementary mode of reality in its entire ramification. Since reality keeps unfolding its internal character and continues to make itself felt interminably, both at the physical and metaphysical domains, it would be futile to indulge in apodictic proofs or denials of certain types of phenomena, most especially when they are encrypted.

This notwithstanding, in most matters relating to the nature and epistemological status of most of these encrypted phenomena, we may agree or disagree as to how we feel or do not feel about their impact. We may agree or disagree about their nature and modes of operation depending on the state of our minds, levels of education, socialisation and indoctrination. However, there is one area where, probably, we would be inclined to agree: That is in the area of the legitimising role which they play in given circumstances. Generally, most spiritual supernatural phenomena, for example, have much to do with alternative paradigms for better ways of doing things in the world. In this role, they seek to satisfy positive expectations, fill desires that are lacking or are summoned towards eliminating those conditions that can be considered repugnant or unpleasant. In the case of Nigeria, for example, such conditions are met by recourse to such phenomena as spirits, charms, mermaid, jujus, divination, consultation of oracles, miracle healing, sorcery, magic, witchcrafts etc. These are those phenomena that continue to play some dominant roles in the lives of people and in faces of challenges. These phenomena fall within the domain of the type of ideal perfect world many always desire. It would be a big mistake to regard these as purposeless, obscure and superstitious phenomena lacking in content and merit. These phenomena seek to make some definite statements about the lives of people and about events. Beyond what is seen, lies something to be comprehended. One of the outstanding underlying purposes that drives and sustains them, is their claims to provide a better world and alternative paradigms for truth, equity, justice, reward, punishment, fair play etc. More often than not, they have the implicit claims of addressing issues in a more perfect, unbiased and non-contradictory ways and in view of the overall well-being of the individual, groups and society at large. As alternatives and more promising means of conflict resolution, for the individual, families, communities and society at large, they are attractive, popular, sought after, and patronised. Hence, they are often seen as alternatives to what many have come to designate as our inefficient, unreliable and corrupt human systems in those issues that matter most. In this capacity, such phenomena are seen as representatives of all the power that be

As extraordinary and alternatives paradigms, their truth claims would naturally depend more, not on those purposes they serve best - on those matters where they excel and are very successful - but on those instances where they fail and are found wanting. In other words, they are supposed to be above board in all matters relating to human overall welfare, as these relate to the harmony of all missing links in their mutual interrelatedness. In other words, to uphold their legitimacy, they are expected to supersede all human insufficient, both personally and system wise. We can then say that in view of validating their claims, they must address the human conditions in the comprehensiveness of their interrelatedness and not in the fragmentation of their otherness. In practical terms, any supernatural instance that stands for justice cannot be instrumental for injustice and should not be manipulated in anyway whatsoever to attain unjust ends. An instance that stands for the protection of lives and property should do so across board and not be selective. Those that stand for vengeance, have to do so in view of upholding harmony between all missing links. For this reason, if the claims of any given supernatural instance are geared towards security of lives and property, justice, peace, prosperity etc, this has to be as comprehensive as possible, otherwise, its claims easily negate the aim establishing it.

Hence, where the modus operandi of any given spiritual supernatural instance or of any acclaimed encrypted phenomena is selective, inconsistent and contradictory, there are reasons also to doubt the foundation on which it stands. Where such a negative moments are in place, we have reasons to believe that these are mere extension of a corrupt social system manipulated by those who have the advantage of power. Such power can be due to better insights into the mode of operation of certain natural laws that remain foreclosed to outsiders. In such asymmetrical cases, those who have the advantage of insight often use it for their own selfish purposes and to the detriment of others. Evidently, there are reasons to assume that in those cases involving inconsistencies, we are dealing with matters of genuine epistemological logical forms, within the range of philosophy, and not with purely supernatural puzzles.

All modes of encrypted phenomena have the capacity to introduce a divide in the human consciousness due to the special claims attached to their modes of existence. When this happens, we are dealing with a typical case of encrypted rationality. One of the greatest challenged we face in such a situation is how to restore human consciousness to a balanced state such that the tension ensuing from this type of rationality can be manageable. In all matters, complementary ontology aims at the re-empowerment of the mind, which may be so challenged in such situations that it easily succumbs to trappings of our raw cognitive ambience, which is restrictive, exclusivist and illusion inducing. This re-empowerment takes place through the process of complementary transcendent existential conversion or *being-in control (ima-onwe-onye).* Without this act, our world turns mysterious, deceitful, incomprehensible, challenging and dreadful. This re-empowerment can hardly happen where actors assume that their raw cognitive ambience is the most real world accessible to them. Thus, restoring this balance ensues the moment actors are aware of the mutual complementary mode of relationship between all missing links and are ready to embrace this. In this awareness can be located *being-in-control* of the ambivalence generated by all human existential situations. This is how to be entails all the processes put in place to ensure that all missing links remain harmonised. Where this complementary awareness is lacking dangers are that human approach to the world would ever remain as divided as ever. In all cases where complementary rationality is absent, the future referential dimension of reality is hardly taken into account.

Since philosophy, as wisdom, has also an unmistakable instructive, illuminative and pedagogical task, it would be very unwise to deny the existence of supernatural phenomena bearing in mind the capacity of the human mind to mutate and transform as the conflux of all missing links. In this capacity, the mind has the capacity to assume any of its numerous modes of expression, including the most benevolent and compassionate. It can at the same time degenerate to the lowest abyss of wickedness and absurdity. Bearing this in mind, our approach to the mysterious unknown has to be done in the mindset of philosophical scepticism and openness all at the same time. It is in this double attitude that all missing links in the comprehensiveness of their interrelatedness can be penetrated, as they remain both open and closed to each other. Here, we approach the unknown mysterious with utmost scepticism, to hold gullibility in check. We approach the unknown mysterious with openness, since reality in its fragmentation has an inherent dimension of surprises. We approach the unknown mysterious with utmost caution, lest we become cheap victims of our scepticism and gullibility. This notwithstanding, those things we do not have sufficient knowledge about would always tend to remain mysterious, awe-inspiring, bewildering and fascinating to us. It is for this reason, that the rule of thumb should always hold sway. First, we should always allow the principle of interdisciplinarity to apply as much as possible. Here, we have to allow the law enforcement agents, psychologists, psychiatrists, and criminologists etc. to do their job when this becomes necessary. I would even say, in majority of the cases. Second, to understand the mysteries behind the modus operandi of most matters we designate as spiritual supernatural would be equivalent to understanding the mysteries behind the active ingredients that give Coca Cola its peculiar taste or demanding that the mysteries behind a well-guarded patent be laid bare. These are well-guarded secrets accessible to insiders and would remain mysteries to untutored minds. Third, no one should underestimate the determination of criminals or very shrewd individuals and groups who have learnt how to manipulate physical laws to their advantage to exploit these to the full in very challenged situations. Fourth, in most contentious situations, we are not dealing with mysteries beyond human comprehension. In such matters, we should never underestimate the impacts arising from stressed and dysfunctional social systems and institutions in dire need of overhaul. The same is applicable to those challenges arising from much stressed psyche brought about by unfulfilled wants and expectations. Finally, bearing in mind the incommensurability of reality, not all matters that have to deal with supernatural forces, and all those spiritual super-sensible conjectures, are truly special philosophical issues. To overcome all forms of world immanent pre-deterministic supernaturalism inherent in commitment to most forms of encrypted phenomena, there is need to create a conceptual framework that guarantees some measure of freedom of action and of reasoning for all stakeholders. As long as the powers of the explainer to give meaning to what is needed to be explained is drawn from the same mysterious foundation, all matters relating to such supernatural milieu would remain perpetually shrouded in mystery. The same is applicable when those seeking information or are in need are totally at the mercy of the explainer.

This notwithstanding, since human knowledge is limited and reality continues unfolding itself daily, there is room always for genuine and pleasant surprises. Such genuine surprises have to be seen as those exceptions that justify the rule and not those rules that defy rational explanation as to be declared supernatural and something beyond the meddling of mere mortals. Thus, it is in mutual complementarity of our efforts that we can address problems arising from encrypted phenomena adequately.

Here Aristotle's observation is very instructive "no one is able to attain the truth adequately, while, on the other hand, we do not collectively fail, but every one says something true about the nature of things, and while individually we contribute little or nothing to the truth, by the union of Perhaps, too, as difficulties are of two kinds, the cause of all a considerable amount is amassed" (*Metaphysica* BOOK a1).

17. On decoding the encrypt, complementary noetic propaedeutic and effective legal system

Momoh's understanding that the main fulcrum of African worldview is that reality is spiritual may even be seen as a statement of fact, which captures very vividly the type of encrypted mindset with which most Africans seek to grapple with the realities of life. Such approach is very common and concerns not only challenges of daily living, but also those relating to more complicated types of solutions involving scientists and specialists. Here, I quite agree with Umorem, who quoting Ukoli observes, "What is more disturbing, and which perhaps may undermine any success in the achievement of the goals of science/technological education in Nigeria, is the fact that even the educated elite including practicing scientists, are still under the influence of their traditional beliefs especially in times of crisis, even when logical and rational scientific explanations are available. ... Those of them who have renounced their traditional cosmology have developed an unquestioning belief and faith in some other supernatural forces as preached by their new religions" (19).Where this challenged bifurcating attitude to reality holds sway, the consequences cannot be underestimated.

Most especially within the African context of consideration, it is important to note that not all phenomena that many seem to project to philosophical importance deserve the attention expanded on them philosophically. In some of these cases, we are dealing with matters requiring rudimentary enlightenment about some natural phenomena and occurrences. More often than not, we are dealing with cases where those who have advantages of insight concerning how to manipulate some natural causes, events and phenomena use their superior knowledge to gain undue advantages over others. These are those cases, where human beings withhold some pieces of information from others to exercise undue power over them. The human nature is such that those who know how to manipulate the laws of nature often use their knowledge for either the benefits or disadvantages of others. Where human beings have not learnt to be in control of the ambivalence of their existential situations, chances are that they seek to exploit the benefit of insight to the detriment of non-initiates. In most asymmetrical situations of power imbalance, those who know often misuse their privileged positions to exploit others. The human consciousness is such that it can always be manipulated time without number for the same mistakes, expectations and unfulfilled wishes, at similar times and places. Not to acknowledge this fact is denying our humanity. This is why in view of this recurrent blunder there is dire need to undertake measures needed to enlighten the mind in view of its own internal constraints and those arising from the outside. This can be achieved by recourse to those measures needed to protect the individual and society from undue exploitation. Here, the roles, which a noetic propaedeutic plays cannot be under rated. In this case, such a propaedeutic has be an integral aspect of mass literacy education. The same is applicable to having an effective legal system and the mechanisms of control needed for law enforcement. All forms of noetic propaedeutic ensuing in the process of mass literacy are fundamental human rights that help to strengthen the mind and thereby embower the subject to attain some level of autonomy, including freedom from undue exploitation. The ultimate aim of a complementary noetic propaedeutic is to prepare the subject to face the realities of life harmonised from within. In the process of such education, thinking subjects learn to define their interests within the framework of totality. Where this type of mindset is prevalent actors learn to set their priorities right and to see each other as aspects of the same totality. In the absence of this form of education, actors would hardly use available resources for the betterment of all. On the contrary, they would tend to see human coexistence as a form of struggle where the feats is destined to survive. Within such contexts, even if governments and communities have all the resources needed to cater for the welfare of their members, those few that are in power avail themselves of any given opportunities to enrich themselves at the expense of the generality. It is in such situations that we are confronted with cases of the paradox of abject poverty in the midst of plenty. This is specifically why a complementary comprehensive type of mass literacy becomes indispensable should subjects acquire the necessary tools towards mastering the challenges of existence creditably.

Now, those who insist that for the African reality is spiritual, indirectly subscribe to the notion that for the African reality is encrypted. However, to ignore the fact that such matters exist in all human societies, and that human beings have always sought ways of handling them, is trying to impose non-human categories on human conditions. It is again not realistic to ignore the fact that there are better ways of handling such matters, where the requisite determination and openness are given. The question in the case of Africa, where we assume that reality is basically encrypted, is by whom and who has the keys to decrypt them? In traditional African societies, it is easier to know whose codes we are following and where the keys are to be found. One of the most difficult problems with contemporary African situations is to know and define clearly who the masters of the keys are, and the types of algorithms they use. This can be a Herculean task. The issue becomes all the more complicated if we remember that within this context of explanation, it is now taken for granted that the knowing subject always needs some external aid in order to know and attain higher levels of self actualisation. Over and above all, it is almost an accepted dogma within this milieu that to address complex human problems, recourse to manipulation and devious means is a valid methodological option. With this, we appear to be giving an old method an official stamp of approval; this is that approach in traditional African societies that tries to glorify the mysterious supernatural and is deeply committed to the efficacy of encrypted spiritual super-sensible, for very obvious reasons. Even then, in our contemporary situation, new conditions have been created and attached to the old order. Within this contemporary situation, both encrypted phenomena and the persons empowered to know the codes have gone tremendous transformation. With this, what we have is a situation where those entitled to explicate the code have assumed such an amorphous character as to complicate the character of the mysteries. In matters of this nature, it is often important to note that the symbols and encryption keys can appear dissimilar but the objectives and the effects they produce remain almost the same. Hence, if we approach old problems with old mindset, not putting into account the new conditions that have been added, we are bound to err grievously in our explanation.

Generally, in the use of these encryption mechanisms, actors seek undue advantages over others in asymmetrical situations of power imbalance. Since this is a human problem and not an African problem as such, they can be addressed creditably when human beings pool their resources together. However, when we assume that spiritual supernatural phenomena are peculiar to African experience, we indirectly subscribe to the idea that such matters cannot be handled based on the resources accruing from the growth of knowledge made possible by the mutual complementary relationship between all missing links of reality. In this case, the African has to find solutions in a world it has created for itself in utter negation of the general human resources. Based on such assumptions, we are led to conclude also that the African consciousness follows a completely different standards and such that deserve very different sets of rules. These are those assumptions that create the impression that solutions to most African problems must be peculiar and that superstitious practices and beliefs are allowable integral aspects of African experience of reality. With this, we are forced to accept that the pool of knowledge available to humanity stops at the doorsteps of Africans because this does not concern them. If a person thinks that he has not laboured for something, it is most unjust to reap from the results. However, we know that our world cannot be thought of except in terms of mutual complementary dependence. Here, Africans have much to benefit from the resources of others and this as a natural right. Likewise, others have a right to benefit from African experience of the world. Where, we do not think this way, all our actions are bound to boomerang either for good or for worst. Where one is not in tune with this mode of complementary attitude to reality, the tendency is always to seek one's own unique ways of solving problems. When this happens, one is bound to live with one's unique types of solutions. This attitude to the problem can grossly impoverish our world and weaken our position. On the other hand, we stand to flourish greatly if we have the capacity to tap into the enormous positive resources of the world. It would be a big mistake not to recognise that we have a stake in the vast pool of knowledge and resources at the disposal of humanity at any given moment. Since we are entitled to this pool of knowledge, we would be undercutting our opportunities as to be living in an impoverished world we have created for ourselves.

Approaching matters of this nature with an exclusivist mindset seems to ignore the natural propensity of the subject to capitalise on the advantages accruing from its faithful compliance to the demands of the moment. This is when actors prefer to act after what they consider as the empowerment bestowed by encrypted phenomena not minding other more refined modes of addressing the same matters. This can explain why the changes brought by Western influence notwithstanding, many Africans prefer those codes of conduct that have the capacity of giving them an edge in asymmetrical situations. In Nigeria, for example, even if people are ready to imitate Western lifestyle in most matters of everyday concern, they still prefer to fall back on those negative forces drawing from their raw cognitive ambiences, in view of achieving some set objectives. Thus, even if many are aware that wealth can be made through adherence to the rules governing market economics, they prefer those acts dictated by the encrypted phenomena based on which they can manoeuvre and manipulate more easily. It is due to this, that one can all the more understand why there is today very high increase in all those practices that have to deal with money doubling, ritual killing, cult activities, secret societies and most acts geared towards the quickest ways of wealth generation, and the overall improvement of the welfare of the individual. Even if people know that money can be made through honest savings, honest investment opportunities, through creativity and hard work, they still assume that there are other ways still quicker and surest, as these are facilitated by encrypted phenomena, supernatural powers, diverse forms of external intervention and manipulation. In very gullible and stressed circumstances, success is often guaranteed which boosts the criminal energies to be creative in devious means needed to dupe and exploit. The same can be said of diverse forms of obsessive behaviour geared towards overall empowerment of the individual. These can be seen as typical cases of embracing those codes that guarantee the survival of the individual, as these serve some pragmatic cognitive postulates.

It is important to remark that spirits and supernatural phenomena as encrypted phenomena can play similar roles in dissimilar contexts, while retaining their characters as encrypted pragmatic cognitive postulates. This is precisely how the role they play in traditional African environments cannot be equated, without qualification, to the roles the play in changed contemporary circumstances. The same is still the case, even if in both cases they serve as pragmatic cognitive postulates. In all cases, the meanings and types of encryption brought to bear on reality may vary, but the overall effects can remain the same. Since in most contexts, recourse to these pragmatic cognitive postulates appears to be the surest and easiest ways of upholding power asymmetry, they would ever remain attractive. Generally, those, who are empowered by means of these encrypted phenomena, would tend to reject and scorn at all solutions that have human origin, as they endeavour to devise more complex ways of keeping the codes secure and intact. This is valid, not only for traditional African conditions, but more so, for contemporary African situations. Thus, our raw primary cognitive ambience is the domain of the obscure exclusivist mysteries, the realm that cordons off intervention, as it condones encrypted phenomena in view of seeking permanent security for insiders.

We can say that in most situations, these near extraordinary experiences and occurrences are instances of deep asymmetry as these concern the relationship of human beings to each other and to the world in general. More often than not, we are dealing with cases of arbitrary incursion into the operations of the mind, in view of steering and manipulating these operations to gain personal advantages and at the expense of others. They can also be cases where we seek to employ our superior knowledge for the betterment of the lot of our fellow human beings. However, due to the promptings of our instinct of self-preservation, we seek to shroud our actions in mysteries and codes to hold sway. Such a supercharged situation has all it takes to create tensions and illusions of all kinds. Hence, a milieu that assumes that "reality is spiritual", without qualification, has all the potentials to create such asymmetrical conditions geared towards personal empowerment. Any milieu that polarises reality, sees the world in the spiritual-material, soul-body, mater-form, intellect-sense ontological bracket only, has all it takes to complicate matters for human consciousness. Where the subject identifies the spiritual supernatural as its main realm, it would invariably also seek spiritual remedies for most challenging problems in total negation of the mutual complementary comprehensive constitution of reality. It is due to bifurcating tendencies of this type, be it of the purely spiritual type, and be it of the purely material type that most human problems hardly find any credible solutions. It is a situation where an artificial division has been introduced into the centre of human consciousness, and such that makes the subject prone to illusions, leads it astray, and throws it off balance.

Thus, the epistemological values of encrypted phenomena and their pragmatic cognitive relevance are better handled within a wider complementary cognitive ambience. It is within this ambience that we have as many keys as may become necessary towards unlocking the meaning enshrined in these hard-to-crack codes. When approached within this wider complementary ambience, and bearing in mind their relevance for all the actors and factors involved, better conditions can be created in view of appreciating the true characters of these phenomena. When this happens, we come to realise that some of these phenomena would turn out to enshrine human genuine longing for the absolute. Others would be cases of hallucination, some genuine cases of psychiatric illnesses, still others clear cases of illusions caused by sheer ignorance and greed. Still others, those rare phenomena and occurrences whose nature need time, resources and perseverance to understand. We find most of these cases in all human cultures fully represented and most cultures have devised means towards addressing them. In some cases very successfully and creditably. It would be a big mistake to assume that these solutions are culture bound and as such cannot be of any use in our own cases. On the contrary, they can always be useful towards solving similar problems within other contexts. Where we assume that ours is peculiar, and as such the method needed to address them must also differ from those obtainable elsewhere, that is the moment we endorse ignorance for knowledge and adopt manipulation and deceit as operational principles of action. Here, philosophy, as wisdom, stands to point out the various ways in which the encoded phenomena can be decoded, and the need to complement our efforts in view of searching for the best keys available, and rejecting those that are not to the best interests of the subject, bearing in mind the deep affinity these interests have for all missing links.

In crucial matters of this nature, it may sometimes be useful relying on some insights and clues provided by insiders themselves. Here the attitude of the Aros in the case of the dreaded Ibinukpabi may be very instructive. Thus "there is a saying by the Aros that Nwa Aro *adighi asi ibe ya Ibinukpabia ajuola* gi – Aro does not intimidate his fellow Aro man by telling him Ibinukpabi asked of you" (Nwala 91). Similarly the Fanti caution 'Nananom npow nyimpa na woyeé (The mysteries surrounding the grove of the dead fathers were created by men) (Oguah, African and Western Philosophy 219). In the case of the Aros, these were the custodians of *Ibinukpabi*, the greatest and most dreaded of Igbo oracles during its time. Aros as insiders knew very well that the whole affair was a hoax design to exploit and intimidate. As the source of Aro wealth, this oracle can be considered their trade secret and to reveal its mode of operation is comparable today to stealing the trade secret of a company. Where such issues are today considered as economic crimes, punishable by legalised sanctions, they were tagged abominations within the context of oracular consultation. Where such matters are today issues of litigation, to be settled by heavy fines, restitution and prohibitions, within the framework of oracular consultation, they are considered as sacred infringements atonable by severest punishments not excluding capital punishment to intimidate and conserve special privileges. When what is considered as supernatural turns out to be a smokescreen for guarding trade secrets, we are dealing with typical cases of world immanent missing links being elevated to the status of the absolute and serving human interests at the expense of other stakeholders. Since the human nature hardly changes, even in changed circumstances, there is need to bear in mind always such crucial cases as those of the *Aros* due to the enormity of its influence and how widespread the lies were believed.

One who has taught metaphysics or epistemology in most Nigerian institutions of higher learning knows that one of the greatest challenges is to find the foundation on which to erect or impact unbiased knowledge beyond the common rumours and beliefs in circulation. This is that situation where the subject and its ambience remain in a relationship of negative mutual reinforcement. The situation is still worst when actors have not learnt to define themselves within a wider complementary ambience but insist on accepting the promptings of their raw primary cognitive ambience as dogmas of epistemology and action. This is that situation where most young people believe that the world is populated by spirits of indescribable kinds, mostly malevolent kinds, just as most adults assume this to be the case and as they hear these circulated in their locations. They believe in most of the fantastic and horror stories they see in most of those movies being circulated today by the nascent Nigerian movie industry, Nollywood. In this case, many are almost unable to make the distinction between fact and fiction. The bias is so strong that questioning these stories is like trying to break taboos or questioning indubitable dogmas. Here, there is hardly any difference between the language of fact and language of fiction and analogy. The same is the lack of distinction between symbols, metaphors and what they stand for. This is when anthropomorphism turns to real conjectures. It is this type of impetuous mindset that prefers the huts and hideouts of witchdoctors, medicine men and women, diviners and seers in the resolution of most complex and knotty problems. This is that mindset that believes in the efficacy of enshrouded phenomena in view of unmitigated empowerment. In this way, cult mentality easily supplants real scientific mindset and cult practices easily mistaken for real scientific culture.

More often than not, most complex matters relating to encrypted phenomena have to deal with a milieu that believes on the advantages that encrypted language and phenomena bestow. These are those forces that many assume bestow unparalleled advantages in asymmetrical situations of power imbalance. Due to its sensibility about its unique position and the privileges these bestow, actors seek to endorse such phenomena. It is for this reason that those who have advantage of power can easily become resistant to any mechanisms devised to break its codes, be this from within or from without. In this case, actors would do anything imaginable to uphold the status quo ante through recourse to more complex algorithms that translate to those mechanisms devised to undermine due processes of law and order. Hence, what is most striking and disturbing about those cases involving mysterious phenomena of the spiritual supernatural type is its disregard and contempt for positive human resourcefulness and exposure of the subject to a wider world in view of seeking solutions. This is its secretive, intransigent and manipulative dimension. Hence, when weighed against the aims driving them, one easily understands the types of encrypted pragmatic roles these beliefs and practices are capable of playing. It is not one reducible to a common denominator as to require a unified pattern of philosophical attention and explanation. In Nigeria, for example, it is stunning that most individuals raised in this milieu are quite open and tolerant to most of those positive changes coming from the outside, most especially from the West. In spite of this openness, there is visible unalloyed loyalty to the internal forces of encryption from which they draw their strength. This is mostly the case, when human beings do not believe in positive ways of changing their existence, but insist on believing that extraordinary achievements and feats can only be attained through fraud and questionable means. Here, recourse to these encrypted phenomena turns out to highly preferred means of achieving success. This is that mentality that hardly believes in attaining great heights through hard work and perseverance, but insists on pursuing set goals through those devious and questionable means that are readily available and home-made. These are those cases, where people capitalise on an already sick social system and exploit some of its weakest points to advance their personal interests. It is an encrypted mode of exploiting the system at its weakest moments and manipulating those means that help the ego attain set objective quickest, with less risks and at the expense of other.

As long as people get what they want, can easily circumvent the laws, are not easily held accountable for their crimes, most phenomena that remain mysterious to us would endure and the mysteries deepened. The same is applicable to those unorthodox problem-solving techniques, where those who make recourse to them cannot be readily summoned and made accountable for their actions. A milieu that condones mystification, both of phenomena and the ego, would very likely do everything imaginable to create cognitive disparity and asymmetry needed to uphold the status quo. In these circumstances, those things we assume are mysterious, spiritual supernatural phenomena, would often turn out to be encrypted cognitive blocks and pragmatic cognitive postulates designed to gain some advantages in asymmetrical situations of power imbalance. This is that situation, where those who have the expertise, have mastered other encrypted mechanisms, misuse their positions, to lord it over the generality and most especially over those they target as cheap victims. Any social system whose legal systems and law enforcement agencies exhibits many exploitable loopholes is bound to contend with mysterious and inscrutable phenomena, since such weaknesses in social order help enormously to create favourable conditions for the emergence of special phenomena and the requisite codes needed to secure them. The same is applicable to a social system where ignorance and lack of exposure to alternative paradigms hold sway. Humans are beings that always seek to turn asymmetrical situations of power imbalance to their own advantages. This propensity gets a boost when actors have the feeling that they can get away with their mistakes and crimes.

In a situation of this nature, positive empowerment ensuing from better educational opportunities that lead to positive self-affirmation, effective legal systems and strong law enforcement agencies, come in quite handy. This notwithstanding, it would be a big mistake to assume that matters dealing with encoded phenomena, as pragmatic cognitive postulates, can be resolved solely by recourse to some of these positive measures of enlightenment, legislation and control. As long as the human person is a being that is caught in the ambivalence of his existential situations, and as long as exclusivist tendencies remains attractive and effective means of conflict resolution, such problems would persist. One can say that putting alternative measures towards reengineering our social systems positively would definitely serve to control and minimise the worst forms of abuses and the dangers ensuing from these encrypted phenomena. Such measures alone would hardly be adequate to eradicate them completely. The aim should never be that of eradicating extraordinary phenomena in our lives, but that of sifting through missing links in view of harmonising them. Moreover, to seek to eradicate all encrypted phenomena completely would mean to encroach into the character of reality, which in itself remains partially encrypted and continues in its journey of ceaseless unfolding. This is that reality that in its incommensurability continues to yield new insights and challenges. Hence, even if all cases of spiritual supernatural share the character of being encrypted, not all cases qualify as constraining cognitive blocks of practical pragmatic purposes worthy of eradication. Some of these phenomena, per se, serve very important functions as active agents of positive social changes and transformation. This is the case with positive forms of organised religion and other mechanisms and institutions that take charge of the spiritual and psychological needs of the human person. However, when these positive means of social transformation are left, unchecked and unmonitored, to the whims and caprices of individuals and groups, they can all the more assume encrypted features more difficult to handle. This is why, issues relating to such phenomena cannot be handled outside of the important position, which the human person takes within such a complex framework.

Since we cannot rule out the positive gains associated with some of these phenomena, it becomes imperative to enact laws towards their regulations, positive exploration and exploitation. Here, conducive conditions have to be created within the legal framework for transparent and responsible exercise of those professions deriving from indigenous African knowledge. Where the rules guiding these professions are know and can be controlled, this would definitely help to decriminalise those that are genuine and motivate gifted individuals and groups to put their special knowledge and services to the use of the community. It is gratifying to note that, in Nigeria, positive efforts are being put in this direction. A typical example is the case of what was once referred to as traditional medicine pejoratively. This is now being refined and its practices adapted to recognised methods of research and development to the extent that these practices are even finding acceptance into the academia as disciplines worthy of study.

It has to be stressed that generally, we cannot talk of spiritual supernatural forces and about the difficult and complex issues associated with them, in isolation of the strategic confluxing role, which the human person plays. For this reason, the validation of claims and character of explanation sought within such frameworks must proceed from what human beings undertake to be in harmony with the world around them. Where we do not take this stand, we may be forced to handle the problem of good and evil, reward and punishment, freedom and responsibility, quite isolated from the central role, which the subject plays in very important matters of this type. The moment this happens, that is when the mind starts to paint pictures of physical and metaphysical evils and realities, as if these can exist in isolation of the thinking subject itself.

18. On encrypted rationality, complementary rationality and being-in-control (*ima-onwe-onye*)

In dealing with encrypted phenomena, one of the most critical tasks subsists in addressing the tension generated by all human ambivalent situations, which can deepen the divide in human consciousness, as to distort our overall perception of reality. Here, the need for the acquisition of a complementary form of rationality becomes inevitable. This is that form of rationality that ensures that our approach to the world remains harmonised and human consciousness equilibrated from within, as to guide actors in their relationship to the world. Thus, one of the major tasks in dealing with any phenomenon in need of understanding and interpretation would ever remain, to know if the claims associated with it can be harmonised with interests of all missing links of reality. Where such has been positively established, we have reasons to assume that a subject who makes such claims is at least in a position to equilibrate the tension arising from within itself which can be very instrumental in distorting the picture of the world. When the subject operates in this harmonised way, we say that it is being-in-control (*ọ ma-onwe-ya*). This is that moment, when the subject always seeks to grasp all missing links from the preceding condition of their comprehensive interreletedness and not in the fragmentation and relativity of their world immanency only. At such moments, the subject strives to see all things that exist in a complementary mutual relationship as missing links. Over and above all, the subject strives to grasp all missing links as aspects of the self-expression of being in its dynamic essentiality devoid of polarisation. It is as missing links that their special significances can be recognised as things having meaning within a universal framework and not as things that serve themselves only. It is at this moment that we seek to grasp them, as not only discrete substances or essences, but more so as beings that are intricately related to each other beyond the artificial divide imposed by the mind in its raw primary cognitive ambience. This is that moment when essences can never be penetrated unless they are related to their accidents in a relationship of mutual complementary harmony. It is for this reason that all missing links, as finite beings, and all experiences, are context-bound, can be penetrated not only in their relativity but also in view of their mutual interrelatedness within a wider complementary setting.

Approaching missing links in this way reveals to the thinking subject that the totality of what missing links represent can never be penetrated unless this becomes accessible to the mind in its relativity, failing which the mind becomes a victim of its striving towards absolute determination. In other words, most matters dealing with adequate representation of reality have to deal with how well the human mind can grasp the world within the confines of the transcendent categories of unity of consciousness, which are the very forms of the mind in its operations. Where the mind pretends that it can do away with any of these indispensable dimensions of its operations, it immediately finds itself in grave difficulty. This difficulty is one that threatens all theories seeking to grasp reality, but insist on doing so only from one aspect of its expression and as raw data of the primary cognitive ambience. Where the mind insists on operating only from a given perspective of its determination, it automatically generates undue tension and negates thereby the fact that anything that exists serves a missing link of reality. In such instances, the human mind in its insufficiency creates artificial problems for itself, since in seeking to penetrate reality, it acts as if some aspects of the same are dispensable. It is the same experience that can give the thinking subject the impressing that some aspects of reality are too important as to deserve special attention. The dangers arising from a distorted non-complementary approach relates not only to matters of epistemology in our representation of the world, but more so to general issues of truth themselves. All attempts at remaining at one side of the ambivalent divide would ever pose very serious problems as this relates to the character of truth. Truth can never be had in fragments, but becomes accessible when the mind is in a position to allow the limitations of being to be the cause of its joy in view of the joy of being, that sustains all authentic inquiry.

Since the human mind is fundamentally structured to perceive reality in a comprehensive complementary fashion, it can hardly work in a one-dimensional mode and uphold its legitimacy. It is rather a faculty of multidimensional determination, which can never be manipulated arbitrarily without very serious repercussions. This is why, the openness to the experience of the transcendent categories of the unity of consciousness enters necessarily into those conditions needed to ensure grasping reality truly and authentically. In this case, all missing links have to be grasped in their relativity but within the confines of comprehensiveness and future reference, which gives them their full worth. Where the mind negates these transcendent categories, it automatically capitulates to forces of distortion. In all cases, the task would always remain how to emancipate the human mind from all forms of arbitrariness, which are some of the major reasons for the distortion of reality and superstitions of all kinds, be this of spiritual supernatural kind, or of the scientific intellectual kind.

Since polarised tension laden situations are subject to historically induced factors, they can be reversed the moment enabling counter measures are in place, recognised and put into use. Basically, though, these counter measures become accessible in understanding the need to reconcile the logic of personal interest with the ontological logic. Where an actor is successful in reconciling both logics, we can say without equivocation that the individual in question is being-in-control (*ọ ma-onwe-ya*). We say this in the sense of a subject having the capacity to equilibrate the tensions arising from the ambivalence of its situation. This is that tension that persists wherever the mind tends to introduce an artificial divide between missing links in view of satisfying some personal interests at exclusion of the interests of other stakeholders. As long as the subject is not in a position to see all missing links as mutual complementary aspects of reality, it would always remain in tension and be drawn into the divide it has created for itself and often to its greatest disadvantage and displeasure. It is in confronting such tension, through the reconciliation of the logic of human interest with the ontological logic, that we can located the act of restoration of harmony within the subject and between the subject and its ambience. Here, the subject learns to understand that reality is immense and that the mind is the very conflux of all missing links in the complementarity of their interrelatedness. It is by so doing that we restore confidence in the mind such that it learns to excel and to transcend positively without tending to extreme poles. In the same way, it learns to embrace reality in its complexity without polarising any of its aspects. In the case of those Africans who seek to enthrone the spiritual supernatural as something supreme, this would amount to restoring real confidence in a battered human consciousness, which has not learnt to grasp the human person in the ambivalence of its tension ladenness and reality in the comprehensiveness of its complementary interrelatedness. Where the thinking subject has not reassured itself as to the important nature of its confluxing role, the tendency for it is to abnegate its responsibilities. This is the moment it sees in external forces as the sole active agents of all events in the world and the human subject as mere toys in the hands of the gods or other forms of encrypted phenomena. As the conflux of all missing links in the comprehensiveness of their interrelatedness, the human mind has the capacity to not only penetrate and harmonise them, it can also distort and misuse them. As that conflux that is both material and spiritual, the human mind can transcend and excel positively, just as it can denigrate and confound negatively. It is not only powerful but can fall into the deepest abyss of its being. In this awareness is rooted *being-in-control* (*ima-onwe-onye*).

19. On ethnocentric reduction, methods of comparison and the character of intercultural philosophical contacts

Those who give the impression that reality can only be grasped from one aspect of its diverse constitution often end up presenting us with a distorted picture of the world due to their compromised mindset. Such distortions ensue due to the type of artificial tension to which they subject what is expected to be grasped and which they have already created within themselves. All modes of fragmented approaches, either as epistemological or ontological paradigms, are bound to present insurmountable difficulties most especially in matters concerning intercultural encounters. Since one of the main causes of this type of bifurcating approach is unintended ethnocentric reduction, it suffices to explore further the implications of unintended ethnocentric reduction most especially for intercultural philosophical contacts. We have to remember that unintended ethnocentric reduction is mostly prevalent where researchers try to create a picture of the world only in keeping with what they think is their own distinct cultural domains; a domain that for them is not in any way coextensive with any other cultures. In this way, they go ahead reclaiming and defending such domains vehemently against those they imagined to be outsiders and intruders. As is often the case in such matters, such researchers seek to reclaim those things they imagine are the excellent achievements peculiar only to their own cultural domains. These they often try to contrast with those of other cultures in view of projecting their image in a discriminative one-dimensional non-complementary exclusivist way. Due to their compromised types of mindset, they ab initio make some of the positive aims driving intercultural encounters difficult. In some cases, they even defeat these aims completely. Worst still is that such researchers often end up negating some of the positive goals they have set for themselves due to the type of divisiveness inherent in their approaches. We encounter such problems amply given in the book edited by Brown "*African Philosophy. New and Traditional Perspec-*

tives". The contributors are eminent scholars of multicultural composition. The target of this book "is to bring Western philosophy into contact with traditional African folk philosophy in a fruitful way" (vii). What is striking about this work is that it creates two distinct, artificial and often confusing thought systems and intellectual domains and seeks a dialogue between them. These two are, a traditional African type of folk philosophy, which is equated with African philosophy or "African thinking" per se. The other is a modern way of thinking which is equated with Western values and civilisation everywhere and every time. This approach, that is definitely very erroneous, is a clear indication of a mindset caught in the worst webs of unintended ethnophilosophic reduction. There are innumerable examples of this type of approach and this is why it is a big problem not only for doing philosophy freely and objectively, but also as this regards human interpersonal relationship.

What the contributors in Brown's book fail to understand is that such expressions as *African traditional thinking, modern thinking, Western values and civilization, Western world, third world, are often mere ideological constructs of convenience* that have their origin in a polarising, antagonistic and elitist type of thinking characteristic of the way most Western thinkers categorise and demarcate the world. This tendency to see things in antagonistic opposites is the remnant of a milieu that has imbibed, is still been socialised and being groomed in a divisive type of ontology that sees the world in black and white. Much time and patience is needed for re-socialisation and re-education in matters of this nature. What most people who think in this divisive category forget is that human civilisation is an ongoing process that is sustained by mutual complementarity of ideas. In this case, most of the distinctions and categorisations used in Brown's book concerning purely Western values and traditional African values are mere fictions of the mind. As ideological artificial constructs and superimpositions, such distinctions can grossly hinder dialogue, since they are some of the worst active agents of concealment of human ambivalent existential situation. Besides, they are forms of encrypted language devised to gain undue advantage and uphold power in asymmetrical situations. Where this type of mindset is operational, philosophy as a science of being in its dynamic relational essentiality is destined to lose those things that give it its significance. By so doing, it can easily turn to a battle-ground for the exchange of prejudices misconceived as comparison of distinct and disjointed worldviews.

Due to the challenges of this ambivalence, inquirers often make recourse to what they identify as dialogue, but, as a matter of fact, they are merely interested in conserving the status quo ante of their highly priced intellectual domains and ghettos. This is one of the main lessons we learn from the heat being generated in some quarters by Martin Bernal's work "Black Athena"." This is mostly the case with those Afrocentrists and Eurocentrists who see in this work reasons to defend folk ideological prejudices in the name of science. This issue is also relevant within the context of what is to-day being propagated as intercultural philosophy, which consider dialogue, and polylog almost as ends in themselves. Here, one starts to wonder how effective these newer devises can be, if thorough their consequent application prejudices are bound to be cemented in the name of mutual encounter. Definitely, philosophy has a higher normative prescriptive vocation, which is dictated and directed by the idea of being in its relational dynamic essentiality. It is in view of this that all approaches that claim to be comparative in orientation have also to strive to make people conscious of differences and similarities, but not as ends in themselves. On the contrary, differences and similarities are inescapable attributes of being which get their full values and meanings within a complementary context. In other words, differences and similarities would always be pursued as ends in themselves where actors have not learnt to see reality as constituted of missing links that are intricately interwoven. Hence, if there is anything which any discourse based method of inquiry should aim at, it is that of giving the human mind a new orientation in view of perceiving clearly the character of the intricate bond existing between all missing links, such that, in the case of humans, they learn to see each other as beings building one harmonious family. What this means is that philosophy has more to it than merely reminding people of their similarities and differences. It seeks to create the condition for defusing the tension, which these distinctions can create for any mindset that is very sensitive about them. It can achieve this noble objective when it succeeds in providing a higher ontological principle of integration needed to harmonise similarities and differences. It is within the framework of such an ontological commitment that both concepts can be grasped as aspects of being without division, polarisation and distortion. That is to say, philosophy has as one of its primary objectives to authenticate, vindicate and grasp what is intended within any given context beyond ethnic boundaries and divides. It is such an undertaking that makes philosophy a second order discipline beyond mere theories and abstract constructs, but one that seeks to inquire beyond the limit imposed by differences and similarities in a way that makes it relevant to human coexistence. Where philosophy is seen as the ground for mutual comparison of worldviews only, it is divorced of its practical pragmatic functions, such that it can easily degenerate to a battleground for ideological tussles and can very easily compromise its ontological vocation.

In matters of this nature, what is demanded of effective intercultural philosophy is easier said or written than done. A careful study of some of the treatises on this matter would immediately reveal how difficult it is to harmonise theory with praxis. More often than not, works of most researchers show the difficulty many encounter in harmonising theory in matters dealing with differences and similarities. Many often assume that there are irreconcilable differences between diverse cultures and conceptual frameworks; and that where similarities do exist, these can hardly be treated within the context of mutual complementary dependence. We encounter a typical example of this in Brown's essay on "Understanding and Ontology in Traditional African Thought" (158-178). Here, he goes ahead comparing and contrasting Western Civilisation with what he identifies as traditional African thought. Interestingly, he equates traditional African thought with *African thought per se*. In other words, African thought past, present and future is nothing other than *traditional African thought*. It is in this sense that he finds it proper to compare "Western Perspectives and African Conceptions of Personhood" (163-167). What is still very striking is that he sees what he identifies as "Western Perspective" and "African Conceptions" as two completely distinct worlds existing side by side each other on two parallel axes. One is therefore hardly surprised if in the course of this comparison he ascribes all the gains of human civilisation to what is usually identified as the West. In this case, both thought systems, even if they have certain things in common, do not belong to a common human heritage in their genesis, but are distinct modes of thought systems in both genesis and development. With this type of comparison, the genesis and development of human ideas are handled as artificial processes that coexist side by side each other without due regard for the natural mutual complementary enrichment that is basic to such an important processes. It is due to disjointed comparisons of this kind, that many, unintentionally, equate modern civilisation to Western values as if modern civilisation and all that goes with it started and ended in the West. Even if we can make references, in time and place, in the course of development of certain ideas and other forms of human endeavours, these remain mere mental constructs devises by the mind to make some sorts of distinctions. In their genesis and development, ideas and human achievements follow a natural process where all the actors and factors that enter into these processes blend into a mutual ontological complementary whole. This natural process is not always perceptible to human consciousness, but remains the very active motor that drives human history itself. Hence, all attempts at introducing rigid distinction between diverse regions of this development and in its genesis would always portend difficulties of ontological practical type. All modes of divisive discriminatory reasoning negate the moment of mutual complementarity without which nothing can be conceived both in genesis and in evolution. Hence, any approach that gives the impression that diverse conceptions and worldviews can be discussed rigidly independent of each other remains a highly improbable hypothesis. This is mostly the case, if we consider the fact that even within identical frameworks human achievements can only be thought of only within the context of mutual enrichment and dependence. If this is the case within such circumscribed contexts, what more within a broader universal framework, where human beings in their insufficiency can hardly evolve to higher levels of self-actualisation without mutual help and dependency.

Relying on the deeply compromised and biased hypothesis of non-complementary mode of determination, most things that are conceived as dialogue or polylog between conceptual schemes, eventually, turns out to be impracticable exercises, because of the antagonistic divisive foundation on which their premises are erected. What type of dialogue does one expect in a situation where people are only interested in presenting their views as if these belong to completely diverse regions of being? Again, what type of dialogue does one expect in a situation where people are interested only in securing specific intellectual domains which they consider as those belonging to them by reason of some special cleavages? People who advocate this type of theory are some of those who have great difficulty understanding that the destiny of the simple labourer in Venezuela, who lifts crude oil under the harshest conditions, those of the business tycoon in New York, who trades the same, those of the engineers who devise means of converting the same to other products, and those of the consumers, who delight in the end products are intricately interwoven. Hence, the story of the crude oil starting with the labourer in Venezuela does not end when the labourer receives his or her meagre pay, it continues even in determining what happens with the crude oil afterwards. In the area of technology, for example, we can say that all the processes involved in the evolution of any product stay to each other and determine each other in a relationship of mutual complementary dependence. As these concern human beings, these processes rest on their sweats such that one can say that their joys and displeasures are intimately and intricately interwoven in a common mutual complementary bond without which nothing can be thought of or realised. In this case, all involved are carriers of civilisation jointly and inseparably. The same can be said of all forms of human encounter that are dependent on each other to uphold their being or to have this diminished. In all instances, there is an infinite mutual dependency between units on account of which no single individual or groups of individuals can claim sole credit or abnegate its responsibilities for anything. This is why all human potentialities, both as individuals and as groups, find full expression within a global context, such that the process of globalisation makes sense when all have the chance to have their needs fully served. It is in this sense that globalisation is the invention of no culture. It is that underlying force that propels our being to new heights in view of making us new and perfect individuals. Hence, this phenomenon gets its full worth, attains its full objective, where human beings have the chances of becoming human. It is undermined in all those unilateral acts that undermine the interests of others.

One of the most severe consequences of any approach that views human achievements and failures in isolation of the totality of human family is its constraining propensities for both knowledge and betterment of human overall welfare. Over and above all, such approaches have what it takes to impede mutual understanding, to foster and harden prejudices and throw the mind into the deepest recess of its own subjectivity in view of upholding the status quo ante. We see some of these severest consequences reflected in the book edited by Brown. Thus, it is not surprising that most of the contributors landed precisely at same position they initially intended to avoid. By seeking "to bring Western philosophy into contact with traditional African folk philosophy in a fruitful way", the contributors in the book indirectly also engaged themselves more intensively with the question if there is an African philosophy different from Western philosophy; a philosophical debate, which, as the editor rightly pointed out "has lost much of its luster" (vi). This form of circularity is unavoidable and has its roots in a method that has lost its foundation in being, as that on account of which anything that exists serves a missing link of reality. By making recourse to exclusivist non-complementary approaches, researchers often succeed in reducing philosophy to an arena for the comparison of themes congenial to specific cultures while negating the unavoidable mutual complementary relationship between all modes of expression of being in history. One can say that, one of the gravest dangers that most comparative methods of philosophical inquiry have to face is the one that has to do with motives of unintended ethnocentric commitment. Since these dangers surface in ways that are not always evident to inquirers themselves, they remain very threatening. Oversensitivity for one's ethnic matters can become a burden if it leads to negation of the mutual complementary dependence between diverse regions of being.

This over concentration on the inside with its attendant unintended ethnocentric commitment can help explain the alleged stagnation in African philosophy.

20. On understanding and impermeability of meaning beyond ethnic confines

Many who focus mainly on the comparison of worldviews and cultural differences as the primary objective of philosophical inquiry quite unwittingly assume that differences make communication of meaning difficult if not impossible. One of the greatest dangers enshrined in this type of reasoning is that of elevating accidental qualities to very significant categories in matters dealing with human interpersonal relationship. That such an approach can complicate human interpersonal relationship is not difficult to imagine. These are those situations when such things as social status, nationality, religion, colour, language, cultural affiliation, earning, achievement etc. are seen as necessary conditions for any sort of effective human interpersonal relationship. It is in view of addressing some of the difficulties such comparative works present that one can assess Franz Gmainer-Pranzl's observation that complementary reflection shares much in common with many theories that are interested in matters concerning the "other" or the "alien" (93). Some of the many problems theories that have to deal with "the other" have to contend with are those relating to understanding and to the communication of meaning between diverse groups. The other is how what is communicated should be understood. Within such contexts, such questions become relevant: Can we and to what extent can we understand the other in contexts of communication? What is the nature of the meaning sought and communicated in such contexts? Most unintended ethnocentric inspired methods of inquiry assume that meaning is accessible only to people who share the same restricted framework of understanding. In this case, all matters of meaning remain perpetually inaccessible to outsiders no matter how hard they try. This is mostly the case when inquirers assume that their raw primary cognitive ambience is the most real world ever.

In reply, I would say that as difficult as the issue of mutual communication and sharing of meaning may appear, I consider the way we handle this matter one of the most important conditions for peace and harmony among diverse peoples of the world. The parameters we erect with regard to grasping what is intended goes a long way in determining the way we view and relate to other peoples who are assumed to be different from ourselves. One thing is certain in this regard: Within multiethnic and multicultural contexts, human beings can never eliminate or demolish biases completely, as they seek close relationship with each other. This is not even possible within the confines of our own homes and families. What more with regard to the larger global family, with its diversities of expectations? Biases enter into the character of human encounter with reality at all levels of determination, as relative historical subjects. At times, biases are even useful towards handling effectively unwanted intrusions. What has been said about biases is also valid for the persistence of variants of tension, as we find these in most situations of life. Even if biases and tensions cannot be completely eliminated in human interpersonal relationship, they can at least be controlled to make effective communication possible. In other words, what is most important is that in each undertaking, those involved should be awake to some of the special types of tensions and biases involved in these areas.

What this entails is that the tensions and biases arising from our different backgrounds notwithstanding, mutual communication and understanding of meaning are possible, even if we come from different cultural backgrounds and speak different languages, wear diverse attires, provoke and annoy each other mutually. In all situations, we have to bear in mind always that it is not only cultural differences that can constitute themselves to insurmountable difficulties in the process of communication of meaning and mutual understanding. There are many more things that can do the same even more intensively, such that to make recourse to some variables always is a clear indication of the arbitrariness of such choices. Admittedly, this matter is not as simple and straightforward as it presents itself at the intimate private levels, but it can help to show that problems relating to lack of understanding between diverse peoples, both at the private and public domains, can be created artificially. This is mostly the case with issues dealing with those we characterise as the "real other", aliens and strangers and where our natural instinct of self-preservation magnifies such things as language differences, cultural differences, mentality, colour, status, achievement and other accidental qualities to the point of making human mutual coexistence difficult, if not impossible based on such differences. What happens in such situations is that the mind easily elevates such accidental categories to absolute categories in view of safeguarding certain interests it considers sacrosanct. This must not be the case, if we come to realise that the dichotomy between substance and accident, matter and form, as articulated by Aristotle is an unfortunate extreme distinction that did not take into account fully the intrinsic mutual complementary bond existing between all missing links. Since the time of Aristotle, this mode of artificial distinction between substance and accidents has unfortunately entered deeply into the way most inquirers relate to reality, such that, they easily become victims of its most severe consequences. These are those, who easily assume that such categories as language differences must be reasons why understanding and communication of meaning should be impossible in human interpersonal relationship, and most especially, in matters dealing with strangers.

This can be seen as one of the many reasons why, at the more advanced level, most ethnocentric inspired methods of investigation assume that meaning is basically incommunicable and understanding practically impossible due to the constraints imposed by accidental qualities and most especially those of language and cultural differences. In this case, the assumption is that to get at what the thing is in itself, there is always the need to rely on the description given by the insider because "there are arenas in which language itself seems to fail us" in our attempts to understand people of other cultures. (Brown, Seeing through the Conceptual Languages of Others 6). This is why "to understand the philosophical perspectives of other cultures, one must come to understand those perspectives from the points of view of those who hold them." (Brown, Seeing through the Conceptual Languages of Others 6). Brown's position is in harmony with that of Peter Winch for whom human action is rule following. It is in this sense that Winch avers that since human action involves meaning, such meaning must be understood "from the inside" (The Idea of a Social Science).

Brown and Winch are not alone in this illusion, which is very widespread as it concerns most presuppositions underlying cultural inquiries most especially from the perspective of hardened ethnocentrists. One thing must be admitted at the onset: There are obvious problems associated with understanding meanings enshrined in thoughts, as these presents themselves outside of the framework of our subjective worlds. However, the issue of impermeability of meaning, as most ethnocentrists paint the horrifying picture, is not such an insurmountable problem as to declare, *everyone to his subjective meaning and all through translators.* This is one of the arguments often used to undermine the interests of those we identify as "the other" "the foreigner", "the queer", the "exotic" etc. with a view to make mutual integration impossible.

Here, almost everyone is more comfortable in the artificial world where he can communicate only with members of his family, with his kith and kin, his race, his town's people, with people of his nationality, and indeed, with those people we feel that we share intimately the same framework of meaning and understanding. One thing is certain, the problem posed by such things as language with regard to understanding is a general human problem that confronts us, as earlier mentioned, even in the very confines of our homes. In some cases, we encounter these problems in these intimate areas still more intense than with those others we think that we do not know very well. This is why its solution cannot be adequately sought in a pure abstract cognitive level or by recourse to a predicative categorial logic of differences and similarities only. Besides, it is not one that has to be approached with a mythological mindset resting on the prompting of commonsense experience. This is the case when we bring commonsense experience to bear on such subtle matters as the foundation on which meaning and understanding are erected. Most approaches that consider meaning impermeable can be said to be subject to some of the difficulties arising from reliance on the promptings of commonsense experience as we find this in Brown's approach. Thus for him "to know what starvation is one ought to have experienced starvation itself". (Brown Seeing through the Conceptual Languages of Others, cf. Footnote nr. 6). In other words, to understand the meaning enshrined in language, one must be an insider or owner of the language in question. In this case, the best doctors to handle certain diseases are those that have actually suffered such diseases. Likewise, only those African philosophers who are really witches or wizards are best qualified to talk about witchcraft, and the magicians and sorcerer amongst them perform best when acting from the inside. Contrary to this form of oversensitivity against the category of *otherness*, we can say that language does not fail us just because we are outsiders seeking to understand what is intended by the insiders. When language itself fails, this may have other reasons that are not to be sought in the character of language itself, but have to do with the type of mindset with which communication is sought

Certainly, some of the points raised by Brown with regard to the private character of language and impermeability of meaning have some relevance, but their truth worth must be taken with a grain of salt. Here, one must admit that the issue involved is not as simple as it appears. One thing is clear, in all matters concerning language, understanding and meaning, we perceive the world differently even in those cases where we speak the same language. Hence, if we insist that original meaning should be made accessible to us only through an insider, who speaks the original language, then communication would be virtually impossible, or at best, we would need an infinite number of translators who belong to the "inside". In this case, we would also have as many rules governing language and meaning as we have individuals in any given location, because of privacy of language. Where would that take us?

What this shows is that there is need to assume the necessity of a common credible framework on which meaning and mutual understanding are erected. *In this case, meaning is accessible and can be grasped only within a complementary comprehensive framework that transcends the mechanistic references, artificial rules of grammar and other artificial linguistic symbols, forms and devises.* The reasonableness of this assumption becomes obvious if we consider other human acts that presuppose such a unified complementary comprehensive frame of reference. This is the case with such human acts as remembering, imitation, association of ideas etc. In these acts that are very essential in everyday encounter and interaction, we rely on an infinite complementary comprehensive common and unified frame of reference, even if we are not always aware of this, to know things and broaden our views about the world. To these basic acts belongs the human capacity to compare one thing with the other without which human life would be impossible. In this act of comparing one thing with the other, a person transcends his own particular world and thereby seeks to grasp into the world of other objects and persons outside of his own private subjective world. In interpersonal relationship, we compare our ideas with those of others outside of our worlds, and in most cases, we are successful. The capacity to represent what is not present here and now and in such acts, rests on the assumption of a more comprehensive complementary common framework of meaning and understanding in the absence of which such acts become futile.

It is based on this common complementary framework of meaning that I can draw inspirations for my comparisons, and say with some amount of certainty that what I am doing has meaning. If not, I would be encased in my subjective world devoid of references and in this case devoid of expressiveness. What this shows is that all matters of meaning are complementarily relational and can be articulated in view of a common foundation from which they ensue. Here, the idea of being as something dynamic in its essential interrelatedness and something that connotes all possible relations because of which anything that exists serves a missing link of reality becomes relevant. It is because of sharing a common horizon as this is provided by all missing links being in a relationship of mutual complementary interrelatedness that meaning is possible, can be grasped and communicated. It is totally another question, if the meanings pursued and obtained, within such frameworks, are accurate or meaningful enough. This is not a matter that can be decided a priori, since the difficulties involved present themselves even within those frameworks where people speak the same languages, and share values and norms commonly.

What this shows is that no missing link taken singly or as a set, outside of the framework provided by the totality, is adequate enough to serve as the foundation of meaning. This matter becomes most relevant in those situations where many assume that we understand each other better because we share certain characterisations intimately. This must not be the case since intimacy is no guarantor for understanding. There is hardly any form of understanding that can be sought outside of the openness bestowed by the mutual complementary dependence between all stakeholders. The difficulties we encounter in the communication of meaning thus transcend artificial differences and similarities. It has more to do with the character of being in its incommensurability, as it seeks expression as an ambivalent experience in most existential situations. In this case, while trying to grasp at the foundation of meaning, we can encounter difficulties posed by the challenges inherent in the character of being itself, and not necessarily because certain categories have absolute significances and pose insurmountable difficulties such that in their absence understanding and communication of meaning become impossible. Where certain categories assume such absolute significances in human interpersonal relationship, these are usually mere inventions of the mind, which seeks always to elevate accidental qualities to absolute categories.

Hence, in all matters involving understanding and meaning, it may be useful to bear in mind always that we are dealing with issues that have to deal with incompleteness as this relates to what is communicated. In the case of meaning, where we seek absolute meanings and look upon language as something that bestows or guarantees absolute meaning, we immediately find ourselves in the way of error. This is the moment we assume that those who share the same linguistic framework with us are capable of communicating those absolute meanings that are not accessible to outsiders. As far as meaning is something that is accessible only in a fragmentary form, all involved are both insiders and outsiders and this is why each has to give the other a chance irrespective of his or her biases, likes and dislikes, cultural and ideological affiliations. The false assumption that only those that belong to specific cultural milieus have the capacity to understand themselves better arises from what I call the fallacy of "the nearer the better and the safer", which is the *super-maxim* that controls most human undertakings. The fallacy enshrined in this super-maxim is not always evident and it is something that drives most ethnocentric inspired methods of investigation and ethnocentric commitments. These are those approaches that have the tendency to look inwards only for the solution of most critical problems.

Another example suffices to make this very important point still clearer. This is with reference to Ozumba's attempt to criticise Wiredu's "How not to compare African and Western thoughts". Here, Ozumba remarks: "Not being born into that [culture] he has not the stature nor the capacity to compare them. …For a person to make such comparison, he has to be versed in the cultures that he is comparing. This is a fundamental limitation as far as the topic how not to compare African thought with Western thought is concerned. …Wiredu being an outsider as far as Western culture is concerned, cannot rightly show how the comparison between Western thought and African thought should progress which is the implication of his topic" (Footmark 129). First, it is important to remark that it is only Ozumba, perhaps, who knows his parameters for judging how "versed" Wiredu is in matters of this nature. He probably knows all that Wiredu knows about Western culture and the quantity and quality of knowledge that qualifies a person to embark on such undertaking. If the prerequisite to engage in such comparison is that bestowed by right of progeny or cultural affiliation, we can as well conclude that anyone born into such cultures, no matter his or her credentials, can do better than Wiredu in matters of such comparison. This is hardly to be expected. Wiredu's right of comparison ensues from the fact of his being human and sharing certain things in common with all actors and factors in communication situations that entitle him to such a comparison. This is that common horizon that opens up the world of the other in a way that brings it nearest to the comparing subject. To deny the rights bestowed by this common horizon of meaning and understanding would entail an arbitrary incursion into the rights of others, and in matters that concern them most intimately. This is the character of all forms of ethnocentric mindsets in their intolerance and arbitrariness.

To avoid relapse to these two extreme positions of intolerance and arbitrariness, we are bound to admit, in goodwill, the existence of a common horizon of meaning and understanding because of which communication and all mutual acts can be established between beings with similar if not identical capacities of knowing and willing. This assumption is reasonable not only theoretically but also practically, should we remain those insufficient beings that are mutually dependent in the process of consummating our reflection and acting responsibly.

In the case of Ozumba and Wiredu, we can say that Ozumba cannot a priori deny Wiredu his fundamental human rights of comparison without serious repercussions. This right of comparison is anchored on Wiredu's natural right of sharing a common horizon of meaning and understanding with those beings similar to himself. If Ozumba denies him this right, he does so only arbitrarily and dogmatically. In the exercise of his natural right of comparison, Wiredu would not be expected to come out with what, in our opinion, might be adjudged the best comparison. Such judgments are restricted on account of the incommensurability of the horizon from which all matters of comparison draw their being. In this case, this horizon is both open and closed, but it is still accessible to those who, in goodwill, accept it as the framework for the articulation of their ideas. In this case, we should appreciate the outcome of those efforts communicators make, in goodwill, in view of making meaning accessible and transparent. In all communication situations, it is the duty of all stakeholders to complement their efforts in view of helping what is intended emerge more clearly.

21. On understanding, meaning, goodwill and a common horizon of being

By articulating reality within a horizon that is complementary in constitution, complementary reflection seeks to do away with recourse to an infinite number of guides or translators in our bid to understand and know what is intended in all situations of communication. The same is applicable as this concerns overcoming the danger of regress ad infinitum in our search for a common ground on which to base our reflection. Likewise, by following a complementary approach, we would be in a position to offer valid reasons for our choices between alternatives, so that cases of arbitrariness in this regard is grossly minimised if not completely eliminated. Over and above all, it is under the assumption of a commonly shared complementary horizon that the issue of communicability of meaning, both at the private more intimate sphere and the more complex public sphere, can be rendered more manageable.

Now, assuming it is true that the only condition for understanding another person is that the inquirer must have access to the framework of meaning, as this is provided by the person concerned, or the insider himself, the decisive question would then be: Why are we hesitant and ungenerous in extending the same rights and privileges to human beings generally, as beings that share those things in common that define them as human? Going by such an assumption concerning the underlying humanness of all in communication situations, it then becomes obvious that all are, somehow, insiders; a status that is bestowed by their fundamental capacity to understand meaning, when this is communicated to them. In this case, it would be proper to assume that as human beings with the fundamental predisposition to understand and communicate what we perceive, we should have the capacity to understanding each other mutually our linguistic, cultural and other differences notwithstanding, and as communicated even by those whose languages we do not understand. In other words, when the requisite conditions are given, human beings have the capacity to understand each other, their differences notwithstanding. Admittedly, those variables that can impinge on mutual communication of meaning and understanding, such as differences in language and conceptual schemes, have the capacity to challenge human fundamental predisposition to communicate and understand each other in a harmonious way in keeping with the special character of their being. This notwithstanding, they do not have the capacity to vitiate the fundamental humanness on which all meanings rest. In this case, we cannot imagine a situation where a person remains completely an outsider in matters that have to do with the constitutive nature of his being. For these reasons, the resolution of issues relating to the difficulties concerning understanding and meaning, as these can be complicated through differences, has to be articulated at another level to be useful and credible.

When carefully considered, these impeding variables are grossly dispositional and not constitutive. In this case, differences in language, character type, culture, can never be converted to substantial issues, since they have their true worth within a wider complementary bracket that legitimises them. Where we isolate them from this complementary framework, that is the moment they start to assume overbearing significances, as if they are things that can be assessed only from the inside. Hence, as partly fundamental dispositional issues, such difficulties arising from understanding and communication of meaning, due to apparently insurmountable differences, have to be handled as general human problems that must not be predicated on linguistic and cultural barriers. Hence, it is important to state that communication is always possible and can always succeed if we consider the mutual complementary link defining the horizon of all stakeholders and the type of wider complementary horizon within which their ideas take full character. We do this bearing in mind that the human raw primary cognitive ambience gets its full worth when articulated within a wider complementary cognitive ambience, as earlier stated. Hence, it is by the acquisition of a complementary type of mindset that all forms of communication and meaning get their full worth. Remove this form of mutual complementary mode of communication, all meanings turn subjective and all actors recoil to themselves as insiders both in the private and in groups. In all cases, the problem has to deal with the acquisition of the requisite mindset needed to change our world positively. Here, such a mindset precedes all forms of dialogue or polylog. This is precisely why complementary reflection is at variance with diverse methods that see discourse as a necessary precondition for positive changes in the world. Where the goodwill provided by the acquisition of a complementary type of mindset is given, all matters of discourse would follow naturally. Where such is lacking, discourse has hardly any chances of succeeding. In the consciousness that all entering the communication act share the same horizon of meaning, much can be achieved, since this gives all stakeholders the leverage to see themselves as human beings first. These are those human beings whose lives are beclouded with ambivalences and who struggle to overcome these as limited subjects. Where such a consciousness is given, all stakeholders come to realise that communication of meaning and understanding are merely limited act that require the efforts of all stakeholders to succeed, such that the difficulties arising from differences would be seen as things natural and not things constitutive and special. Hence, the common horizon that is shared by all is one that bestows the insight to confront differences and not one that emboldens to absolute otherness.

Arguments in favour of the impenetrability of meaning made possible due to cultural and linguistic differences ensue the moment we consider missing links as irreconcilable units existing side by side each other and not as complements that share a common horizon that is complementary in constitution. Thus, the sensitivity concerning the existence of a common mutual complementary ontological horizon is needed to address the issues of differences that might arise in most communication situations. It is in the absence of commitment to such a horizon that actors can make claims, often unintentionally, to certain areas they consider special to them, and which remain foreclosed to other stakeholders. As beings that share a common ontological horizon that is complementary in constitution, all participants in the process of communication have an inherent moment of insufficiency. This is not fundamentally a disadvantage because this is the character of all missing links, including the nature of all stakeholders. This insufficiency makes them mutually dependent on each other. This being the case, the issue of access to meaning and matters of understanding can be articulated on the plane of human insufficiency to attain full worth. Due to this insufficiency, it is then understandable that what can be obtained in situations of communication is mostly an imperfect representation of what is ultimately intended and such that is in harmony with human relative historical conditions. This is why communication, and what is intended in communication situations, must not always be perfect. In most cases, in seeking to express ourselves we are successful, and at other times, we are less successful, due to the incommensurability of what is enshrined in meaning. This fact is obtainable even within apparently homogenous conditions. Here, all concerned are bound to each other in a relationship of mutual service in complementarity, in view of making communication succeed and the meaning intended accessible. Due to this insufficiency and the dangers of failure, stakeholders have to allow the limitations of being to be the cause of their joy, should the process uphold its worth.

Thus, all human acts, including meaning enshrined in thought, as they seek perfectibility draw their full expression from a common complementary pool that makes apparently unbridgeable difficulties manageable. This is the joy of being as that complementary horizon that makes the communication of meaning and understanding always possible, our insufficiencies notwithstanding. Incapacity or refusal to share meaning and communicate in this way with an absent other could have very serious consequences, not only for interpersonal relationship, but more so for any philosophy that seeks to be intercultural in orientation.

22. On language, philosophy and expression of meaning

Another area where the issue of impermeability of meaning presents itself as an acute problem is in the area of the relationship between philosophy and the language needed to express the meaning thereby intended. This is mostly the case in African philosophy, where most practitioners of philosophy make use of foreign languages as the language of choice for doing their work. Many seem to assume that unless a philosopher uses his or her native language or mother tongue to communicate meaning, it is highly probable that his capacity to express what is intended would be impaired. In the worst cases, his meaning would even remain incommunicable and his aim defeated. In this case, a philosophy is vindicated, gains in importance and authenticity, remains original, the more its vehicle of expression is the mother tongue or native language of the philosopher concerned.

This is another way of saying that language bestows authenticity and through language truth and meaning emerge. Over and above all, this implies that to get at the original meaning intended by thought, it is not even enough that communicators, as foreigners, speak, write and understand the language of communication. In other words, the ideal thing is that communicators should be natives who are born into a given system of thought. They should be natives who are naturally clad with the sophistications of the language through which meaning is expressed. In the case of African philosophy, many assume that for one to speak truly of African philosophy, and one that impacts African meaning, the philosopher concerned must be a native-born who uses his or her mother tongue or native language to write and speak on philosophical issues. Among those who share this view is Ogunmodede, who informs us also that Wiredu shares his view and champions it (African Philosophy in African Language 3-26). Ozumba's claim that because Wiredu is not born into Western culture, "he has not the stature nor the capacity to compare" it with African culture, is committed to such views by implication. Since many things are involved in this matter, I shall discuss only an aspect of it now and reserve the rest for another section of this book where this matter shall be discussed in connection with conceptual decolonisation.

Without denying some of the gains and advantages that might accrue, were we to do philosophy only in our native languages, and in tune with the conceptual schemes of our cultures, these gains can hardly compare with some of the major advantages thereby ignored where the reverse is the case. Some of the main difficulties posed by the apparent impermeability of meaning, as occasioned by language differences, is easily overcome if we allow the limitation of being to be the cause of our joy, and know that being which is ultimately enshrined in meaning is accessible only indirectly and via the medium of missing links of reality in their relativity and otherness. In this case, it pays always to have a mindset that is open to the use of any language to express meaning. Where this openness is not present, we would always try to pick quarrels with those who are trying to communicate meaning through languages other than their mother tongues. Meaning does not become clearer just because something has been spoken or written. It does not become clearer just because those speaking share some common languages as their native languages. Other factors must be considered. One is the character of the thing being communicated. Another factor is the level of interest invested in an enterprise, then the expertise needed to master what is being communicated etc. This merely goes to confirm that what can be had in any communication situation is not perfect. It is not every native-born French person that has the capacity to understand "very clearly" what Descartes intends *in the "Meditations on First Philosophy"*. Neither has every German the wherewithal to follow Hegel's complex reasoning and logic. Here, provision has to be made for training, expertise, and ability to master certain sets of vocabulary, technicalities and use of certain expressions. What this means is that at a certain level, we speak in coded languages and here symbolic and orthographic modes of expression assume very different character and play different functions. In some cases, we do not even need to make full sentences before what is intended becomes evident to trained ears. In this case, all languages are open and closed and in the use of language, we are all insiders and outsiders, "natives" and "strangers" as situations demand. In order that what is intended does not get lost all together and remain obscure, another approach is needed in a matter of this nature such that all stakeholders remain beneficiaries of what is intended and communicated. For this reason, all stakeholders can be participants of the meaning intended where the requisite mindset is given. Such mindset can be acquired through the process of complementary noetic propaedeutic, which reveals to the subject that anything that exists serves a missing link of reality. Being born into a language is no guarantee that communicators are already equipped with this type of mindset. This is why grasping of meaning and understanding in the real sense of the word transcend mere possession of languages and those observable means of exchanges that go with these. Even if these acts can build on these variables needed for their expression, they supersede them. In the case of meaning, this unfolds within a more complementary comprehensive framework where all the actors, factors and all missing links needed for meaning to emerge must be put into consideration.

Hence, it pays to bear in mind that in all situations involving human beings, no understanding is complete or perfect and the same can be said of meaning thereby intended. This incompleteness ensues from the character of the source through which understanding and meaning derive their being. This source is immense and can only be penetrated only partially at any given time and locations. On account of this, not even if a person were to communicate fully in African languages as Kai Kresse extols Okot p'Bitek as "the first modern African writer who wrote in an African language" (Third Way, 218), does what the thinker intends become obvious, even to his or her own native audience. Likewise, what the thinker seeks to communicate does not become less clear just because this person makes recourse to another language.

What we can infer from this is that every language situation is a situation of interpretation of meaning where some basic dispositions are needed. Hence, meaning can never be artificially enforced but can be made accessible only under the assumption of the sharing of a common horizon of being, which strikes interlocutors in their fragmentation and makes evident to them the fact that their insufficiency notwithstanding they can still be a part of what is ultimately intended. In this case, all who are involved in a communication process always leave out something un-communicated and always have something to learn from each. The greatest of what they can learn from a situation of this nature is that the full meaning intended in all cases has future referential dimension. Hence, all that is fully intended has to be fully grasped in patience, our differences, linguistic similarities and dissimilarities notwithstanding. Where we approach each other with a prejudiced mind, thinking that similarities bestow authenticity, what is intended in communication would often remain inaccessible. Even at the most elementary level, it would be a mistake for a person raising a child to think that the child does not know what is intended, going by the imperfect way the child tries to express itself. Even if the requisite vocabularies and techniques of expression are not fully given, it would be sheer foolishness to stop communicating, just because we cannot fully delve into the world of the child. Both the child and the coach depend on each other, day in day out, and learn mutually from each other, by some unique ways needed to make communication succeed.

Often one encounters prejudice just because one is speaking or writing in a foreign language. Worst still is when, the meaning a piece of writing has to convey is perceived differently depending on whether it is written Kofi, Kofi-movich, Kofi-stein, Kofi-nsky or Kofi-berger. In many cases, the tendency is for the possessors of certain languages to imagine that foreigners do not know what they are talking about, and here, they know the category of foreigners they have in mind. I would say that those foreigners we think do not know what they are talking about, in most cases know. This is why we should give them a chance to be heard. This is the type of thinking behind the irritation that might be felt by the owners of a given language when a philosopher is expressing himself in a foreign language other than his own. The feeling is that he cannot do this properly. If a person is engulfed by such doubts and irritations, this person should never regard it as empty moments. They are those moment when our finitude should become clearer to us in a more intensive manner, as to understand that to be is to be in mutual complementary service. In this case, philosophy becomes very interesting when what is intended becomes difficult to comprehend. Here, it entails all the efforts we make and all the mechanisms we put in place to see that communication succeeds as part of the service we render each other, as beings in need of full authentication.

When we think that we can understand what a person writing or communicating in a foreign language intends, chances are that we would not have any axe to grind with the person involved. When we actually think that we have understood what this person intends to communicate, we would also not have any problems with the person concerned and there would be no need raising some problems. If on the other hand, we think, for whatsoever reason(s), that what is being communicated does not harmonise with what we expect, then, either a new way of reasoning has been introduced, that is (un)worthy of attention. Where we consider the new way of reasoning worthy of attention, we give it the attention needed. Where on the other hand, we do not consider it worthy of attention, we discard it, not because the person communicating has not the capacity to use a foreign language correctly but for reasons better known to us. What is demanded in such a situation is that we readjust to the new way of communicating that is peculiar to the person communicating. It is not to be expected that all communicators should be fully satisfied with what happens in communication environment. This is not a tragedy, provided we allow the limitations of being to be the cause of our joy. There is often something left over to talk and speculate about and this belongs to the character of the relationship between thought, meaning and language. In order that philosophy can be that wonder that it is supposed to be, there is need to allow the limitations of being to be the cause of our joy. To do otherwise might amount to rashness.

In other words, the actual thing that is intended in our attempt to grasp meaning, in the use of language, transcends language itself. It is never complete and keeps unfolding. This is why what is intended is at the root of all scientific endeavours and drives them at all times and all places, towards more discoveries and better insight. The moment we claim full access to meaning, under whatsoever pretensions, that is the moment we kill inquiry, reflection, creativity and invention. Hence, any attempt to restrict meaning necessarily and arbitrarily, to any specific language or mode of expressing it, is an attempt to curtail its richness. In all matters of linguistic differences, therefore, we should allow the limitations of being to be the cause of our joy, bearing in mind that being gets full authentication when brought into our historical conditions, as missing links in mutual complementary relationship. This is why genuine commonsense experience, which is not all that very common, and is in some cases even difficult to come by, teaches that a person who speaks a particular language, as his or her mother tongue, is likelier to tell us what is truly intended by the use of the language in question. However, there is no guarantee that this person would actually tell us this. Likewise, genuine commonsense experience teaches that a person who has learnt the language and at the same time has the capacity to make the same experience is better than the person who has the language but has not made the experience. It is for this reason that we should not disqualify, a priori, a person who has premonition into the ultimate character of the content of meaning, but is not very conversant in its vehicle of acquisition and expression. In matters of this nature, mutual forbearance and support in patience is needed. Hence, issues relating to problems of this nature can never be resolved arbitrarily by recourse to uncritical observation of commonsense experience, which urges us on that *the nearer the better and the safer.*

23. On understanding as exercise in complementarity

In matters of interpretation, as this concerns the issue of meaning, at least three things are involved. These include the material to be interpreted, the interpreter and those receiving the interpretation. For meaning to be communicated effectively, these three basic regions have to cohere and complement themselves. This coherence in complementarity cannot succeed where the faculty of *obi/mmụọ eziokwu (harmonising faculty)* is not active. This is the seat of *obiọha or obiọra* (complementary totalising mindset or global mindset) needed to make communication of meaning succeed. Within this context, this faculty is where the phenomenon of basic trust and confidence is erected, as this is enshrined in the experience of transcendent complementary unity of consciousness as aspect of *obi nwanne* or vicarious feeling of compassion. These dimensions of human interpersonal relationship are indispensable in matters of this nature. These are those things that make possible the experience that helps us bridge the difficulties posed by differences as these relate to the use of different languages to understand and communicate meaning. Wherever the dimension of mutual trust in aforementioned mode is absent, what is intended becomes remote, and all forms of meaning turn subjectively unbridgeable.

Not even when people speak the same language and share most things in common can we guarantee that they communicate meaningfully. We see this in those cases, were communicators, for very utilitarian reasons, decide to misunderstand themselves. Hence, meaning is not something that is pre-given, but something that can be grasped when the requisite conditions are given. Such conditions have a transcendent character deriving from the fact that those who share meaning do also share a certain horizon that can guarantee transparency of meaning, when it is made available. It is based on the presence of this transcendent horizon that we can assume that a person that is not a native can understand meaning communicated to him, just as the person seeking meaning has to trust that what is communicated to him has the capacity to approximate what he intends. Here, all concerned share the same inseparable horizon of being that is complementarily given and which makes communication possible irrespective of language barrier. This is the transcendent complementary philosophical horizon that is sought in all questions regarding culture. It is in this process that what is intended takes character and shape, in so far as it has the capacity to validate or invalidate the subjective worlds of all involved. This is why, I maintain that attending to most of these issues depends on the goodwill ensuing from this horizon and which all stakeholders bring to bear on the matter. Where such is given, what is intended in language can never differ from what is communicated and vice versa, due to the type of intimate mutual complementary relationship existing between units within the framework of the whole.

Due to this inherent mutual complementary relationship, the issues arising from them can never be degraded to culture-specific matters. They are issues that touch on our humanity and have to be viewed as such. Besides, they are issues that have a dispositional dimension and here, what is ultimately intended transcends all language barriers. In this case, sharing a common language can even be a hindrance towards gaining full access to what is enshrined in meaning, if we consider such languages as having the source of their legitimisation somewhere outside of the common horizon that validates all missing links of reality.

Philosophy in order to be relevant to the situation of the world today should never ignore the fact that meaning is actually communicable even if human beings speak different languages. For meaning to be grasped within a wider communication horizon, understanding has to be taken as an exercise in complementarity. This entails exploring all possible relations as an aid in seeing meaning emerge. There are today innumerable resources that can help make communication of meaning easier and successful. However, the problem is that human beings are often too lazy, proud, ignorant, careless and negligent to make recourse to these resources. Many are satisfied with the little advantages bestowed by their worlds. Hence, why the communication of meaning is at times difficult is that human beings fail to explore all the resources available to them and thereby restrict themselves only to those known and convenient means of understanding. Like most things human, bridging differences remains a theoretical exercise and not a practical one. In view of understanding meaning fully, reference to some sources can be very helpful, where we succeed, it shows that meaning is communicable, our doubts notwithstanding. Fortunately, there is every indication that a common global language deeply embedded in vicariousness of meaning is emerging. This is what one learns in the way human beings are now in the position to bridge most linguistic and other artificial barriers, as they meet virtually to chat from very remote locations of the globe, often with completely unknown individuals, at most internet forums. In some cases, these mutual interactions relate to very intimate matters that in some cases find good solutions. Here people seek to understand each other, often richly and more deeply, with the help of the little common language at their disposal. In this way, they demonstrate that there is more to communication than sharing common artificial linguistic signs and symbols. That this is happening in an interconnected world that paradoxically remains more polarised than ever shows the complex character of the problem.

In this sense, one of the most important tasks of any philosophy that has the interest of humanity at heart today should consist on how to deepen this interconnectivity and not on how deepen the divide. Here, a complementary comprehensive approach would definitely serve some purpose. This is all the more the case, if we remember that being in its dynamic essentiality can be grasped and articulated in diverse modes of its relative fragmentary historicity as missing links that are in infinite mutual future referential complementary relationship. In other words, the philosophical perspective is not solely the localised perspective. It is rather a transcendent perspective, which is characterised with digging out or excavating being in its most dynamic essentiality, as missing links of reality in mutual complementary relationship with each other. This can still be achieved by recourse to a language that is not our mother tongue.

Therefore, in depicting his localised perspective, the philosopher should always embark on transcending it simultaneously and herein can be located the act of philosophical self-definition or self-understanding, which is more than that of a mere spectator. Hence, to get at the meanings attached to language entails not only the capacity to depict or describe the content of the language itself. It entails the capacity to bring this into contact with all the possible relations that determine meaning ultimately. Here, the meaning enshrined in languages of the past can be understood in relationship to what they ultimately intend and this is better regained by reference to all possible relations in a complementary comprehensive future referential perspective. Here, there is one important measure for all that is intended, that is reality itself which keeps unfolding, and which supersedes all the subjective meanings we can ever impute to our world.

24. On understanding of meaning as joy in complementarity

To understand any phenomenon entails the openness to communicate our experiences as it occurs to us within that framework that ensures mutual understanding. At all levels of determination, the philosopher listens to what is being communicated to him based on the problem situation. This he handles within the context of a complementary comprehensive future reference in view of apprehending what is really intended. Granted that all finite beings have those things that give them their form, these can hardly be penetrated within the framework of their specific differences outside of the framework provided by all missing links. Hence, all matters get their full meaning, can be articulated and legitimised adequately, only when viewed and measured within the framework of the totality of reality. Here, all cultures obtain their legitimacy in the process of co-authentication and mutual enrichment, due to their relative characteristics as missing links. That is to say, they are worldviews in constant dynamic mutual complementary relationship, such that the more we strain ourselves to get only at those thoughts we consider locally relevant, the more we are alienated from the foundation that sustains them. What this means, is that, there is something around which all worldviews anchor irrespective of their differences. This is why, in our bid to compare them with each other, we should never be surprised if similar and even identical questions are raised within different cultural milieus. The same can be said with regard to the answers sought and obtained. It is for this reason that it should never be surprising if complementary reflection, for example, arrives at conclusions that Kimmerle adjudges useful for handling issues that have been raised elsewhere in philosophy about subject-object dichotomy. While I share his enthusiasm and joy, in this discovery, I caution that such should never be overshadowed by that type of attitude where people easily gets irritated or surprised when they discover that some of those values they cherish are equally found, reflected and even replicated in other cultures; at times, almost exactly. This is precisely those moments when we hear such comments as "even they do so so and so like us". This can occur where the mind has been educated to see itself as the norm and measure of all good things. In all matters, we have to be humble and know that, in spite of all, we are still humans. In most practical situations of life, we arrive at certain conclusion and insight, not necessarily because we belong to specific cultures, speak certain languages, but because we are human beings. The same thing is applicable to the philosopher who occupies himself with a human problem and not with those problems that relate only to his culture. This is still the case, even if his reflection is culture bound. His reflection is culture bound, not only with regard to specific problems of his culture, but more so, insofar as this his culture happens to be in unavoidable mutual relationship with all missing links, with all actors and factors that help to determine his ambience. In this case, the answers and insights provided prove useful in a universal general sense, irrespective of the cultural affinity of the thinker. This is again a sure indication of the existence of that common horizon from which all contents ensue, and without which all answers remain blind and all manners of striving remain aimless. This happy discovery should be a cause of joy for all stakeholders who seek closer contact with each other.

What this means is that human beings are capable of encountering and handling similar, if not the same problems, irrespective of diversities in their cultural locations. They do so because they share a horizon of being within which they can articulate their meaning and seek to understand themselves mutually. This is why, in the face of most daunting problems of existence, the answers provided may be fundamentally similar, if not identical in some cases. This, to some extent, reveals the fundamental structure of our being, which is structured toward a unity of consciousness. It is because of this that mutual understanding is always possible, when we strain ourselves a little. We can enhance this possibility of mutual understanding, if we put more efforts to eradicate some of the artificial barriers we erect against each other and know that we can be richer if we endorse fully the gains accruing from the insufficiency, fragmentation and openness of our being towards a future that is uncertain. In its uncertainty, this future demands mutual complementary enrichment. Besides language, some of the artificial barriers that make the grasping and sharing of meaning difficult, if not impossible, are those that concern those conceptual ideological superstructures that the mind devises to make itself exclusivist and special. To master our situations successfully, we must be committed to this fundamental character of our being in its insufficiency, which calls for mutual complementation of all our resources. Where we are committed to mutual complementary interdependence, we are committed to mutual sharing of our joys, failures and all that our world has to offer. In this case, we see the need to consider all the achievements or failures of humanity, not as things that can be credited to any particular sets of people or cultures, be it the Western world or any worlds of our creation and imagination, but things that belong to a common human heritage, where each unit makes its honest contributions in its own ways.

What this means is that each individual stands to impact on our world irrespective of ethnic and cultural localisations, as we share the same horizon of being. Here, philosophy has the task of outlining some of the conditions needed to make this mutual dependency work. In this case, it should be more than an avenue for recounting achievements, exploits, victories and defeats. Thus, in complementary mutual dependence all entities involved stand to gain fully through the augmentation of their potentialities, since commitment to complementarity is commitment to variety and multidimensionality, which in themselves are strength and not limitation. Any form of discourse between different cultures would hardly take place in an atmosphere where each individual is afraid to relate to the other lest what one considers the splendour of one's achievements get lost and unrecognised in the sea of mutual complementary anonymity. Such fears are often fired by our primitive instinct of self-preservation of the selfish egoistic type, which enhances our inordinate thirst for self-esteem and recognition in view of being considered special with the privileges that go with such special status. It is specifically due to such unfounded fears that we seek to hang onto those things we consider our specific intellectual terrains and devise those obnoxious habits that give us some special air of importance to appear different.

In consummating our reflection, it is often useful to remember the undeniable fact of unavoidable mutual indebtedness and inter-dependence in complementarity of all finite beings, at all times and places. This concession creates the necessary leverage for philosophy to investigate its subject matter truly and freely, irrespective of local constraints, and with regard to the universal structure of reality. This universal commitment has always characterised philosophy in its self-understanding as wisdom. It is based on this characteristic that it seeks to understand reality in its most sublime form. Where this complementary structure of reality is forgotten, there is often the tendency to elevate the alleged little privileges conveyed on us by relative historical circumstances to absolute advantages. Worse still is when we seek to raise such alleged privileges to ideal paradigms for the judgement of others. This is when we also seek to recount such privileges triumphantly and to compare them with the thought systems of others, imagining that this is the main target of philosophical inquiry. Where this form of philosophising is prevalent, it would succeed, probably, in deepening the divide between diverse cultures, due to its obvious localised, elitist and exclusivist pretensions. In matters of cultural philosophy, it may be worthwhile allowing those issues we imagine to be culture specific to be ringing loudly in our minds' ears continuously, with a view to forestalling cases of undue false claims and avoidable reductionism.

25. On suspicion of dogmatism and imposed orthodoxy

Let us now focus on another issue raised by Kimmerle when he observes, with reference to complementary reflection, that "on the one hand, scepticism and relativism, which undermine every true statement, would follow from that. And on the other hand dogmatism and imposed orthodoxy could not be avoided". This conclusion would be inevitable were one to pursue complementary reflection as an end in itself. This is when its basic presuppositions would be understood in a way that is absolute as not to admit of any other alternative models of investigating reality. However, by its self-definition and understanding complementary reflection admits of alternative ways of seeing the world; this is why it is complementary and not dualistically polarising. For this reason it can be characterised neither as sceptic, relative, dogmatic or a tendency towards arbitrary imposition. Complementary reflection sees itself as a complement to other systems, and the same can be said of its presuppositions that can never be complete outside of the framework provided by the whole. In this case, it has room to accommodate all other positions, which are committed to mutual coexistence of units within any given framework. However, it emphasises the fact that all statements geared towards penetrating reality can be articulated creditably within a relative-absolute brackets. Naturally, such an insistence evokes the feeling of dogmatism, but a dogmatism of a comprehensive mutual complementary type. When now Kimmerle hints at relativism, dogmatism and imposed orthodoxy, as recurrent themes in complementary reflection, he captures a very significant dimension of this mode of doing philosophy. This is that dimension of complementary reflection which seeks to harmonise conflicting moments of our existential living and conceptual formations. The most fundamental of such conflicts is that which relates to the absolute – relativity tension evident in most situations of life. I strongly contend that it is within this absolute-relative bracket that the issue of dogmatism/imposed orthodoxy and arbitrariness can also be handled creditably. To lay all doubts at bay, in this important matter, I wish to state clearly my position, as it concerns the absolute–relative dichotomy, on the one hand, and tendencies to extreme forms of dogmatism/imposed orthodoxy and arbitrariness, on the other. In complementary reflection, I affirm the capacity for all units and thought systems to cohere and give us a harmonised picture of reality. It is a commitment to comprehensiveness, which creates the enabling conditions for all forms of absolute determination to be handled adequately within the framework of relativity, as this is consistent with all complementary modes of determination.

A careful look at the main trust of complementary reflection would show its devotion towards highlighting the dangers enshrined in what I have identified as the forgetfulness of the ambivalent nature of all human existential situations. This is the inherent tendency of human reason to tend towards extreme poles. Here, I join all philosophies to seek credible solutions concerning this tension, as it is prevalent in most multicultural and multiethnic environment today. One of its most radical modes of expression is in unintended ethnocentric commitment, as that tendency to take unilateral steps in resolving issues, quite unintentionally. Admittedly, finding solution to this problem is a difficult undertaking. As a serious matter, it requires all the resources at our disposal towards its resolution. Where this does not happen, we risk not building a peaceful and harmonious world, where each missing link should find a place it calls its own. Hence, one of the main targets of complementary reflection is to seek a way towards addressing this fundamental tempestuous issue adequately and creditably. Its principles and method are geared primarily towards forestalling relapse into extreme forms of relativism and absolutism. By so doing, it seeks to inquire into those conditions needed for the coexistence of all stakeholders, notwithstanding their diverse credentials. Due to the care taken to construct the principles and imperative of complementary reflection, in a systematic methodological way, most cultural philosophies might be tempted to interpret this approach as denial of differences in their over-sensitivity and fear with regard to relapse to what they see as a dogmatising, doctrinal type of system-building. Most especially those neo-liberal theories of democratic humanistic type, as they are practiced today by many so-called Western philosophers, believe that we can do philosophy and relate with each other better by abandoning system building altogether. By taking this stance, they think that they ought to have salvaged their image from the anvil of criticism concerning a dogmatic, domineering, doctrinal type of system-building characteristic of the way philosophy has hitherto been done in the West. The problem is not with systems themselves problem is not with systems themselves but with the type of mindset a person approaches the issues at stake. Whenever the mindset is polarising, dualistic antagonising and exclusivist, all modes of system building turn hegemonic. It is this hegemonic mindset that has to be addressed and measures devised to put its excesses at bay. This is precisely what the noetic dimension of complementary reflection targets as its primary function. An advocacy that foresees the eradication of system building in the way philosophy is done hardly shows any good understanding concerning the fundamental nature of human consciousness, which always seeks to grasp reality in a comprehensive systematic absolute future related fashion. This must not be a disadvantage. This inherent capacity of the mind to be systematic is something that needs to be well guided. By advocating the abandonment of system-building altogether, these neo-liberals find themselves in another extreme position of dogmatic anti-dogmatists of a fundamentalist intolerant type. Likewise, most position that seek to banish all forms of absolute commitment from their radar screen hardly realise that they are tending towards another extreme position. This they do without understanding that the human consciousness is fundamentally constituted to strive towards absolute unity.

Complementary reflection seeks to overcome this extreme position and is resistant to all forms of fixed-focus type of predetermination, be it absolute or relative. The reason for this is that for complementary reflection, all aspects of human experience form part of the totality of the flow of consciousness, at all levels of determination. In this case, the issue would ever remain how to uphold harmony in every situation in which we find ourselves, such that units are fully integrated, without contradiction – both formally and materially, into a totality as they form dimensions of the dynamic self-expression of being in history. Naturally, this is not an easy undertaking, where the issue of unity in diversity is easily interpreted in the sense of arbitrary hegemonic tendency. In this case, whoever talks of unity is immediately suspected of embarking on a journey that seeks to negate human freedom. This must not be the case, since unity does not automatically translate to arbitrary imposition but a response to a fundamental need in human nature that is genuine.

That a thinker makes a systematic methodological recourse to an issue does not automatically mean that the person in question is dogmatising. On the contrary, such approaches ensue from the character of the problem, which demands a systematic comprehensive answer. In complementary reflection, my point of departure is that any aspect of our experience of being in history that proves exclusivist makes itself inadequate towards addressing the issue of harmony of differences within the framework of the whole. It is within a system of complementing units that I think that most problems of differences and similarities can be addressed adequately, bearing in mind this fundamental human tendency towards extreme poles, which can make the fundamental tendency to harmonised coexistence unrealistic and in some cases almost unachievable. By recourse to this systematic methodological approach, complementary reflections seeks to understand the mechanisms involved in this tension, and such that make the subject always seek its autonomy outside of the framework provided by the whole; again, such that makes stakeholders always tend towards opposite directions in seeking solutions to their problems. Most approaches that wear a liberal democratic mask appear to be negligent of the character of the problem, since they seek to address it in a straightforward manner. This is precisely why in their eagerness to combat absolutism, they inadvertently revert to relativism and vice versa. In their eagerness to sound democratic, they inadvertently assume the paraphernalia of the worst types of despots. Unfortunately, many of them are hardly aware of the consequences of their position because of the phenomenon of concealment that complicates matters for them.

In matter of this nature, it suffices to emphasis that all forms of world immanent predeterminations have an inherently relative fragmentary character that can never be overlooked. The tendency of the human reason, in all ambivalent situations, is to negate this relative fragmentation and to render itself absolute. Here, complementary reflection seeks to restore a balance in human reason, which often seeks its autonomy outside of the framework provided by the whole. This loss of balance is caused by excessive selfishness, which is grounded in our passion for self-preservation. For complementary reflection, therefore, self-transcendence and authentic existence entail those mechanisms and measures we put in place to rid ourselves of the passion for exclusiveness and to harmonise our personal interests and dysfunctional expectations with those of all missing links of reality. Here, complementary reflection makes recourse to those tools designed to combat this ambivalence. These are the tools that cater for the unity of being and consciousness, as they find expression in the transcendent categories of unity of consciousness, These transcendent categories include *fragmentation (relativity), comprehensiveness, totality, unity, wholeness and future reference.* Through recourse to these transcendent categories, a complementary mindset always seeks harmony in differentiation in all historical situations, without the danger of falling into extreme positions. In this case, human reason can uphold its autonomy creditably, if it is in a position to concede to its relativity and abdicate the passion for absoluteness, as an aspect of its destiny in given historical situations. This is why complementary reflection finds it fitting to elevate the injunction to its truth and authenticity criterion, which states: *never elevate a world immanent missing link to an absolute instance.* While commenting on the importance of this injunction, Esu, Thomas Ijemot rightly pointed out that it is a "link between the relative and absolute, [as it] upholds the character of each in a complementary harmony" (unpublished M.A. Thesis 99). This position can hardly be designated as absolutist.

Since one of the main reasons for a loss of equilibrium in human relationship is human reason becoming exclusively hegemonic and absolute, complementary reflection foresees the acquisition of that faculty that is responsible for the unity of being and consciousness and for the harmony of differences, as a necessary condition for this harmony of differences. Here, we are thinking of the need to acquire a complementary type of totalising mind *obiọha*, which is firmly grounded in the harmonising faculty of *obi/mmụọ eziokwu* and this in all matters relating to harmony of differences. Thus, *obi/mmụọ eziokwu is* the seat of aforementioned transcendent categories of unity of consciousness. Hence, no form of rational act deserving its name is adequate, which negates the operations of this totalising faculty and the acquisition of its diverse practical modes of expression. Again, no form of human act can be considered adequate or authentic and complete that is executed in the negation of the applicability of these transcendent categories.

The implication of faithful adherence to the demands of these transcendent categories can be specified more concretely as follows: Through commitment to fragmentation, all missing links concede to their relativity and inadequacy. Through commitment to wholeness, comprehensiveness, unity and future reference, they become aware of their relativity and the need to refer all claims and assertions to the ultimate future referential foundation of their validation. Through consistent habitual internalisation of the demands of these transcendent categories of unity of consciousness, the mind always seeks balance in its inherent tendency towards extreme forms of relativism and absoluteness, and thereby becomes conscious of the danger these entail. The worst and severest of this danger is the negation of mutual complementary relationship between units within the framework of the whole.

Complementary relationship has nothing in common with those theories that preach total identity without differentiation, neither does it set any premium on any claims towards absolute differences. It merely claims that anything that exists serves a missing link of reality, because of which all units are mutually related, such that a negation of this inherently necessary mutual complementary relationship invariably leads to self-negation. Therefore, it is in full commitment to these transcendent categories, that the mind becomes fully conscious of the implications of a complementary relationship, as to concede to the fact that anything that exists serves a missing link of reality, in view of the joy of being. In all existential situations, this joy of being sustains our actions, such that to negate the mutual complementary dependence between units would amount to negation of those necessary conditions needed to uphold our joy and happiness as beings seeking full authentication. In this way, adherence to the demands of the principles and imperative of complementary reflection, as these specify the minimum condition for the acquisition of the joy of being, guards against relapse into worst forms of exclusiveness, arbitrariness, contradiction and self-alienation.

This approach is definitely a formidable bulwark against relapse into extreme forms of absolutism and relativism, as it guards against all manners of dogmatism and arbitrary imposition, bearing in mind that it is firmly anchored on the demands of the principle and imperative of complementary reflection, as aspects of the principle of non-contradiction and the truth and authenticity criterion. In proposing the principles and imperative of complementary reflection, I am therefore not making a one sided claim with regard to the relativity or absoluteness of reality in general. On the contrary, in complementary reflection, I am fully calling for a comprehensive commitment to wholeness, which makes recourse to one-sided dogmatism or arbitrary imposition, as methodological principle, impossible. In all contentious situations, we are therefore challenged, in the process of *existential conversion*, to act in such a way that the transcendent categories of unity of consciousness become existential categories, through our awareness of their binding character, and as a way of overcoming all ambivalences posed by our existential situations. As insurmountable a hurdle as this may seem, it can only be achieved under the assumption of a common horizon of meaning that is binding on all, and not on the platform of a framework that advocates parallel coexistence as this is typical of most discourse based methods of inquiry.

26. On the *arụsi* controversy and critical thinking in African philosophy

We now turn to Kimmerle's very important observation that according to Achebe and Oluwole, "in African thought 'nothing is absolute'"; an opinion about African experience of the world, which Kimmerle himself appears to espouse. Whereas I strongly contend that the expression "African thought" is borne by unintended ethnocentric commitment, I shall reply to this observation because of its strategic importance in African philosophy. In other words, such sweeping generalisations, which are at times unavoidable, can be considered remnants of unintended ethno-philosophic commitment and a mindset, which tries to see the world only from one perspective. This is that situation where for the subject, reality is either absolute or relative and there is no other alternative way of seeing it.

Even if some cultural theorists, for example those of intercultural brand, imagine that their position is different from this extreme way of seeing the world, they are mistaken. They take to this extreme one-dimensional position the moment they are unable or unwilling to recognise the incontrovertible role, which the absolute plays in human experience of reality. Any theory formulation that seeks to do away with the dimension of the absolute finds itself battling with fake problems. Therefore, it is important to accord the absolute its rightful place within the framework of any theory formulation. The fact that commitment to absoluteness belongs necessarily and positively to the structure of human consciousness is something that escapes most theorists. The question is not whether the structure of human consciousness is fundamentally geared towards absolute commitment. The issue is how to assess or handle the absolute within a framework that tends towards extreme poles. The problem posed by this difficulty can easily spin out of control. We see this in those cases where people wish to be humanistic but gloss over some of those things that help the human person uphold his being. Where a person wishes to be humanistic and does not address adequately the human craving for absoluteness, this person does so at the high risk of sounding strange and even absurd.

In this matter, Achebe, apparently has some difficulty assessing correctly the status of statements that have to deal with ultimate realities within the context of Igbo existential experience. His conclusion that for Igbos "Nothing is absolute" (Achebe "Chi in Igbo Cosmology" 68; Method 171), can be said to touch on Tempels' proposition that the Bantu cannot "conceive the transcendental notion of 'being' by separating it from its attribute". Why Achebe's position is significant is the weight behind his authority. Many have been misled by his position, as to generalise about the Igbo on this matter. A typical example is Ogugua, who echoing Achebe on this matter, without actually quoting him, states, "In Igbo-African Ontology, there is rejection of absolutes, hence the rendition of Being as negation. We say in Igbo world 'ife kwulu ife akwudebe ya' – when something stands, another stands beside it" (77). What has been said of Achebe can equally be said of some other Igbo intellectuals who command much influence. A typical example is Nwoga who gave the 1984 Ahiajoku lectures of the Igbo intelligentsia. Deriving his conclusion from Nwoga's, rather curious claim that "Igbos see reality in complementary dualities" (22), Ekwuru avers that "for the traditional Igbo, there is a kind of cosmological relativism; the universe in which contrasting forces constitute the dynamic constituents of being, is devoid of absolutes" (62).

Even if Achebe and his ilk are writing specifically with regard to Igbos, Kimmerle's observation, in the case of Achebe, seems to suggest that his observation can be generalised for all Africans. This is typical of what can happen when one approaches cultural matters with unintended ethnocentric mindset. Here the assumption is that there is a way of thinking congenial to all peoples of certain cultural areas at given times. For complementary reflection what many have come to characterise as "African thought" is not something homogeneous, since there are clear indications of the existence of identifiable systems of thought within this traditional African ambit. Both private opinions of individual thinkers and groups of thinkers are well documented within this ambit. Given that there are worldviews that can be characterised as community thought, the task of philosophy is not to go about documenting such but to probe, for example, into their epistemological and ontological foundations. In doing this, philosophy is invariably taken to the level of critical appraisal of the ideas of those individual thinkers and groups of thinkers whose opinions constitute the corpus of this existential living. It is hardly to the interest of philosophy merely to document them and dogmatise on these ideas, as worldviews beyond reproach, as if they are immutable dogmas. If we did, this is the moment we arrive at such odd conclusions that for the Igbos "Nothing is absolute". By taking this position, we are led to believe that all Igbos are of this opinion, whereas there is enough evidence to show that not all traditional Igbos, what more all contemporary Igbos think this way. In matters of this kind, philosophy has the task of probing the validity of such generalisations based on good insightful reasons.

To start with, Igbos, like other human beings, are critical in their approach to the world. Generally, there is every indication that the so-called community thoughts and worldviews provided the foundation for further reflection in keeping with the exigencies of life. This is precisely why within the rank and file of African philosophers themselves, there is hardly any agreement as to a common dominator to which the worldviews of any given sets of people can be reduced. Some refer to African worldviews as holistic, other write in terms of a unitary worldview, still others write in terms of dualistic, universalistic etc. It is in view of these differences and nuances that Anyanwu reminds us that "The Igbos assume, for example, that every person has his or her own 'Chi', and that no two 'Chi' are identical, but they will or may differ about the significance, function and implications of 'Chi'" (The Problem of the Method in African Philosophy 64). What Anyanwu is saying is that among Igbos, even in such fundamental ontological matters as the concept of "chi", there are shades of opinion. In keeping with this critical and varied attitude to reality, Nwoga claims that Igbos see things in "complementary dualities". Meaning that dualism is not ruled out as one of the ways Igbos see the world. On his part, Nwala, more cautiously, designates traditional Igbo ethical attitude as "flexible" and not as one devoid of absolute commitment as Achebe appears to be insinuating (Nwala 58-62; Asouzu, The Method and Principles 348). When these thinkers refer to Igbos as having diverse opinion about the same phenomenon or the world in general, they merely suggest that individual Igbos and groups of Igbos have varied opinions about reality. The same is applicable to other Africans. This is precisely what we can infer from Godwin Azenabor's position, who in reference to Lancinay Keita targets *holism as* "an African philosophical tradition" (Azenabor, Understanding the problems in African Philosophy 77).

Going by their own self-understanding, Igbos never tire of pointing out the important status of individual critical reflection as is pointedly captured by the Igbo aphorism *uche bu akpa onye ọbula nya nke ya* (thought is like a bag and each person carries his own). Evidently, this is a commitment to criticality and not a sure sign of relativity. Going by this insight, most Igbos have the flair of arguing and pondering their points of view such that they can hardly be designated as conformists. This flare to insist on individual private opinion is even one that is often misunderstood as Igbo intellectual arrogance. This is most especially the case with many early anthropologists, who came in contact with Igbos. A typical example is Leith-Ross who writing about the Igbos says: "I never cease to wonder at and be a little disturbed by, their lack of reverence… Admiration, respect, prestige, were dead words to them, either when used in connection with the white man or with themselves…The Ibo men and women are so continually in the right and so busy proving that everyone else is in the wrong." (Sylvia Leith-Ross 357, quoted in Akogu 103). Even Achebe himself captured this critical character trait of Igbos in one of his novels, as this is epitomised in the person of Obiako. In the novel "Things Fall Apart" Achebe tells us that the Oracle told the man Obiako that his dead father demanded a goat from him as appeasement sacrifice. Irked by what Obiako considered as an inordinate request, Obiako requested the oracle to ask his dead father "if he ever had a fowl when he was alive" (Achebe, Things Fall Apart 15). Referring to traditional Igbos, one of the earliest missionaries in Igboland, Joseph Shanahan, has this to say "They insisted on bargaining and arguing to their hearts' content before agreeing to anything definite" (Congregation of The Holy Ghost, Short Life of Bishop Shanahan 82), This attitude to take a personal critical stand cannot be designated as a sign of relativity, but a sign that this ambience had provision and respect for diversity of opinions.

Hence if Achebe and Oluwole uphold that "in African thought 'nothing is absolute'" as Kimmerle rightly pointed out that Achebe does, they are entitled to their opinions, which along with others show that there is more to what many designate as homogenous and conformist African worldviews. In this case, the position, which Achebe and Oluwole hold, can be understood alongside mine. This merely goes to reinforce my assertion that there are diverse currents of thought in traditional African philosophy of which the complementary current is only one. However, should Achebe and Oluwole insist, as Kimmerle makes us understand, that generally in African thought "nothing is absolute" and that "I am the truth, the way, and the life would be called blasphemous or simply absurd", (Achebe 68), I would say that their understanding of this way of relating to reality is far from being accurate.

To start with, most ethnophilosophic-induced methods of investigation espouse a non-dynamic, stagnant, un-progressive type of thinking. It is for this reason that they make us believe that what is called "African thought" never changes and never evolves. In this case, they see African philosophy only from the perspective of traditional African life that belongs to a distant past. For them, what contemporary day Africans do as philosophy is in no way different from the way philosophy has always been done in the past. In other words, "African thought", for them, is immutable, it never changes, and it is stagnant. If "African thought" should be "African thought", and one that spans the past, the present and tending towards the future, we can then understand why most present day Africans would welcome the statement with joy "I am the truth, the way, and the life". These are those Africans who through education, socialisation and indoctrination have other ways of seeing reality. Definitely, such Africans would hardly call such a statement "blasphemous or simply absurd" as Achebe claims that they would, just because they are Africans. As philosophers, we have the task of probing the epistemological status of such statements based on available facts and in adherence to the rules of clear reasoning. What this means is that Achebe's opinion, in this matter, should be taken with a philosophical grain of salt. In this case, what might interest us would be how the truth content of his position can be validated, if only empirically. With reference to his claim that for the Igbos "Nothing is absolute", I would say that his claim can hardly be generalised for all Igbos, nor can it be firmly substantiated by available evidence. In this case, his claim is highly improbable.

Contrary to Achebe's claims, Igbo world is characterised by an ubiquity of phenomena that demand absolute allegiance. By every indication, many Igbos are actually committed to the demands of these absolute phenomena. Over and above all, Igbo vocabulary has a very prominent place for the concept "absolute commitment". This is when Igbos use the term *alụsi or arụsi* to designate *the absolute or absolute commitment.* This concept is one of those that command the greatest significance in Igbo existential experience. One of the greatest problems concepts present is to reduce them to what we think is their unaltered significances within the context of our raw primary cognitive ambiences. Since such ambiences are by nature resistant to changes, it hardly occurs to us that words can have other meanings beyond the impositions accruing from this raw primary cognitive ambience. It is in this sense that Idowu calls our attention to the diverse senses in which the Yoruba use the term "God" (Olodumare). According to him, the Yoruba word "Olodumare" can be used in the sense of "Olodu-Omo-Ere" (The Supreme one, off-spring of the boa); "Olofu Ma Re" (The supreme one who remains constant); "Olodu Mo Are" (The supreme one, wearing the crown); "Olodu Kari" (The perfect one), "Olodumare" (The one to whom I must return) (Idowu cited in Onyewuenyi African Belief in Reincarnation).

Within the context of Igbo vocabulary, we have cases of words that can be used in diverse senses beyond restrictions imposed by our raw primary cognitive ambience. To such, belongs the word *alụsi or arụsi,* which for many refers to *deities,* without qualification. In this case, we are dealing with lesser deities (*arụsi or alụsi*) in contradistinction to the supreme deity (Chukwu). Notwithstanding this rigid way of using this term as to refer to the distinction between an absolute supreme being (Chukwu) on the one hand and other lesser deities (*alụsi*) on the other, there are other ways of using the word *arụsi or alụsi.* This concept *alụsi or arụsi* can be understood in at least two major senses. First, *arụsi/alụsi* translates to a command, a warning or an injunction. To convey these meanings, it is written thus: *arụ si* or *alụ si (*do *not violate*!); *arụ si* or *alụ si* (you are commanded, do not violate!); *arụ si* or *alụ si* (you are warned, do not violate). The second sense is when this command is object-oriented, as to designate what is being commanded, warned about or enjoined. Within this context, the word designates those deities that demand absolute allegiance. It is in this latter sense, that any of these deities is equated with the literary meaning of what is commanded, enjoined or warned about, as to connote "the inviolable", "the indubitable", and "the absolute instance".

In such cases, the word *alụsi or arụsi,* as the inviolable, denotes an absolute instance. It is as the absolute *(alụsi/arụsi)* that Igbo deities serve a very important judicial function, as the point of final appeal in matters of arbitration. This is when a person is challenged to take an oath as *ita arụsi or ita arụsi* (chewing of the absolute or taking an oath). As final instances of arbitration, these deities demand absolute allegiance when, for example, oaths are taken in their names. It is for this reason that if oaths and covenants are made in the name of, say, the *arụsi/alụsi* "Ala", such oaths and covenants "must be fulfilled" (Abanuka, Philosophy and the Igbo World, 32). Since we are in the realm of the ultimate or absolute experience, violations of such covenants or oaths are supposed to attract very severe punishments, including even the ultimate punishment, which is the death of the transgressor.

We can then understand the importance attached to such famous oracles as – *Igwe-ka-Ani, Agbala* and *Ebulu-Okpa-Bia among the Igbos.* The verdicts of these oracles were considered as absolutely binding and *here something is absolute.* Since these oracles enjoyed the status of absolute instances, they generally enjoyed much prestige and patronage. It is for this reason that they were ironically also grossly abused (Asouzu, The Method 217-219). The oracle *Ebulu-Okpa-Bia,* for example, was unmistakably identified, by most Igbos, with the supreme absolute deity *Chukwu*. It is for this reason, that the custodians of this oracle the *Aros* enjoyed unprecedented privileges in Igbo-land, since they designated themselves as *Umuchukwu* (the children of the supreme deity) and were understood as such.

27. On *arụsi* within missing links in their tension-ladenness

Having now established the fact that one cannot state categorically that for all Igbos "Nothing is absolute", as Achebe claims, I dare to propose that the dimension of absolute commitment is something consistent with fundamental human experience of reality. Thus, all forms of extreme commitment, as we have these in most human affairs and conditions, in loving, hatred, in the desire for the liquidation of one's enemies, in diverse forms of fanatical acts have implicit dimensions of the absolute. In other words, to be human has an inherent moment of absolute commitment. With this, we can now turn to another dimension of the relationship of Igbo to the absolute that can help us understand the intricacies involved in this matter. The insight we get from this would be needed to show more clearly how human experience of reality can be articulated more creditable within an absolute–relative bracket, and not with respect to a one-dimensional absolute or relative axis. Taking into account the ever-present tension within this absolute-relative type of relationship can help us appreciate the need to address the difficulties this tension poses, by recourse to a complementary logic. This type of logic seeks to equilibrate this tension. It is not one that tries to polarise it even more. Most irreconcilable conflicts in human interpersonal relationship arise when stakeholders take only to one side of this tension, be this to the absolute, be this to the relative. When this happens, actors can easily err in their judgement of the status of the absolute in given matters, which they can regard as the only thing that matters.

The way the concept *arụsi* or absolute is used by many within the context of Igbo existential living can help us understand its wide-ranging ramifications in view of avoiding some of the most severe excesses ensuing from the use of the concept itself. Within most contexts of Igbo existential experience, one of the greatest mistakes is to assume that *alụsi/arụsi* (the absolute*)* has a very straightforward connotation as to designate the absolute without further qualifications. On the contrary, the concept has paradoxically also a deeply relative dimension that is not always evident. This becomes most clear when the human mind is caught in the web of its ambivalence; a lesson we learn from the attitude of most Igbos to some of those deities that many approach with trepidation as absolute instances. A typical example is the case of *ikenga,* an ubiquitous deity of utility. When things are moving on well with an average traditional Igbo, for example, this person approaches this deity with utmost devotion and reverence. If on the contrary, this person has the feeling that *ikenga, his or her personal god (chi),* has outlived its usefulness, the person goes to any length to deal with *ikenga*. The most radical form of this dealing with an individual's personal god is to discard it completely when a person has the feeling that his *ikenga* or personal chi has reverted to a good for nothing deity that consumes sacrifices without commensurate performance or reciprocity. This is when the individual concerned avers: *Ikenga adigi ile awaa ya nkụ;* it is again the saying*: ikenga waa anya agwa ya osisi eji tụọ ya* (if Ikenga has outlived its usefulness, it must be converted to firewood or if *Ikenga* becomes stubborn, it must be told that it is merely carved out of wood). In such moments, when people have the impression that ikenga has outlived its usefulness, *Ikenga* is actually forced to shed its absolute characteristic. Consequently, the *ikenga* concerned is immediately rejected and converted to firewood. Yorubas have similar attitude to their deities. Thus, within the Yoruba pantheon, "A god who fails in his duties towards his adherents may be threatened or even abandoned by such devotees" (Balogun The Role of the Gods 56).

Over and above all, there is a high concentration of deities seeking breeding space within the context of the Igbo pantheon, within the same location. This does not make any one of the *alụsis* less an *alụsi* or an absolute. This is very typical with my people the Aros of Arondizuogu (The Method and Principles 29). Thus, their commitment to the absolute deity *Chukwu* notwithstanding, they never tire of invoking their numerous other gods, in full awareness that they are arụsi or alụsi (absolutes). Thus, in invoking them the Aros of Arondizuogu exclaim *alụsi nine di na Izuogu na Iheme* (all the deities resident in Izuogu and Iheme).

One of the greatest mistakes again is to interpret this attitude of these Igbos that relate in this fashion to their deities (*arụsi or alụsi*) as an evident sign of his thoroughgoing relativism. Here, we are dealing with a typical instance of divided allegiance of the mind. It is a situation where the human mind is torn between relative and absolute commitment. It is a case of an internal tension and divide within the subject itself, as it seeks to reconcile the two basic logics that direct human action. These are, the logic of human interest and the ontological logic. Here, the human mind has the tendency to swing between two poles, one absolute, and the other relative. We are dealing here with typical cases of how the human consciousness reacts to the internal struggle to which it is subject. Here, the mode of flow of consciousness of an average traditional Igbo, for example, is not an exception. On the contrary, it follows the general rule regulating the flow of the consciousness of all mortals. We can say that human consciousness is subject to challenges of an internal absolute-relative tension. In this internal struggle, a subject has the tendency to heed the call of the moment, the logic of human interest, when its most cherished interests are at stake, oblivious of the totality of its determination, as this is epitomised in the ontological logic. When the logic of human interest takes the upper hand, the traditional Igbo, for example, discards *ikenga,* in its absolute significance as *arụsi or alụsi,* for whatsoever reason(s), and follows those interests that appeal most to the actor.

Among some Igbos, this tendency is clearly again shown in their discriminative categorisation of human beings into *osu* and *diala* for very pragmatic and egoistic purposes. In this case, the *diala* is the free born, with full rights of a person, whereas the *osu* is the untouchable or outcast. As cult slaves, such outcasts are more pointedly "called *ndi agọlu n' alụsi* (those consecrated or dedicated or offered to a spirit)" (Arinze, 59). Although most communities cannot do without their *osu,* who is dedicated to their deities, and who performs indispensable functions, the *osu* is nevertheless ostracised from the community. Thus, his person is an embodiment of the tension existing within human consciousness. Due to this tension, we can then say that the *osu is an indispensable outcast,* who is treated with the paradoxical mixed feeling of acceptance and rejection, with reverence and scorn all at the same time.

For this reason, it is very important to stress that *this swinging between absoluteness and relativity, acceptance and rejection, reverence and scorn, trepidation and joy, should never be interpreted as a sign of thoroughgoing relativity, as many hastily conclude.* On the contrary, *this vicissitude between absolute commitment and relativity is indicative of the internal tension, which is generated within the subject because of the ambivalent condition of all existential situations.* We can then say that the human consciousness often finds itself in a position that can rightly be described as a *commitment to both the absolute and the relative at the same time.* Here we are dealing with typical cases of *alụsi* within missing links in their tension-ladenness.

28. On the *arụsi* controversy and the moral sense: The categorical imperatives versus the universal imperatives

One of the severest consequences of the denial of commitment to the absolute is that this automatically impinges on the moral sense. Within African philosophy, those who are saying that African experience of the world is thoroughgoing relative are nothing but unapologetic disciples of Tempels. Even if they are not fully aware of this, they lend credence to Tempels' wrong thesis that, "We [the West] can conceive the transcendental notion of 'being' by separating it from its attribute, 'Force', but the Bantu cannot" (Tempels, Bantu Philosophy 50). Bearing in mind that many who reason this way have all Africans in mind, we can then see how unintended ethnocentric commitment can complicate matters for them. This is the case, not only with Kimmerle, but more so, with Achebe and Oluwole, who, according to Kimmerle, shares this opinion. The fact of absolute determination in relativity is the ontological precondition needed should we think of real freedom and happiness for any human action. What this means is that even if our freedom is relative, it is fully realisable and can be upheld only in consideration of the consequences of our actions vis-à-vis all possible relations, as missing links, that are mutually dependent on each other. For this mode of relationship to be complete, we must assume that it is interminable and absolute. In the absence of such absolute mode of determination, chances are that there is yet something left unattended to because of which the happiness we seek becomes unachievable. Hence, where this form of mutual relationship is not absolute in constitution, the chances of realising human freedom would remain perpetually restricted and unachievable. In other words, for real human happiness and freedom to be thinkable, this must be done under the assumption of an absolute foundation that guarantees such. Even within a relative framework, we see why this assumption makes sense. Any action we perform that does not take into account all the possible and imaginable relations, in their mutual complementary interrelatedness, leaves something unattended to which can always threaten and challenge the genuineness of such an action. This becomes most obvious in all those cases where we act in view of realising only our interests.

When now we focus only in realising our interests only, it is obvious that we can hardly attend to the interest of all stakeholders through this egoistic way. Where the interests of these remain unattended to, they can always turn around to make life insecure and unbearable for us and thereby undermine the ultimate end driving our action, which is the attainment of happiness and contentment. Hence, inability to attend to the interests of all comprehensively and absolutely, even if only theoretically, would restrict our freedom of action massively. In other words, by acting in an egoistic way, we would hardly address the needs of all concerned. Those, whose needs and interests remain unattended to, would pose perpetual dangers to us. In this way, our original intention to realise only our interests would be defeated, since this is perpetually under jeopardy and threat arising from those whose interests we neglected.

Besides, all acts of selfishness are driven by the ulterior motive of absolute possessiveness, which can only be possible when all possibilities of threat are eliminated. For actors to be truly selfish in the real sense of the word, they have to reckon with a situation where they perform such acts for themselves and for themselves alone without any form of challenges and infringement. This makes the presupposition of an absolute point of reference necessary, as this is equally the guarantor even of such negative cravings as selfish acts. What this shows is that even to be morally depraved, in the real sense of the word, actors have to presuppose the absolute to accomplish that nefarious feat, where they should remain unchallenged in their depravity. Likewise, to be truly good and benevolent, this has to be done under absolute conditions, where our goodness does not risk being challenged by any relative conditions that would undermine its inherent positive character. What this means is that, to be actually moral beings, either positively or negatively, we must act in such a way that takes into consideration all possible relations, as missing links in their mutual complementary interrelatedness. We can then say that morality is the capacity of the subject to be aware of the absolute cravings of human consciousness, which the mind intuits in the mutual dependence and interdependence in complementarity of all missing links.

Therefore, in all cases, there is need to assume an absolute instance because of which the human person can be said to be a moral agent. This is that absolute instance towards which human reason and will are directed and which directs and authenticates human action. These are those acts that we designate as moral acts which both in their deficiency and goodness need some absolute point of legitimisation. To uphold this legitimacy, such acts must be absolute to deserve their name. However, because of the challenges arising from human ambivalence situations, we are persuaded that acting in absolute manner is not possible, because the subject is internally challenged. This notwithstanding, for morality to be possible all acts seeking to be truly good must be total and absolute. The same can be said of all acts that really seek to be bad. They do so at least theoretically.

Hence, in order that morality and freedom can be possible we must assume this absolute foundation. Yet, it is within an absolute-relative bracket, in its swinging, that we can actually define this freedom and happiness due to the restrictions arising from human relative condition. It is a freedom and a state of happiness that are torn between egoism and altruism, as this is induced by our instinct of self-preservation, which instigates us to be selfish, but warns us, at the same time, to be cautious and considerate, lest in being excessively egocentric, by absolutely negating the interests of others, we risk losing our interests also. It is therefore on account of the ambivalence of all human existential situations, that we are again persuaded internally that it is possible that matters of morality can be defined within the relative region of this tension alone and that we can make do with half measures.

What this shows is that moral laws have an unmistakable absolute, binding and categorical foundation. This notwithstanding, the type of perfection achievable is only that, which is reserved to mere mortals. These are mortals caught in the ambivalent pendulum between absoluteness and relativity. It would be most unrealistic to uphold the opinion that moral laws, at this ambivalent level, is binding absolutely categorical as to demand that we must act *from duty* (The Metaphysical Foundation of Morals 528-537) Such a demand merely pretends to ignore the tension attached to the human condition, which, in all fairness, can make accession to such absolute duty-bound demand, difficult if not impossible. In obeying moral commands or imperatives, we must always bear in mind this precarious human condition. It is inconsideration of this precarious human condition that all modes of deontological ethical commands appear not to be taking the human condition seriously.

In complementary reflection, for moral laws to be really human, they have to be seen as binding in a comprehensive sense and not in an absolute categorical sense. This is why for complementary reflection, imperatives are not categorical, in the sense of absolute commands, but comprehensive, in the sense of relating to all human beings. This is precisely the point of demarcation between Immanuel Kant's categorical imperative and the imperative of complementary reflection. Whereas for Immanuel Kant and most deontological ethical systems, imperatives are categorical and absolute, for complementary reflection imperatives are not absolute but universal. Hence, we talk of *universal imperatives* in the case of complementary reflection as opposed to categorical imperatives. When now Kant approaches matters of ethical relevance with the mindset of *acting from duty,* this aims at the realisation of absolute imperatives as paradigms of practical living. Here, we talk of *categorical imperatives*. As relative historical beings, trying to achieve this categorical feat, which for Kant is a pragmatic viable option, is hardly in harmony with the type of tension to which human consciousness is exposed. For this reason, the realisation of all forms of categorical imperatives would remain mere utopia, since no human person can act in such a categorical absolute sense. Should we, in spite of the dangers posed by this precarious situation, insist that the human person acts *from duty*, we risk negating what actually makes us human in our relativity. In this case, acting moral, has an inescapable compulsive pathological moment. To forestall this, complementary reflection prefers addressing ethical imperatives from the point of view of their universal relevance, in view of grasping the human person in the fragility of his condition. By so doing, we recognise that the ethical subject is a human being, whose moral acts can only be realised based on human conditions and in reliance on those things that enter into defining our humanity. To these belong, not only our intellectual faculties, but also all possible relations in their complementary mutual interrelatedness. This is why, morality cannot be possible unless subjects invest all their resources including their emotional life, and all modes of inclination in those things that demand their attention. In view of this, complementary reflection does not subscribe to those positions that make moral imperatives dependent on obeying the promptings of what can be identified as those laws ensuing from the intellect alone. We are moral subjects when acting from the provisions of the totality of our being, while thereby being aware of the precariousness of our ambivalent existential situations. It is in response to this awareness that the universal imperative of complementary reflection demands, "Allow the limitations of being to be the cause of your joy." By this imperative, we are commanded always to think global and be human. This imperative merely demands that we act as human being destined for the joy f being, our fragility notwithstanding. It is in the act of existential conversion, that this human act takes concrete shape as all that is needed to be in control, in the sense of *being-in-control* (*ima-onwe-onye*) of our tension-laden existential situations.

In other words, complementary reflection arrives at the formulation of its imperative bearing in mind human relative condition, which must not be seen as an undue encumbrance or an insurmountable burden to authentic existence. On the contrary, to act ethically authentic, the human person has to do this in keeping with his nature that is both passionate and rational and at times irrational to the point of self-contradiction.

Hence, it has to be stressed that although imperatives, in the ideal theoretical ontological level, are absolute commands that demand absolute compliance, at the practical existential level, they demand universal compliance that is not absolute but complementarily binding. Their universal complementary binding character derives from the fact that any actor that seeks to negate them, risks not achieving those objectives he or she sets for himself or herself. In our relativity, we know that any measures undertaken to subvert the interests of others, would invariably make the realisation of our own interests difficult, if not impossible. For this reason, acting rational entails all those measures taken to preserve one's interests in the process of which the actor ensures that the interest of other stakeholders are upheld. This can happen where our actions have universal applicability. Hence, to this realisation is attached an imperative that is universally binding, but not categorically absolute, since actors are free to undermine laws dealing even with their interests. However, they would refrain from subverting such laws if by so doing they risk not getting what they want. In other words, if they value their interests and those noble goals they set for themselves, which we assume they do, they would do everything possible to refrain from undermining these, through undermining the interests of others. A clear demonstration of their rationality and good will towards themselves, is rooted in what they undertake to uphold their personal interests as these are coextensive with those of others. In this case, the imperative is universally valid but not absolute.

Hence, although complementary reflection recognizes that *uwa ezu oke* (the world is insufficient) and for this reason keeps asking *onye ka ozuru? (Who is perfect?)*, it is aware that *ibuanyidanda* (in complementarity we subsist and endure). This being the case, there is dire need to complement our efforts in our insufficiency. This can be done through those positive measures we take towards true and authentic living that seek to approximate the binding character of this absolute on which all imperatives rest, both those that claim categorical status and those that claim universal applicability. It is within this bracket that the imperative of complementary reflection can be situated. It is within this bracket that this imperative makes sense and draws its meaning, when it urges us to allow the limitations of being to be the cause of our joy. Where we are able to turn all missing links to sources of joy, we have the chances of living a relatively contented existence in our untiring efforts to be good which resembles what is absolutely demanded in all cases of morality. Within this framework therefore, it is only when we include all possible relations in the calculus of our actions, in a comprehensive complementary fashion, that human happiness and the freedom of the individual can be thinkable. These create the conditions for approximating what the mind seeks to grasp in its tendency to be absolute as a guarantee even of its own existence. Where this absolute foundation is not fully attended to, the human mind is exposed to all forms of threats. It is for this reason, that it seeks the absolute as an end in itself even if unconsciously. Hence, to assume the forcefulness of this absolute, in all matters human, is, at least, theoretically binding, since this is what gives us our moral sense. Practically, we may chose to act otherwise. What this shows is that it is only those persons who scorn at a complementary type of relationship that can be said not to desire real happiness.

We can therefore say that even if moral laws are binding absolutely, perfection is not achievable by any mortal subject in human relative condition, due to this tension that characterises human existence. Hence, any paradigm that a priori negates an absolute determination in human action ab inito negates morality as something fundamentally characteristic of the human person. In this negation, such a theory abdicates its rights to be human, since it questions the very foundations of the moral life of the individual. We can then see the precarious situation in which Tempels' position has brought us as this is further propounded by Kimmerle and Achebe. To say that the worldview of Africans is *merely relative*, as Kimmerle makes us believe and with particular reference to Achebe and Oluwole, is equivalent to saying that Africans are not moral beings. I assume that this is certainly not what they wish to say. However, the implications of their position are bewildering. This is precisely what can happen when researchers go about their work with ethnocentric mindset. We can rightly say that in all ambivalent situations, the human mind or human consciousness is torn between absolute and relative commitment, within the same framework, as an indication of its freedom that is not complete and as a clear indication of its determination to seek and share this freedom with others. This tendency to be committed to the absolute within human relative condition is not abdicable should humans remain those beings that are moral, rational and have the capacity to seek freedom and happiness. Hence, in matters of this nature, all human actions, no matter their character, have an aim guiding them, which is the realisation of a certain desirable objective that is worthy of attainment. This is that dimension of apparent goodness attached to every action that draws its character from the absolute goodness that determines all actions. This tending towards our objective in this manner is a clear manifestation of a moral sense and our ability to act rationally, which we carry within us by reason of our being human, and being destined for the good. To uphold this moral sense means all the efforts we make to equilibrate the tension arising from our ambivalent situations, without which we can never achieve any objectives we set before for ourselves, no matter their character. It is by reason of this equilibration that we demonstrate that we are human beings, who are reasonable and who understand that their desires can be realised based on the character of their being, which tends towards two extreme poles. Our commitment to this equilibration takes most concrete shape in our dealings with the opposite other most especially with other human beings. The capacity to define ourselves within this absolute-relative bracket as to give others a chance marks us out as rational moral beings.

Hence, any paradigm that a priori negates an absolute reference, which determines human action, in view of which its relativity becomes clearer, ab initio negates morality and the usefulness of moral laws. In this negation, such a theory abdicates its rights to be human, since it denies the most fundamental condition that bestows humans beings with a special place in the cosmos. The same is applicable also with regard to the subject upholding its moral responsibilities as a being that necessarily tends to ultimacy, its relativity notwithstanding. This commitment to an absolute instance must be seen as something very important and binding, at least theoretically, since it serves as a reminder that we have an obligation towards each other that is binding. Were we to say that a worldview is relative without qualifications, that is to say without any form of absolute commitment, then the grievous consequences are more than obvious.

We can then see how this moral sense has strong bearing to the principles and imperative of complementary reflection, the truth and authenticity criterion, as they form an indivisible unity with the principle of non-contradiction. It is therefore in consideration of the full implications of the relative-absolute relationship that the need to assume the applicability of the intrinsic connection that exists between these principles and the imperative of complementary reflection can be appreciated. In this case, this intrinsic connection lays out clearly the conditions for harmonious coexistence between missing links within any given framework, in view of performing their functions well and satisfactorily. In other words, we can rightly say that in all ambivalent situations, the human mind or human consciousness is torn between absolute and relative commitment within the same framework as an indication of the limitations imposed on its freedom, which nevertheless has a total, comprehensive and future referential dimension. This manner of understanding the situation of the human person, in given historical conditions, is not abdicable should human beings be those special rational creatures we all assume they are.

It would therefore not be proper to designate a worldview in such a tension-laden situation as either relative or absolute, without qualification. Here, reality presents itself to the mind not merely from one side, but from all sides of its constitution, all at the same time in its ambivalence. This is that reality that presents itself as something inviting and terrifying, agreeable and disagreeable, all at the same time. In this case, should we try to grasp and depict the structure of the human consciousness adequately and accurately, this can be done in the depth of its ambivalence, and not in the polarisation of its extreme expression in relativity and absoluteness. This swinging between absoluteness and relativity is not something peculiar to African experience of the world. This is precisely the point which Tempels also misses with his cumulative theistic evolutionary depiction of the Bantu when he claims: "Bantu of the present day have maintained their faith in what were originally theistic elements of their religion, yet we see them today at one and the same time ancestor worshippers, animists, dynamists, totemists and believers in magic" (Bantu Philosophy 34). Tempels came to this conclusion naturally on account of the heavy ethnocentric spectacle he was wearing in his consideration of the Bantu of his time. Were it not for this bias, he would have known that the phenomenon he was describing is not peculiar to the Bantu, but one that has relevance for the way all human beings relate to reality. All human beings tend to misrepresent what they consider as the absolute, and this is why they tend at one time towards polytheism, at another time towards monotheism and at other times towards animism, dynamism etc.

This vicissitudinous tendency towards absoluteness and relativity, theism and atheism, animism and dynamism and other forms of religious commitment can hardly be interpreted as evolutionary or signs of thoroughgoing relative commitment. This is something that accompanies the human consciousness, wherever human beings start to ask questions and seek comprehensive answers. It is merely a common phenomenon that characterises the structure of the human consciousness in its ambivalence and one that transcends all cultures. Besides, there is no doubt that the traditional Igbo experience of reality admitted of the dimension of absolute commitment, since Igbos, like all human beings, are deeply aware of the forcefulness of the principle of non-contradiction.

In other words, this tension captures the situation of the mind in its confusion between what things are in themselves and what the mind imagines them to be, as situations demand. This tension, which gives us insight into the character of the problem, does give us at the same time full insight into the type of solution(s) or approach(s) needed to address them. If any brand of intercultural philosophies thinks that it can avoid the moment of absolute commitment in its theory formulation, it does so at the risk of misrepresenting the human situation and this can have very grievous consequences.

From the foregoing, one can say that the human mind, in its fragmentary relative constitution, has an unmistakable dimension of ultimate absolute determination, which must be addressed, should we uphold a balance within the subject. In all matters human, this mode of ambivalent determination must always be borne in mind, should reflection not get lost in the tension the human subject is exposed. Should such occur, human reason easily finds itself on the way to extreme poles of either relativity or absoluteness. It is therefore necessary to state now: *Complementary reflection is not claiming that human experience of reality and the world in general is absolute or relative without qualification. It is rather affirming that human experience of reality can be situated within the bracket of the tension generated by all human ambivalent situations. Such ambivalent situations have both an absolute and a relative dimension all the time and at all places.*

In this sense, the whole matter revolves around the reasons underlying the subject-object tension such that the subject seeks its autonomy outside the foundation of its unity. In other words, it is a problem of the challenges of human ambivalent situation and the processes needed to confront this challenge, as this forms the focus of the principles and imperative of complementary reflection. *This position would give us a very important clue towards answering many questions that may be raised concerning some of the basic presuppositions of my position in complementary reflection.*

This complementary transcendent approach is all the more inevitable because, in our encounter with reality, there is always a moment of uncertainty, and here, we remain ignorant of some aspects of the totality of our world, no matter the efforts we make, and no matter how hard we strain ourselves. The issue of absoluteness or relativity depends therefore, on the readiness of a subject to be realistic to itself, and its world, and resubmit itself to the character of its true nature, as something relative striving towards wholeness. Here, the subject is better committed to the guidance ensuing from the demand of truth and authenticity criterion; a criterion that captures all missing links in their nature and adds nothing more.

Complementary reflection thus, sneers at all forms of exclusive, absolute, extreme hegemonic forms of reasoning, be it absolute or relative, that seek to resolve this issue arbitrarily on the platform of an ideal absolute or relative hegemonic form of rationality. The way we handle this issue determines the type of philosophy, conception of human being, and society we are capable of evolving. It is for this reason that I insist that all meanings and references get their true worth, and can be validated, only in a comprehensive, whole and future oriented manner. The reason is that, reality does not evince itself fully in singular historical instances, but only complementarily comprehensive. In this sense, wholeness, unity, comprehensiveness, fragmentation, and future reference remain those transcendent ontological categories of authentication for all forms of knowledge and experience. Although these categories are intrinsic forms of the mind, they can be invalidated due to the challenges of our ambivalent existential situation. On the other hand, they can be regained experientially in the process of *existential conversion,* where we render these transcendent categories concrete. It is on account of commitment to these transcendent categories and based on the resultant mutual experience of transcendent complementary unity of consciousness that most knotty issues can be explored.

29. On the ontological foundation of true and authentic knowledge and action and being-in-control (*ima-onwe-onye*)

Since the idea of relative character of truth is one that hardly goes away, most especially among African philosophers, it suffices to elucidate this matter from another angle. This exposition has to be read along with the erroneous claim that "in African thought 'nothing is absolute'". For complementary reflection, the ultimate foundation of true knowledge and experience of reality is ontologically founded in being, insofar being is that on account of which anything that exists serves a missing link of reality. Here, we are dealing with the idea of being in its essential interrelatedness without bifurcation. Conceptualising being in this form can not even do away with the idea of the absolute. On the contrary, this makes the assumption of an absolute foundation of all missing links not only impelling but also indispensable. Here, being is that on account of which all missing links are thinkable in a harmonious future referential way. Conceptualising the foundation of true and authentic knowledge and experience of reality in this way is important bearing in mind the relative and fragmentary nature of missing links whose existences always seek permanency. Take away this dimension of an absolute future reference, and this fundamental permanence becomes shaky. It is in view of this absolute future referential dimension of our experience of reality that our genuine efforts to seek harmony as contracting units gets full meaning and can be defended. *This holds true, not only for traditional African experience of reality, but more so for human beings everywhere and every time.* It is because of this absolute reference that all modes of inter-subjective experiences can be defended, all modes of constituted authority, every type of reason, theoretical and practical, legitimised.

Without this form of absolute indubitable commitment in future reference, which for complementary reflection is the ideal of reason seeking full authentication in history, both practically and theoretically, no certain knowledge would be possible, even at pure subjective level. The same can be said of morality, which is grounded, on the feeling of an absolute indubitable foundation, as earlier shown. Such an absolute ontological commitment is inevitable if we are honest with ourselves when we aver that the "modest dream of philosophy [is] to speak the truth (even if, as the case may arise, such truth needs be spoken to power)" (Eze, In Search of Reason's Traces 40). To speak, think of, and even possess such truths, which are binding, and on account of which we speak to power fearlessly, belongs to the natural cravings of the human mind. We can then understand why Eze makes this statement in his advocacy of the philosopher's right of exercise of his natural freedom of criticism against despotic form of reason that can impinge on this natural craving to possess truth in its purest form. However, bearing in mind Eze's consequent aversion for an absolute type of ontological commitment, and in consideration of his determination to speak the truth, no matter whose ox is gored, it is to be assumed that what he has in mind with the above statement is that capacity of the philosopher to speak the whole truth and speak it fearlessly and thoroughly. In this case, if truth needs be spoken to power, and spoken thoroughly and fearlessly, a dream which we all cherish, it must be spoken cautiously, lest in our eagerness to speak the truth, we usurp power.

What this shows is that there is always a moment of absolute commitment in all those matters that we approach with utmost passion, such as speaking the truth fearlessly and thoroughly. Hence, the greatest challenge in all situations is how to address our innate cravings for truth, objectivity, fair play, freedom and justice *in an absolute ideal fashion.* This merely goes to demonstrate that the actual problem is not located on the necessity of an absolute foundation towards which all things are geared. The main problem touches on how to grapple with this indispensable absolute dimension of our experience of the world. What this shows is that the craving for absolute commitment is always given in our passionate relationship to reality and can be concealed from us. Where such absolute cravings are concealed from us, the potentialities for error are always given, even in those matters we adjudge most straightforward. In order not to mistake arrogance for courage, fundamentalism for genuine vocation, and unbridled quest for freedom and fair play for passionate concern for truth, there is need to inquire into the conditions of possibility for all valid claims, most especially in asymmetrical situations of power imbalance. Here, the question of the epistemological foundation of true knowledge and of all claims to certainty becomes an indisputable matter of utmost importance. This can never be resolved arbitrarily by recourse to an unmediated absolute or a relative type of reason. Where we insist on commitment to this mode of unmediated type of rationality, be it relative, be it absolute, all attempts to bring reason under one relative or absolute roof turns arbitrary and hegemonic. This is why all forms of unmediated truths of reason spoken to power, even in the best intentions, easily revert to usurpation of power. As genuine and challenging as the issue involved in matters of this kind can be, they can be resolved only when the inquirer bears in mind that philosophy, as wisdom, is that science that guides us in our eagerness to speak the truth in this latter sense of caution. Here, it reveals to us the dangers concealed by the ambivalence of our situation, such that in speaking the truth, we do not overstep the bounds allowable to mere mortals. It is only from this background of caution that we can address the complex issues arising from such questions as: Whose truth? Whose reason? And: who sets the standard for truth and authenticity? Is there such an objective truth that regulates and binds human actions generally and universally?

To be honest to ourselves, it is important to observe that there are hardly thoroughgoing straightforward adequate rational answers to these questions, since they strike human reason in the depth of its ambivalence, and in the tempestuous nature of its relativity. One thing must however be admitted, any answer(s) that must be adjudged adequate in this direction has to be comprehensive, in the sense that it has to encompass the human person in the totality of his being, as a missing link, bearing in mind the uncertainties that need to be addressed. In this case, it must try to capture the human person in the fragility and insufficiency of his rationality, while bearing in mind the ultimate comprehensiveness of all modes of determination. It is in this sense that this matter can be said to have an inherently socio-psychological dispositional dimension that is often ignored. To tackle such an issue requires therefore recourse to a regulative instance that mediates in ambivalent tension-laden matters of such concern. Here, no finite subject(s), for obvious reasons, no matter how cute and audacious, qualifies for such an enormous undertaking of providing such a comprehensive clear and evident answer. This is why, any truths that must be spoken to power, in a manner that is honest, must be regulated by an instance outside of reason's own domain; *but one that carries reason along with it.* It is within the ambit of such a mediating regulative instance, within which the cravings of the ego and all missing links can be creditably harmonised, that matters of this kind can be handled. This is that complementary ontological horizon where substance and accidents are duly harmonised, such that, all stakeholders making claims to power experience themselves as mutually related in a binding absolute way. Such a regulative instance must be ontologically transcendent in nature, but intricately related to all missing links, as it shares their horizon of being. It is based on these characteristics that such an instance can play this function well.

The necessity of assuming such an objective ontological horizon of mediation, that has the outlook of this absolute mutual complementary mode, and one that offers us the foundation for the legitimisation of all claims about truth and objectivity is not only reasonable but also pragmatically demanding. This fact ensues from the nature of the matter, and can never be wished away, just because we want to do philosophy modestly and humbly. On the contrary, modesty and humility even demand that we submit ourselves, in our relativity and insufficiency, to such an overarching control mechanism, lest reason gets lost in its craving for a self-devised autonomy outside of the legitimacy provided by all missing links. This challenge to be devoted to the legitimacy ensuing from an absolute complementary horizon is unfortunately the philosophical burden as philosophy seeks to grasp the joy of being in all fragmentary historical situations.

Hence, the passionate disposition for truth, as is characteristic of and expected of the philosophical mindset, does not elevate the philosopher automatically either to a "high priest" or a "sovereign", as Eze fears it might (In Search of Reason's Traces 40); it is rather the unfortunate consequence of the vocation of a philosopher, either as a scholar or as a layperson, and in whatever position or duties such a philosopher may find himself or herself. In all these instances, the philosopher is challenged to be committed to truth and authenticity in its most radical, objective, absolute and ontological constitution. Yet by being so committed, the philosopher always remembers the mutual complementary character of all missing links. It is by so doing that human reason remains circumspect and is fully conscious of the dangers posed by the ambivalence of its existential situation. This is what characterises philosophy as wisdom and makes the philosopher, irrespective of his or her standing in life, different from all human beings. This philosopher we all are and can become, depending on how we strive to handle the ambivalence of our situation. This is why I insist that "*All those scientists, pseudo-philosophers, theologians, politicians and ideologists who generate and propagate ideas, and have refused to become philosophers are some of the greatest dangers and challenges to the new world order*" (Asouzu, The Method and Principles 46). It is for this reason also that philosophy, when articulated as a discipline, is nothing other than the science of being through which the thinking subject seeks to address the ambivalence arising from his world, as a being-in-control. This is why for complementary reflection, to be is to be in control and this is the moment human reason seeks truth in its entirety. Here, any philosophy that is articulated outside of the framework provided by all missing links, in their complementary interrelatedness, merely seeks to distort the idea of truth itself. We can then understand why the epistemological foundation of truth and authenticity remains mediated in this mutual complementary mode, in a way that leaves no one in any doubt as to the harmonised nature of the relative and the absolute.

30. On coexistence of contraries and contradictories; the dual fundamental human rights to err and to know reality with certainty

One of the major difficulties which a philosophy that is complementary in orientation has to face is that of having to address those situations that are "Non-complementary, that which is endemically contradictory, that which is negative and that which cannot be integrated as decisive life experience" as pointed out by Franz Gmainer-Pranzl (93, Translated from the German original by me). Gmainer-Pranzl's observation in this connection is one that draws from day-to-day experience, as we have this in most practical situations. These are those situation where actors may be inclined to reject those modes of coexistence they consider unpleasant to them. Within such contexts, a complementary mode of coexistence may even be found most disagreeable. Here, we must concede to human fundamental right to freedom of association and choice between alternatives. It is like addressing those interests which stakeholders consider too sacred to integrate into alternative systems. We have such situations in religion, in commerce, in international relations, in private and public life, etc. The same is applicable to those matters dealing with diverse modes of alternative life styles and revolutionary ideas that challenge the status quo. As this matter concerns complementary reflection, it is important to state that as a philosophy of integration and social progress, it is fully committed to the coexistence of opposites and contraries, as we have this in most situations of life. However, the issue of coexistence of contradictory opposites is another matter. Here, it has to be observed that the freedom of association and choice between alternatives are not absolute modes of freedom.

Most contradictory problems of mutual coexistence among human beings have very serious dispositional dimensions that cannot be ignored. For this reason, such matters cannot be addressed only by making recourse to proofs and demonstrative logical reasoning and arguments. In all cases, all forms of logic have their limits, since they share in human relative insufficiency. In matters of this kind, we are dealing indirectly also with issues concerning absolute truth and who has the right of ultimate insight and adjudication. As earlier pointed out, such matters can never be decided a priori as to be subjected to the legitimacy ensuing from the autonomy ensuing from the subject only. In other words, it is not something that can be decided based either on a relative or an absolute type of rationality only. Here, such matters are not easily resolved solely on claims of who is absolutely right or who is absolutely wrong. To start with, issues involving absolute truths are not matters that can be decided like all matters of experience, because of the limitations imposed by human insufficiency. On the other hand, human consciousness shows an inherent determination towards certainty and one that seeks to know things wholly and absolutely. This cannot be ignored just because we wish to do things our own ways. It is within this relative-absolute bracket, and not outside of it, that such matters can be handled creditable. Similarly, such matters cannot be handled adequately within a context where the ego, in its relativity, arrogates to itself the capacity of acting arbitrarily, as if it is its sole lawgiver. In other words, no matter how highly we cherish our points of view, no positions are absolute as to represent the truth in its totality. Truth emerges within an ontological bracket that has a complementary absolute dimension. This claim makes sense because no human person can exist alone and call this existence. This is why we say that to be is not to be alone (*ka sọ mụ adina*).

As this matter relates to human subjects, one can say that all attempts at grasping the truth are mere approximations of its ultimate objectification but one, which cannot be approximated unless all possible relations are put into account. What this shows is that, the ideal character of truth as the guide that determines human actions, remains undisputed and is reinforced, in all acts seeking full authentication. However, this fact can never negate the moment of human insufficiency. It is this insufficiency that gives truth its absolute significance and character and makes it possible to identify it in its otherness as such. This is why for complementary reflection, truth is communicable through a complementary logic, which makes the absolute and relative dimensions of truth mutually authenticating, as they need each other to be grasped. This is still applicable even to those truths of reason that have an apparently necessary, analytic and apodictic character as we have these in the areas of pure and applied mathematics. Here truth becomes evident indirectly through the instrumentality of synthetic judgements. The same is applicable to the forcefulness and apodictic character of the first principles and the principle of non-contradiction, which become evident in practical moments. The same is applicable to law of causality whose forcefulness is mediated in practical situations of life.

One of the commonest mistakes is to think that these principles and laws can be penetrated directly in their raw forms only. The same holds true when we think that the principle of non-contradiction is applicable in its raw form without taking into account the relative human condition through which it becomes evident. This being the case, in all matters dealing with the human person as a relative subject, the principle of non-contradiction, its apodictic character notwithstanding, can never be enforced, wholly and entirely, without impinging on human freedom and autonomy. Were we to enforce this principle in this raw form, we would be infringing on the fundamental human right to err. This right is co-extensive with our humanity. The same thing is applicable to the human fundamental right to know things with certainty. Hence, it is always important to bear in mind the coexistence of these fundamental natural rights in the same thinking and acting subject. Failure to be concede to this insight would immediately negate one of the most fundamental constituents of what it takes to be a human person. In other words, both the fundamental human rights to err and to know things with certainty are co-extensive with our humanity. Remove these rights and the human person loses his freedom and autonomy. It is therefore within this bracket of our right to know and not to know, our right to strive to perfection and to be limited, to say yes and to say no, all at the same time, that all issues concerning the right to be different can be situated.

In such situations, we are dealing with the human person in the totality of his being and not in the fragmentation of his relativity. Within this bracket, each human being is endowed not only with the fundamental right to err but also with the attendant obligations to live up to those expectations ensuing from his limitations. The most radical form of expression of this obligation is to know that there is a form of certainty to which all reasons are subject and on account of which our rights to err should never be turned to licence. In this case, the right to err translates to the capacity to blend this right with the obligation to realise that the other persons may be certain in those matters that concern them most intimately. It is on account of this realisation that stakeholders should be tolerant and cautious in their dealing with the world around them. Where they repudiate this responsibility to be tolerant and cautious, they risk losing their rights either to know or to err. This is what it entails to be human, failing which stakeholders in conflict situations risk losing their rights and being respected as humans. Where such mutual respect is absent, stakeholders risk degenerating to a state not in keeping with those higher ideas we ascribe to being human and a situation where the exercise of their freedom would be grossly restricted if not revoked completely.

Within any complementary framework, the right to freedom is bestowed by a horizon that legitimises human acts mutually. Within such a horizon any units that dares act outside of the legitimacy provided by the mutual complementary relationship existing between all stakeholders, must reckon with its actions boomeranging. Unless a person decides to live completely alone, in this case, his decision becomes inconsequential. But there is hardly any such miserable human creature that exercises existence in complete isolation. Since it is in community that we define ourselves and make such demands as having our rights defined other ways, we cannot eat our cake and have it. It is then understandable that for complementary reflection, to be is not to be alone (*ka sọ mụ adina*). Hence, to be entails all the processes needed to be in mutual complementary relationship, failing which we cannot say that a person exists. Where a person seeks to exist but does not undertake those things that define his state as existing, we cannot take the person serious. Where he claims to exist but does not take the measures to secure his existence in the sense of defining himself within the framework of all missing links, his action is bound to boomerang. Here, we talk of ontological boomerang effect. A typical example is when a person claims to exist but always seeks his interests at the exclusion of the interests of others. Naturally, this person would not get his interests, unless he sees the need to recognise the interests of others whose existence enter into the definition of his own. This is specifically what we have in mind when we say that consequent or consistent self-interest is anti-self interest. This boomerang effect is enshrined in the insight *egbe bere ugo bere nke si ibe ya ebena nku kwaa ya* (let the kite perch, let the eagle perch, whichever denies the other the same rights, let its wings break). What this implies is that in any given situation where units do not endeavour to uphold some measure of restrain with regard to those rights they consider inalienable, they would hardly also be in a position to enjoy such rights. In other words, it is only when stakeholders are tolerant enough as to recognise that they need to answer to the obligations enshrined in their rights that they can be free to act the way that pleases them.

Even if we are not always aware of the applicability of the inherent necessary relationship between such rights and the obligation that are attached to them, at an abstract ideal level, it has the character of a universal necessary natural law, because it is the foundation on which our rights as free autonomous subjects are grounded. One can therefore say that the capacity to recognise that the rights to err and to know things with certainty belongs fundamentally to the character of the human person in the relativity of his existence and by reason of the absolute form of his determination. From here derives that there is an inescapable mutual relationship between both rights that cannot be ignored or negated. The moment we seek to ignore or negate either of both rights, and the attendant obligations attached to them, that is the moment we abdicate our right also to be human. *It is only in view of respecting these two rights that we can say that the principle of non-contradiction comes in full force, because it does not allow us to be human and not to be human all at the same time. Here we must choose. In this case, this principle is binding absolutely in view of our self-definition.*

If we are able to approximate the demands of the principle of non-contradiction thus in our actions, we can say that acting under the impelling force of its applicability, in the manner stated above, is equivalent to intuiting into the absolute ideal form of its demands and applicability. This grasping into, and having a foretaste of its applicability notwithstanding, all forms of perfection achievable at the level of human coexistence remains incomplete because of the dangers of the challenges arising from human relativity. However, at the ideal absolute level, the validity of this principle remains unchallenged and apodictic as a postulate both of practical and theoretical reason. It is precisely at this level of ultimate applicability that differences give way to absolute unity; complementarity gives way to absolute harmony, such that all missing links in their search for legitimacy find their unity in one absolute foundation that knows of no contradiction. It is in this sense that one can say that "*This ultimate foundation of unity does not admit of any differences and is ultimately exclusive. This is the only moment where in seeking complementarity all entities and interests unite in one ultimate entity whose nature is unity and non-contradiction per se. This is the point where all differences disappear and all forms of ambivalence give way to clarity* (The Method and Principles 312).

It is in view of this absolute ideal state, which can be approximated, even momentarily in the experience of transcendent complementary unity of consciousness and through the act of *existential conversion* that one can say that the idea of co-existence of good and evil as co-existence of moments of being and non-being, within the same framework of meaning is not in consonance with the basic assumptions of complementary reflection. If we view the matter from this ideal absolute perspective, we can then understand why the co-existence of contradictories is not thinkable.

This notwithstanding, due to the special character of the human condition in its relative-absolute determination, all ideas and values, that lay claims to certainty and validity, are inherently subject to authentication in all existential situations. The same thing is applicable to the caution we bring towards them, lest they are true and valid. It is in this openness that the principle of non-contradiction plays itself out, at the concrete practical level. Here, all cases of apparent contradiction between human beings can be handled in patience and tolerance. This is why complementary reflection never ceases to highlight the dispositional dimension of this problem, which must also be handled not purely at a logical abstract level, but more so on the basis of mutual tolerance, backed up by the disposition of mutual vicarious feeling of compassion (*obi nwanne*).

The moment this lesson has been internalised, that is the moment we start thinking of the coexistence even of those matters that appear to us to be contradictory, which in actual fact are matters belonging to those unresolved regions of our being, on account of our determination both to relativity and absoluteness. On the other hand, the moment we ignore the special character of the human situation as something ambivalent, that is the moment also the issues appear insurmountable, which are raised by Gmainer-Pranzl concerning the coexistence of "Non-complementary, that which is endemically contradictory, that which is negative and that which cannot be integrated as decisive life experience"(93). Thus, it is in the simultaneous full affirmation of the fundamental human rights to err and to know things with certainty that the individual upholds his autonomy and not in its denial. This is an insight that easily escapes us in all those situations where we insist on seeing contradictions. Naturally, such contradictions will persist and need to be eradicated, but through the act of positive self-affirmation. This act of positive self-affirmation entails commitment to our humanity, which makes provision for the coexistence of errors. Here, all human beings are subject to error, and this is why we say that to err is human. Anyone who does not subscribe to this age-old adage is not likely to enter into any type of relationship; but there is hardly any such mortal who does not err.

31. On the pedagogy of reason or noetic propaedeutic

In other words, the moment human beings come to realise this important point about the character of their being, as something that has both a relative and absolute determination, that is the moment they unite to seek truth and certainty as a common patrimony, their differences notwithstanding; this is the moment also they cherish such virtues as patience, tolerance, truthfulness, equity, justice, readiness to forgive, ability to love, as things worth aspiring towards. However, the full attainment of this level of consciousness does not come per chance. The natural character of this insight notwithstanding, it needs to be backed up by a form of pedagogy and this is the pedagogy of a complementary comprehensive type that addresses the human person in its entirety. It is a noetic type of propaedeutic that is at the foundation of any action that seeks to be human. This is the main thrust of complementary noetic propaedeutic. It is through this type of propaedeutic that actors come to appreciate the practical worth of the truth and authenticity criterion, as this is an aspect of the principle of non-contradiction. This truth and authenticity criterion, which demands that we never elevate a world immanent missing link to an absolute instance, is nothing other than the main foundation on which the pedagogy of reason, rests, as it keeps reminding all stakeholders about the innate character of their constitution, which is one that plays itself out within a relativity - absolute framework.

What this implies is that the apparent contradictions we sense in interpersonal relationship are not sufficient reasons to make recourse to extreme measures in view of resolving differences. If we do, we are elevating ourselves to absolute instances in total negation of our relative historical condition and in total negation even of our own fundamental right to err. Hence, the awareness concerning the existence of such perceived contradictions is a call to duty, since it offers us the opportunity to understand that exclusiveness and polarisation, as is enshrined in contradictory relationship, is not the ultimate destiny of missing links, as they strive towards full authentication. The existence of such exclusive tendencies is occasioned by the uncertainty surrounding all human ambivalent situations, and such that harbour the phenomenon of concealment (*ihe mkpuchi anya*). This phenomenon hinders the mind from understanding fully its precarious situations. Besides, it is the same phenomenon that hinders the mind from realising that its ultimate destiny has a future reference. Hence, an unflinching commitment to the demands of the principle of non-contradiction indicates a positive commitment to the pedagogy or propaedeutic to which human reason in all historical situations is subject. The aim of this pedagogy is to continue reminding human reason of the character of its ultimate determination, which subsists in the harmony of differences, through which actors attain full autonomy. It is in this sense that all missing links share the same foundation of being, as this is guaranteed by the same indivisible principle of non-contradiction. In this sense also, my position is fully in harmony with the ideas of traditional African philosophers of complementary system of thought for whom the principle of non-contradiction is as valid as we have this in all human communities. I feel that this explication should also help to elucidate the issue, which Esu Thomas Ijemot appears to have misunderstood with regard to my position, as it concerns the principle of non-contradiction and its bearing to the teachings of anonymous traditional African philosophers (Esu 67). All human beings are subject to the dictates of this principle in the way I have explained, and it is by recourse to the demands of such a principle that we can mediate successfully in seemingly difficult cases involving disagreements and differences in opinion. My position, as it concerns African philosophy, cannot be taken for granted if one considers the fact that some people like Onyewuenyi seem to suggest that the principle of non-contradiction is alien to African thinking. As earlier pointed out, this misconception has much to do with Tempels' "vital force" theory.

Since issues relating to most differences and disagreements have usually an inherently dispositional dimension, efforts to offer viable solutions to them must be regained anew. For this reason, such efforts have to proceed from experience, both at the individual and collective levels, as they have a comprehensive outreach, and are anchored on the ontological ultimate foundation of reality. That is to say, the issue concerning how to get at the objective truth that guides our knowledge, actions and decisions, in all critical situations, can never be complete unless its ontological foundation is brought to bear on the totality of all missing links, as these seek comprehensiveness and authenticity in all historical situations. This is why this matter can be articulated fully and adequately as an aspect of truth and authenticity criterion. In this case, as relative historical subject, we seek comprehensiveness, wholeness, universality and future reference in all our actions as ends in themselves, as we make conscious efforts to convert the transcendent categories of unity of consciousness into lived existential categories.

Where this happens, all missing links reveal themselves as veritable sources of joy to any objective actors set for themselves. This is that situation where all stakeholders come to realise fully that they all share the same horizon of being vicariously, and one that gives fulfilment to their aspirations such that anything undertaken to undermine this horizon immediately appears to all stakeholders as self-contradiction. What this implies is that by strict adherence to the demands of the method, principles and imperative of complementary reflection, the mind is imbued with the mechanisms needed to confront the challenges posed by extreme forms of relative and absolute commitment, which surface in situations of contradiction. By reliance on those mechanisms provided by complementary reflection, it becomes evident to all missing links of reality that their sharing of a common horizon of being goes with it an inherent moment of mutual responsibility, the negation of which is inherently also consequent to self-negation. What this implies is that the sharing of the same horizon of being invariably leads, not only to the mutual communicability of transcendent subjective experiences, but more importantly, it leads also to a vicarious sharing of the consequences arising from such experiences both theoretically and practically.

32. On the transcendent categories of unity of consciousness

An issue that deserves more attention is how the transcendent categories of unity of consciousness relate directly to the ideas of anonymous traditional African philosophers of the complementary system of thought. This is precisely the issue which Kimmerle raises when he asks how one should understand my assertion that "the worldview of the traditional African shows…strong moments of the transcendent ontological categories of unity, totality, universality, comprehensiveness, wholeness and future referentiality as authentic dimensions of thoroughgoing complementarism". It is important to remark that what I have in mind with this assertion is precisely the system of thought of anonymous traditional African philosophers of the complementary direction; this assertion follows from the context of the statement. To be more precise, this statement has to be interpreted within the context of anonymous traditional Igbo philosophers of the complementary system of thought; a thought system that finds parallel in other traditional African societies. This being the case, my position refers to complementary system of thought as it might be found in traditional African societies, be this among the traditional "Fulanis, Ibibio, Masai, Hausa, or Fulani, Pygmies, San or Khoi".

There is sufficient evidence, as I have demonstrated in my attempt to rehabilitate this traditional African ontology, that the thinking of these traditional Igbo philosophers shows very strong elements of these transcendent categories, to which belongs the dimension of *fragmentation* as moment of relative future commitment.

With regard to the dimension of relativity, we see this mostly given when traditional Igbo philosophers of the complementary system of thought seek to capture all missing links in their insufficiency in the evident insight that *uwa ezuoke* (the world is incomplete or insufficient). Similarly, they conceptualise being within the relational ontological bracket of *ihe nwere isi na ọdụ* or something that has head and tail-end. This is why these philosophers keep asking: *onye ka ozuru?* (Who is perfect?). This awareness concerning human insufficiency notwithstanding, the resolution of some of the major challenges of this human insufficiency was for these philosophers not an insurmountable task, bearing in mind how the future is very constitutive in their thinking. We can infer this from the influence of these philosophers on the overall way Igbos relate to the future. This is why for most Igbos, *ihe ukwu kpe azụ* (the greatest events are in the future). In other contexts, the same thought is expressed as *nke iru ka* (the future event is the greatest*)*. In the expression *onye ma echi* (who knows tomorrow) we are dealing with the fragmentary uncertain character of existence in its future relatedness. Furthermore, relying on the insight of these traditional Igbo philosophers, Igbos never tire of saying or cautioning: *eche di ime* (tomorrow is pregnant). This saying captures that dimension of the future that is not only real but also uncertain and in which human insufficiency plays itself out. It is in view of confronting the challenges and uncertainties arising from this future referential dimension of all events that these traditional Igbo philosophers insist that *njikọ ka* (togetherness is the greatest virtue). Fundamental to all these lies the horizon within which reality can be creditably articulated when these philosophers insist that *ibuanyidanda* (in mutual complementary dependence, and interdependence we endure and subsist).

In the concept *ozurumba,* traditional Igbo philosophers of the complementary system of thought seek to capture the moment of totality as dimension of universal comprehensiveness. The same thought is enshrined in the concept "obiọha" (complementary comprehensive mindset or philosophical mindset). For Achebe, the moment of totality is further captured by what he calls "double-headed phrases ("Chi" in Igbo Cosmology 71). To these belong such expressions as *"ikwu na ibe"* (the entire community of kinsmen and women; "nta na imo" (odds and ends), etc. Besides, we see the preponderant place which traditional Igbo philosophers assign to the concept of totality as dimension of comprehensiveness as this stays at the very foundation of what Iroegbu characterises as "Uwa Ontology". Uwa in Igbo language denotes the world in its entirety. Using "uwa" as his idea of being, Iroegbu avers, "uwa is all-inclusive" (Iroegbu, Metaphysics 339). What is remarkable in Iroegbu's recourse to "uwa" as the idea of being is not so much so its exactness, but more so the fact that this concept seeks to capture the attitude of traditional Igbo philosophers to reality in general.

All these instances give us insight into the idea of traditional Igbo philosophers of the complementary system of thought for whom being can be grasped from the preceding condition of its all-inclusive complementary comprehensiveness, wholly and entirely. When now these traditional Igbo philosophers of the complementary system of thought recognise the preponderant place of the future in view of grasping being from the preceding conditions of its whole relational essentiality, they do not consider the content and character of this future as a mere theoretical construct. On the contrary, they see the future as a reality that must be reckoned with in view of handling adequately most challenges resulting from human insufficiency. This commitment to a future referential foundation of all possible relations takes a very radical shape for these traditional Igbo philosophers in the ensuing experience of life after death. This took for them, as for most traditional African philosophers of the complementary system of thought, the form of what has come to be characterised as "ancestor **worship**". It is important to highlight the word "worship" to indicate the centrality, intensity and constitutive character of this experience or phenomenon.

It is the same experience that underlies belief in reincarnation and above all the idea of continued existence of the human person in the spirit world after death. This place of continued future existence is designated by Igbos as *ala mmụọ* (land of spirits). Since acceptance into *ala mmụọ* connotes the fullness of human existence in a future related perspective, we can then understand how this belief constitutes the main fulcrum of traditional Igbo existential living. As an idea that rests on the insight of traditional Igbo philosophers of the complementary system of thought, the grips, which this phenomenon has on the psyche of traditional Igbos, remains phenomenal. Thus, we are informed by the anthropologist Basden, when alluding to the importance of the future in traditional Igbo existential living, that:

> For a father to chastise his son is quite unusual; most fathers would not entertain such a proposal. They will not punish even in cases where their offspring thoroughly deserve a sound thrashing. One has known instances where boys have been terrors to the household and still the parents would not take a strong line to bring the young rascals to order. The explanation is that the father stands in mortal dread lest he should incur the lasting displeasure of his son –especially of the eldest one- for on his son depends his own salvation. If his son hates him how is he to be given an honourable and worthy burial? With what marks of distinction will he enter the 'Land of Spirits' if his son remains at enmity with him? This being the case, the father endures the misdemeanours of his son rather than risk incurring that son's displeasure, and thereby putting in jeopardy his status in the future life...The Ibo will endure everything demanded of him in this life, will put up with hardships, the misbehaviour of his children, indeed anything, in order to insure that his burial will be properly performed. His whole future welfare depends upon this, and hence it takes, at all times, a most prominent place in a man's calculations (Basden, Among The Ibos of Nigeria, 85-86, 117-118)

What Basden is describing is that aspect of the ideas of traditional Igbo philosophers of the complementary system of thought that provides a unified consciousness in view of surmounting most radical existential difficulties. This is the idea of life in a future referential perspective. Thus, for the traditional Igbo, human life revolves around a unified consciousness, provided by this belief in a future life, which determined most of its important rites and symbols. Thus the idea of complementarity, in its most complex expression as a transcendent unified conscious act encompassing all areas of life and is geared towards a future that is uncertain, yet intelligible enough as to sustain meaningfully the totality of human existence. This belief forms an integral part of the ideas of traditional Igbo philosophers of the complementary system of thought. Hence, by recourse to the forcefulness of the transcendent categories ensuing from this ontological commitment, these philosophers were able to shape the worldview of their contemporaries and beyond, just as the ideas of eminent philosophers everywhere shape the worldview of their contemporaries and beyond.

In this sense, I quite agree with Kimmerle's observation that it is worthwhile searching for concrete names of these anonymous traditional African philosophers. However, I contest heftily his assertion that "Asouzu does not and/or cannot give their names". In page 24 of "Methods and Principles", I mentioned Mazi Okoli Idozuka (Methods and Principles 24 cf. Igwegbe R. O., *The Original History of Arondizuogu*). I do this bearing in mind that philosophers were to be sought mostly within the rank and file of "medicine men, priests, rulers, military leaders and sagacious elders whose position in the group corresponds roughly to the position occupied by the scholars and thinkers in modern societies" (Momoh quoted in Okoro Problems of African Philosophy 23). Besides the case of Okoli Idozuka, I provided enough clues to other concrete historical individuals that might be designated as such traditional African philosophers. A typical case is. Ewenetem (1728-1820) the Eze Nri in Igboland (Method and Principles 148). In matter of this kind, there is need always to remember the distinction I made between *"anonymous by choice"* and *"anonymous by incapacitation"*. Anonymous by choice is that situation where individuals and communities chose to conserve and document their intellectual heritages anonymously as a premeditated act. In the case of *"anonymous by incapacitation"* we are dealing with a situation where this act of free choice is not given such that intellectual materials are scattered unaccounted for in a haphazard manner. When taking into account the accepted methods of documentation and preservation of intellectual materials in traditional African societies, one would definitely appreciate some of the enormous advantages accruing from the method of *"anonymous by choice"* (Asouzu, Ibuanyidanda 223-224), as this forms one of the most important ways traditional Igbo philosophers adopted in conserving their intellectual heritages.

This notwithstanding, the existence of these traditional African philosophers is no longer a matter of serious academic debate if one were to go by the works of Odera Oruka, Hampaté Bâ and Sodipo/Hallen. One is gratified to note that Yacouba Konaté is devoting his life's ambition to collect more names. Here, he has our full support. With Claude Sumner as the first English-speaking scholar to introduce the thoughts of Zara Yaquob, the Ethiopian philosopher to the philosophical world, a giant step has also been made in this direction. These findings merely go to reinforce my assertion about anonymous traditional African philosophers of the complementary system of thought. This system of thought is definitely not the only one prevalent in traditional African societies, if we are to go by Masolo's reference to *Ogotemmeli* phenomenon among others. I think that Masolo is right in this connection and should not be castigated as is implicit in Kimmerle's comment of "the (not quite correct) story". In other words, I am personally more interested in the ideas and systems of these anonymous traditional African philosophers, than in putting up a comprehensive catalogue of names of traditional African philosophers. The clues I provided are enough to sustain my thesis about the existence of anonymous traditional African philosophers of the complementary system of thought.

The ideas and systems of thought of these individuals are amply represented and accessible to us through numerous literary sources and cultural materials, on the basis of which one can very credibly reconstruct what they stand for, as I have done in detail in the work "The Method and Principles of Complementary Reflection in and Beyond African Philosophy" (155-223). I think this is what is important. Central to the ontology of these anonymous traditional African philosophers is what I have characterised as the idea of transcendent categories of unity of consciousness as these are constitutive for the experience of transcendent complementary unity of consciousness. These transcendent categories of unity of consciousness are forms of the mind or what we call in Igbo *akara obi/mmụọ*. These forms *(akara obi/mmụọ)* attune the mind naturally to be receptive for truth, both formally and materially, at all levels of experience and determination. Furthermore, these categories belong to the nature of the human person in its true and authentic form, since human reason by its very nature although relative, always strives to ultimate certainty. In reliance on these categories, the human mind is capable of the knowledge of missing links of reality as pure means and pure relational essences.

The mind can achieve this because, imbued with these transcendent categories, it has the capacity to adhere to the demands of the principle of non-contradiction, which is an integral aspect and expression of the truth and authenticity criterion. Where the mind is under the influence of these transcendent categories, it is disposed to know things truly and authentically. Furthermore, whenever the human reason acts naturally, that is to say, under the guidance of these transcendent categories, there is the likelihood that it intuits the foundation of its legitimacy. In such cases, the human person is under the guidance of a harmonising faculty *(obi/mmụọ eziokwu)* which finds practical expression in *obiọha* (complementary totalising mindset) and other allied acts. This harmonising faculty makes it possible for the mind to grasp reality in its most authentic constitution. It is precisely due to the guidance ensuing from this harmonising faculty that we can read Ejizu's comment with reference to traditional African societies. Here, Ejizu avers that, "they strove with religious zeal to formulate good and lasting policies, promulgated just laws, settle disputes and dispense justice promptly since they well knew that any infringement, even if it escaped the notice of members of their community was likely to provoke the wrath of the ever-attentive gods" (Ejizu 83). Even if the subject can act under the impelling force of this harmonising faculty, it does this as a free autonomous individual that can work against the promptings of this faculty. The traditional African condition is a very challenged one where the subject, due to the ambivalent tension of this environment, had to contend fiercely with the impairment ensuing from the phenomenon of concealment (*ihe mkpuchi anya*). This is a milieu, where world immanent pre-deterministic way of thinking was very predominant and the dictates of the transcendent faculty of *obi/mmụọ eziokwu, greatly under the challenges of negative wisdom (obi/uche akọlọ* or *obi/uche aghụghọ).* This sheds some light on why in spite of the high ideals professed by members of these traditional African societies, individuals and groups were caught in the web of the worst types of contradiction and paradoxes. These are those instances where commitment to extreme forms of relativity or absoluteness is elevated to those habitual principles that guide human action. In other words, even if relativity is an integral and necessary dimension of our experience of the world, it is not ultimately constitutive of human experience of reality; not even that of traditional African societies. In this point, the traditional African world-immanent pre-deterministic concomitant tendency is as critic worthy as this is everywhere.

33. On the origin and nature of ideas

When challenged in a situation we perceive as unjust, exploitative and oppressive, or in most extreme situations of life, one of the most natural things to do is to defend ourselves. In extreme situations of challenge, we tend to defend ourselves with all the means at our disposal. There are even cases where recourse to the use of excessive force or other extreme measures may be considered legitimate, as is the case of what has come to be called "just war". This is one of the circumstances surrounding the notion of just war as propounded by St. Augustine (The City of God, Book 21). A phenomenon that many have come to regard as having the character of unjust war is colonialism. We can then understand why for many, it is a force that has to be resisted with all means at one's disposal not excluding counterforce. This is when anti-colonial vanguards metamorphose to diverse radical brands of anti-interventionists movements like, anti-neo-colonialists and anti- neo-imperialists movements. This same thing is applicable to brands of anti-globalisation activists, anti-multinational activists etc. These are united in one ideology as it relates to advocating the use of extreme measures, when this must be, in view of combating what they identify as excesses arising from external incursion. As this matter concerns Africa, it is not uncommon when we hear or read about such recommendations that advocate outright rejection of colonial values, due to the fundamental dangers these pose to African survival. This is when many believe that the best way to counter further spread of colonial influence and the loss of African identity is by clenching assiduously to certain things identified as unique to African culture and ways of life. This clarion call for the search of what many consider "conceptual schemes" congenial to African culture belongs to this type of restorative and conservative understanding. Advocates of this approach make us believe that there are original ideas and conceptual schemes, which may after all be a part of African heritage, but which have been suppressed by colonial influence. In this case, what remains is to dig into the past and have them restored in their pristine condition. It is in this sense that one can read the basic recommendations of Wiredu's grand project of "conceptual decolonisation in African" which is in harmony with Kimmerle's understanding of the project of conceptual decolonisation, as the processes and mechanisms needed to include "original African thought into the worldwide philosophical work of today" for the purpose of making them "influential in present debates". By "original African thought", we are thinking of those pristine ideas that their proponents assume are necessarily constitutive of the African identity, as to help distinguish African pattern of thinking from those of other peoples. Due to the difficulties associated with this conservative approach to African conceptual schemes, there is need to investigate into the basic tenets of this grand project of conceptual decolonisation. This is a project that definitely has unmistakable ideological implications and relevance for the overall progress and development in Africa.

Some theories that have to deal with intercultural affairs seem to suggest that, because cultures and human beings are in unavoidable state of competition, there is the need also for each culture to brace up in view of showing what makes it unique. This is at least one of the major impressions one gets when reading the issue Kimmerle raises in connection with Wiredu's grand project of "conceptual decolonisation" (Wiredu, The Need for Conceptual Decolonization in African Philosophy). Thus, Kimmerle informs us that "Actually Wiredu endeavours with this project to include original African thought into the worldwide philosophical work of today. To decolonise the mind does not mean to go back to traditional ways of thought, but to make them active and influential in present debates." In other words, in making them active, we have first to identify them, which by implication means resuscitating conceptual monads lying somewhere, if possible in the past, in view of making them influential. This is the major mindset behind this type of project as it seeks to dig into the past in view of recouping conceptual schemes in their pristine condition. Here, we are dealing with unintended ethnocentric commitment. Thus, one can justifiably say that to "include original African thought" derived from "traditional ways of thought" in view of making "them influential in present debates" is one of the major motives at the foundation of most approaches that understand the world today as a clash of civilisations. It is this type of reactionary thinking that has come to characterise the way most Islamic extremists conceptualise the world today as a clash of civilisation and values where some ideas and values are destined to supersede each other in the process of dialectics of mutual influence. What is especially striking about this understanding of the character of ideas and thoughts is that it imagines ideas or thoughts as discrete quantities or a priori categories lacking in any form of mutual relationship to each other in their genesis and development.

Considering the context within which Wiredu's project is born, as it involves "guarding against the uncritical assimilation of conceptual schemes embedded in foreign languages and cultures" one can, without equivocation, describe his mindset as reactionary, even if Kimmerle appears to disagree. This is all the more the case when one remembers that this project was conceptualised in the spirit driving most anti-colonial reactionary rejectionist movements.

As an idea that has a philosophical significance, it is better handled within a wider philosophical context to help bring to light some of its obvious implications. These are those implications that are not always evident immediately. It is by so doing, that some of the difficulties that weigh heavily on this project, both theoretically and practically, can be appreciated. There is need therefore to explore the full implications of this type theory as to warrant a vociferous call for its complete overhaul. To achieve this, it would be essential to go back a little to the age-old problems underlying some of its basic assumptions as these concern the nature and origin of our ideas. In this sense, I wish to recall that one of the main problems associated with this project of conceptual decolonisation is that it creates the impression that ideas and thoughts, in their genesis and development, are not in mutual complementary relationship. Unless this fundamental illusion is exposed, all the things we call "original African thought" and "original ideas" are bound to lead us to error. Over and above all, the conclusions deriving from such errors can hamper human interpersonal relationship enormously. The basic question then is, what is the nature of ideas in their genesis?

i) The illusion of non-relational character of ideas and thoughts

Most classical theories of knowledge, notably rationalism and empiricism, handled the question of the origin of ideas in the most straightforward manner without due regard for the dynamic character of the mind, which always strives to go beyond known boundaries. This restricting classical bias stays at the foundation of most theories designed to explain the nature of the origin of ideas. In many cases, practitioners of philosophy take sides unintentionally and this arbitrariness in seeking explanation to the origin of ideas can be heightened by our education, socialisation and indoctrination. This is mostly what happens in most ethnocentric inspired methods of investigation, where practitioners of philosophy have not learnt to overcome their biases but carry this into inquiry as remnants of those constraints arising from our raw primary ambiences. One of the major difficulties arising from this constraint is the illusion of the non-relational character of our thoughts and ideas in their genesis and further development. Most ethnocentric inspired methods of investigation take it for granted that there is no how we can start thinking that ideas in their origin and further development can be complementary. Fired by the passion to safeguard what they consider the special character of their cultural patrimonies, they consider these so precious and sacrosanct that for them, this must have something to do with the special character of the origin of their ideas. This is when they devise all sorts of special mechanisms to safeguarding jealously those cultural privileges and patrimonies they have identified as unique to them. Definitely, ideas and thoughts, in their genesis and further development, can hardly be considered as constituted of discrete units or monads that never meet and are merely artificially joined or separated from each other. If this were the case, even at the pure private subjective level, they would hardly lead to true and authentic knowledge. Where they to be seen as such discrete monads or units that are disjointed and in a state of ceaseless internal agitation and conflict within the subject, they can hardly be basis for perceiving reality in a coordinated, systematic, coherent and harmonic way.

When dealing with thinking, thoughts and ideas we can **theoretically** distinguish between *uche* (kernel of thought) and sense impression or sensation (*ihe ahụ na anya ekwe*) in this complex act as these can be clearly spelt out in Igbo language. Yet, in the dynamic process, thinking (*echiche*), leading to knowledge or cognition (*amamihe*), both kernel of thought (*uche*) and sensation or sense impression (*ihe ahụ na anya ekwe*) relate to each other in a harmonised mutual complementary mode, in the most natural way, to yield knowledge or object of knowledge (*amamihe*) itself. This process proceeds without distortion, bifurcation and without division. Here, the whole process of cognition or thinking (*echiche*), as an act within the same subject, can hardly be said to be constituted of isolated discrete quantities, patches or mode of *uche* (kernel of thought) and *ihe ahụ na anya ekwe* (sensation). No, it is a process that flows naturally within a subject. In the whole process of cognition, both *uche* (kernel of thought) and *ihe ahụ na anya ekwe* (sense impression) build a mutual complementary harmonious whole. This harmony ensues due to the dynamic character of the mind. This dynamism relates to both the kernel of thought (*uche*) and sense impressions themselves (*ihe ndi ahụ na anya ekwe*). This dynamism is made possible by certain features of the mind itself. On the part of the intellect, this dynamic feature is called *amumauche* (intellectual intuition) and on the part of the senses, it is called *onyinyouche, (*sensory intuition). Both *amumauche* (intellectual intuition) and *onyinyouche* (sensory intuition), at their diverse levels of occurrence are spark-like phenomena comparable to lightning (*amuma mmiri*). In the case of *onyinyouche*, we are thinking especially of a shadowy, glow-like form of the mind. It is due to this character of theirs that both, *amumauche* and *onyinyouche, as* forms of the mind (*akra uche or akara obi*), can stimulate it and hold the flow of consciousness, such that it remains dynamic and mutually complementing. Hence, in the process that yields ideas, we can never think of *uche* (kernel of thinking or thought) in isolation of *ihe ahụ na anya ekwe* (sense impression or sensation), bearing in mind the dynamic character of both *amumauche* and *onyinyouche*. Both, *uche* and *ihe ahụ na anya ekwe* get fully harmonised, through the agency of *amumauche* and *onyinyouche*, which as forms of the mind (*akra uche or akara obi*) are the very active agents of the mind, as they induce the act of complementation in the process of which true knowledge (*amamihe*) results. Where we entertain the illusion that in the whole process the kernel of thought (*uche*) and sensation or sense impression ((*ihe ahụ na anya ekwe*) are discrete quantities that impress on the mind of a passive subject, quite unrelated to each other, we would invariably also imagine them to be discrete quantities or units that impress the mind at different times. Without intuition, consisting of *amumauche* (intellectual intuitions) and *onyinyouche* (sensory intuition), which is a complementary harmonious whole act of the same thinking subject, no knowledge is possible, and no ideas or thoughts conceivable.

In other words, *amumauche* (intellectual intuitions) and *onyinyouche* (sensory intuition) are the forms or very active agents of the mind, which stimulate it to yield knowledge in a complementary harmonious whole manner. Hence, one can say that ideas are products of indeterminate relational forms of sensations (*onyinyouche*) and intuitions (*amumauche*) which the mind moulds into a coherent whole. Therefore, in the process of their excogitation, ideas or thoughts can be said to arise from apparently indeterminate modes. However, these modes impress on the mind of the thinking subject simultaneously as relational sensory intuitions (*onyinyouche*) and intellectual intuitions (*amumauche*) seeking full expression and articulation. These modes can hardly be viewed as pure isolated forms or monads in their relationship to each other and to the subject that moulds, coordinates or synthesises them to a comprehensive cognitive whole. It is the same thinking subject that harmonises and synthesises, within itself, these forms of its mind, not as purely discrete quantities, but in their inherently relational indeterminate interrelatedness.

One can say, that we perceive the world meaningfully in quasi-relational complementary indeterminate forms. That is to say, in so far as both sensory (*onyinyouche*) and intellectual (*amumauche*) intuitions are not completely determined, but in view of the internal harmony that characterises them in their fundamental mutual interrelatedness. In this way, both the intellectual and sensory intuitions, *(amumauche* and *onyinyouche*), as the foundational forms of the mind (*akara uche or akara obi*) remain the latent active ingredients that stimulate both the kernel of thought (*uche*) and sensation or sense impression (*ihe ahụ na anya ekwe*) to yield true knowledge.

Creativity (*nka*) or the capacity to have original ideas, if we can designate it so, and as this concerns human beings, entails what we make of these forms of the mind (*amumauche and onyinyouche*) in their quasi inherently indeterminate mutual complementary form. What it takes to be creative can be very decisive for what we make out of the whole process of cognition. In creativity, the subject takes the process of cognition a step further beyond what is naturally implied in this whole process. Yet, this does not mean that such original ideas take place in void. They can be thought of only within the context of kernel of the mind (*uche)* and sensation (*ihe ahụ na anya ekwe*) in their mutual interrelatedness, as they remain the raw materials that get stimulated by intellectual and sensory intuitions (*amumauche and onyinyouche*).

It has to be noted that already in their relational indeterminate form, both the intellectual and sensory intuitions (*amumauche* and *onyinyouche*) have an inherent moment of ambivalence. These can easily turn to a burden to a mind as it becomes creative. It is due to this ambivalence that the thinking subject, in being creative or original, can misuse its innate capacity. It is precisely due to this ambivalence also that the subject can be misled into assuming that the whole process of cognition has to do with a process concerning discrete determinate forms of impressions. In other words, the subject remains challenged in the whole process of cognition, as this is its own act, within it. Due to the inherent indeterminate character of the whole process as it relates to a self-conscious subject, the thinking subject is always challenged to prove that it is in control of the whole process. This is when the thinking subject is challenged to demonstrate that it is indeed a being-in-control (*ọma-onwe-ya)*. It does this by identifying the whole process in its fundamental mutual complementary interrelated character. It is a being-in-control insofar as in its creativity it does not allow this cognitive process to get out of hand as to suggest that *uche* (kernel of thought) and *ihe ahụ na anya ekwe* (sense impression) belong to diverse regions of the same cognitive process or that they are acts within a divided subject. Where this happens, the subject finds itself battling with illusions that can have very serious consequences both practical and theoretical. In view of this internal tension within the subject and in consideration of the dangers of misrepresenting this process, complementary reflection emphasis the fact that this process leading to acquisition of knowledge (*amamihe*) is characterised by two very important mental states, *uche ochiche* (anxiety), and *ụjọ ọtụtụ* (fear) which the subject has to learn to deal with creditably (Asouzu, Method and Principles 410-415). This is that mental tension we encounter in all efforts to depict accurately what is involved in all processes of cognition. How we manage this tension-laden situation, and the challenges thereby involved, can go a long way in determining what we make out of the whole process, as this concerns the origin of our ideas. Certainly, this process can hardly be said to be a static, disharmonious, non-complementary one.

We can then say that the thinking subject exists, when it is being-in-control (*ọma-onwe-ya*) of its tension-laden existential situation as this relates to the processes involved in cognition. The highest form of being-in-control (*ima-onwe-onye*) in this regard is to be aware that this process involves all missing links that enter into what it takes to know, and outside of which nothing that has being can be conceived. Thus, the way we view the process involved in cognition has grievous implications for the way we conceptualise existence itself and vice versa. Where we see this cognitive process as something that is rooted in disharmonious type of relationship of the cognitive elements involved, we are bound to approach the wider world and human interpersonal relationship the same way. When we fail to grasp the moment of mutual internal complementary relationship involved in the process of cognition, we are bound to have the illusion that there is no intrinsic mutual relationship between the ideas of diverse peoples in the world, both in their origin and further development.

To avoid relapse into this form of extreme type of exclusivist bifurcating epistemology, there is need to assume that all ideas and thought are complementary, not only in constitution but also in genesis, form, excogitation and in application. It is in this manner that thought has a deep relationship to the entirety of all missing links including also to language, insofar as the latter is the vehicle for the articulation, expression or execution of all ideas and thoughts as things meaningful and made possible by aforementioned intellectual and sensory intuitions. Due to the close affinity existing between ideas or thoughts and language, their elements are fundamentally complementary such that what we consider the most original thoughts and languages can be thought of only as a result of interplay of complementary forces in an infinite and often imperceptible mode. This is why, the issue of language touches necessarily on the issue of the fundamental intimate mutual relationship existing between all ideas and thoughts, as these form a complementary harmonious whole. Thus, for complementary reflection, the origin and nature of our ideas and thoughts can be articulated only within the framework of all the actors and factors that give rise to them. This is why, beside our raw primary cognitive ambience, complementary reflection insists on the legitimacy bestowed by our wider complementary cognitive ambience. Here, our world is a world of ideas that can be depicted, not in the purely intellectual or sensory polarising forms. On the contrary, it is one that ensues in a mutual complementation of all possible relations that enter into its genesis.

The whole problematic can still be elucidated from another

angle. This is when we ask directly and pointedly the questions: What is the character of "original thought"? In what sense do we have or can speak of "original ideas"? Certainly not in the sense of excogitatio ex nihilo i.e. conjuring them out of pure nothingness devoid of relations.

The issue of concepts and ideas, within the context of finite beings can be articulated meaningfully, only within the framework of relationship of units to each other. Hence, original ideas, in the sense of pure personal intuition, even as isolated cognitive blocks, in given locations, is difficult to come by. In this sense, we can know, at the level of personal subjective experience, only in the mode of apperception; that is to say, only as aspects of our cognitive experiences occur to us. What this entails is that in the process of cognition, only aspects of sense impressions are moulded by the mind to what we consider true pictures of our world, as we know it, since we see the world from diverse angles. Even then, this cannot happen if the mind were to separate the matter and form of perception in such a process; it is a process that takes place in a harmonious complementary way, even if this is not immediately evident to the thinking, perceiving and knowing subject. If this were not so, we would be running the risk of having to assume pure forms without content or pure contents without form.

What appears to us as original ideas and thoughts can therefore be seen as forms of apperception. They can be so designated on the condition that we bear in mind the manner of their genesis, which entails mutual internal close relationship between the matter and form of all modes of impression both sensory and intellectual. It is in this mutual complementary manner that we can show our creativity and define our cognitive freedom as individuals who are primarily located and grouped into subjective worlds peculiar to us. It is at this level of cognition that we can localise what we can designate as the human capacity to invent. However, such inventions do not happen in isolation but are thinkable only in view of all possible relations that enter into their genesis. On account of this dependency of the mind on all possible relations, one cannot in the strict sense of the word designate thoughts and ideas, arising from this process, as things that arise from pure personal intuition or creativity devoid of any kinds of relation, as to be designated "original", pure and simple. What actually happens is that we often tend to forget that this our so-called inventions, that belong to what we identify as the fruits of our raw primary cognitive ambiences, are not as untainted, novel, unique and original as we assume and imagine. As long as we forget this fact, that is the moment we also forget that dimension of mutual dependence and indebtedness in complementarity that is characteristic of all cognitive processes. This forgetfulness is at the root of our tendencies always to ascribe the genesis of our individual world of apperception, unintentionally, solely and entirely, to the achievement of our personal private insight. This is precisely the point at which we imagine that all credits should go to our efforts. It is when this happens that we see ourselves armed with those thoughts and conceptual schemes that we believe are special and unique to us in view of influencing others, converting them, and subjugating them to conformity.

Hence, the challenge about the illusion of non-relational character of knowledge will ever remain one of the biggest challenges any ethnocentric induced conception of the world has to contend with. Basically, we carry this illusion within us due to our ethnic and other biases. This is that tainted and compromised mindset we often carry into the world. One of the severest consequences ensuing from this is that it induces us to imagine an ideal world made possible only by our own personal achievements, with its special types of laws, values and privileges. This is that world, which *does not admit of alternative life styles and which must co-exist with other cognitive worlds, in a parallel, if not exclusivist modes of paradoxical co-existence.* This is the world of differences, the tribal and racist world of differences and parallel co-existence. Unless the mind overcomes the illusion of a non-relational form of the origin of our ideas, all the things we call "original ideas and thoughts" will ever have all the potentials to lead us to grievous errors and to heat up unnecessary and unending tensions in society. One of the most severe forms of expression of this error is the situation where we labour unduly, and often vain gloriously and triumphantly, to make one system of thought influential against another and thereby forget the mutual complementary structure of all thoughts in their genesis.

We can then say that the most original thought is reflection itself, but insofar as in this act, the subject seeks to transcend itself and overcome the challenges of division between missing links of reality. It is for this reason, that we say that reflection in a complementary sense entails the act of conscious sorting and sifting of missing links in view of the harmony that reflects the unavoidable mutual relationship that sustains all forms of thoughts and ideas. Thus, all forms of original ideas, as these are represented in reflection, aim at superseding all forms of artificial symbols, which the thinking subject imagines that it can concoct to represent a special type of non-relational world of its own. Original idea or reflection is therefore the life spent in complementation of all missing links in view of the totality. Whenever we seek to articulate original ideas outside of the framework provided by the totality, we are merely acting under the dictates of our passion for self-preservation, in view of upholding some of our most cherished interests against outside intrusion. Here we are evolving defensive mechanisms to uphold thoughts that are no thoughts at all, but mere figments of our imagination aimed at perceived external intrusion. How we address this passion for self-preservation determines the use of words and concepts in given locations. In the tendency to preserve our interests, we develop those exclusivist hegemonic categories of thought that can render human reason absolute in its operation.

For complementary reflection, authentic knowledge means the reaction of the mind to the indeterminacy of sensory and intellectual intuitions, in all ambivalent situations. In this reaction is rooted what it means to be, since to be is to be in control of all tension-laden ambivalent situations. This is that moment when the subject, in full awareness, affirms all missing links as aspect of being seeking full expression in history. This is why we said that being is that on account of which anything that exists serves a missing link of reality. By implication, to be is to be in mutual complementary relationship of all missing links in the sense of *Ibuanyidanda or ka sọ mụ adina (that I may not be alone)*. Hence, in the process of cognition, impressions in their indeterminacy can conceal their dynamic mutual complementary character from the subject and assume the false character of discrete quantities existing side by side each other, outside of the legitimacy bestowed by all missing links. The main task in such a process is to give full meaning to this indeterminacy in their apparent non-relational character. The subject can achieve this in the awareness that our self-definition is possible only within the framework of all the actors and factors that enter into this process of definition. For complementary reflection, therefore, we build concepts and ideas, and these are thinkable, only in ordering all missing links critically into a comprehensive whole, devoid of contradiction, both formally and materially in a future referential manner. This is the only thing that matters and here, all conceptual schemes resemble themselves. Here, units find full authentication and are vindicated and validated harmoniously irrespective of what many assume are their diversities of credential and origins. It is within the framework of complementary mutual relationship that all forms of languages, conceptual schemes and ideas can be thought of validly as human acts. Here, the only ontological criterion towards the determination of the effectiveness of any conceptual scheme, idea or language, as to impact positively or negatively on others, is its capacity or incapacity to harmonise missing links as aspects of the totality.

Thus, what is ultimately intended in the use of language and conceptual schemes can be achieved only in the process of complementary mutual act, which entails a universal critique of language and meaning as to determine their complementary adequacy or inadequacy. A philosopher relates to issues from the comprehensiveness of his intellectual reservoir, and this he or she does as they come, not because he or she belongs to specific cultural milieus. Since what it takes to be continues to evince itself in a complementary future dimension, the wider the horizon of an inquirer is, the better are his or her chances of shedding useful light on questions that might be raised. What this entails is that all inquirers operate fruitfully from the consciousness that all concepts, ideas and meanings are critique worthy at all levels of excogitation, and this can be achieved in a complementary comprehensive future oriented manner. Hence, the excogitation of what concepts and conceptual schemes actually designate takes place at a transcendent level where the philosopher scrutinises their adequacy and applicability, and from the background of ultimate determination. In this case, we are probing their adequacy towards ultimate representation of meaning beyond ethnic biases. Only those ideas and concepts can be influential that help us represent reality in its most authentic and sublime form and not necessarily those that are "original" in the sense of representation of our world in the way they appear to us in our native habitats, in our raw primary conceptual ambiences and ghettos. All original ideas or concepts outside of the framework provided by the whole remain un-thought. Where they are un-thought, they are no ideas.

The consequences of an epistemology that considers the origin of our ideas to be rooted in non-related discrete quantities that are in mutual dialectical opposition is that it sees interpersonal relationship as a competition between those ideas that are unique to each conceptual scheme. It is within such a context that one starts thinking of making uniquely different ideas influential as Kimmerle suggests. This mode of thinking is reminiscent of a milieu that knows no other way of understanding interpersonal relationship except in terms of mutual eliminative type of competition. We encounter this in the mindset underlying most of what is today characterised as intercultural dialogue, where contestants seek to supersede each other by showing their importance and proving the uniqueness of their cultural heritages. Ironically, they endeavour to package these in one form of discourse mechanism or the other. Ideas gain in importance and influence naturally within the framework of dialectic as is to be expected of units that interact with each other. However, such dialectics can hardly be subsumed into an eliminative type of logic of the categorical elitist type. It is when we think, in this discriminative eliminative mode that the issue of "guarding against the uncritical assimilation of conceptual schemes embedded in foreign languages and cultures" arises. This is precisely when Wiredu never tires of insinuating that there is need for us to mount such conceptual and cultural sentinels. For there to be harmony and cohesion within any system, there is need to overcome this type of logic of mutual ceaseless confrontation and suspicion.

ii) Background information concerning the search for original ideas in African philosophy

Before analysing Wiredu's project of conceptual decolonisation in detail, it might be rewarding to give some background information as to some of the factors that facilitated it. I do this bearing in mind some of the possible consequences such a theory of knowledge might have to the overall developmental processes in Africa. This is all the more the case since most theorists of decolonisation see their work as major contributions towards bringing much needed positive changes in African. To start with, the demand for decolonisation stays at the foundation of most theories geared against colonialism and imperialism, as perceived negative force militating against authentic African identity and the self-expression. Most of these theorists and movements view the process of decolonisation as one through which the authentic African identity can emerge, bearing in mind the repressive effect of colonialism on the overall African personality. Since the project of decolonisation can be situated within a context of oppression and struggle, its protagonists assume that there are certain legacies that belong originally to Africans by right of cleavage, which must be guarded and preserved against foreign domination, lest these are lost all together. To these include traditional norms and values along with conceptual schemes. By implication, these cultural activists assume that there are certain patrimonies that are congenial with African identity quite removed from the rest of humanity. Where this ethnocentric mindset is operational, the impression created is that ideas, in their genesis and development, are discrete quantities without a necessary internal mutual complementary linkage. This is the absurd of the otherness that makes the claimant look strange, incongruous and dissimilar when compared with the rest of humanity.

It is in this conservative restorative sense that we can read the mindset of the novelist Ngugi Wa Thiong'o who writes about "decolonisation of the mind". Kwame Nkrumah's theory of "Conciencism" serves as the socio-political equivalent of this advocacy. The same can be said of the motives behind the activities and writings of most critics of colonialism like Franz Fanon, Senghor, Aime Cesarie, Nnamdi Azikiwe and Mbonu Ojike. Ojike is famous for his dictum "boycott all boycottables" and Azikiwe believes in self-affirmation through "psychological aggression". Afrocentricism as a methodology has as its primary objective, a refocusing on Africa in view of restoring African identity badly marred by Eurocentrist and colonial, imperialist propaganda. In this sense, it has a deeply tainted restorative agenda. Similarly, Theophilus Okere and Tsenay Serequeberhan, in the name of hermeneutics of culture propound a philosophy of decolonization that has restoration of original ideas and conceptual schemes as its underlying motive. In keeping with this hermeneutical restorative constraining approach, Oguejiofor, bemoans, in the case of Igbos, "the pristine concept which today is certainly lost to vast majority" (Oguejiofor, The Universal and Particular 25). Okere, who in one of his essays underlines that "unassimilated imports emphasize loss of pristine purity" (Okere, African Culture 11), probably misled him. In these cases, we are dealing with clear instances of unintended ethnocentric reduction that make us believe that ideas are discrete quantities devoid of an inherent moment of relation in their genesis and further development.

Here, I quite agree with Makang that "By reducing African traditions to a fixed past and to a nostalgia for an original state, the ethnological discourse strips African people of their historicity" (326). What is hereby implied is that African history does not lie only in the past but has a present and a future. Hence, realising the fact that the project of conceptual decolonisation can be situated within the context of struggle and restoration of African identity would be very helpful in assessing its epistemological merits and demerits. Here, Wiredu's caution concerning "guarding against the uncritical assimilation of conceptual schemes embedded in foreign languages and cultures", can be seen as the main thrust of his project within the context of such a philosophy born out of struggle. This clarion call towards "guarding against the uncritical assimilation of conceptual schemes embedded in foreign languages and cultures" qualifies for what Makang and Oke refer to as "nostalgia for an original state" and "cultural nostalgia" respectively. This is that nostalgia that permeates Wiredu's thinking and determines largely his style of theorising, as he insists on returning reflection to its pristine traditional African roots. Thus, "With specific reference to politics and governance, Wiredu ...prescribes a return to the indigenous method of decision-making in traditional African life in which, rather than by the methods of Western or other alien forms of democracy, 'governance was, as a rule, by consensus'" (Oke, Cultural Nostalgia 334). One can say that Wiredu's is that type of philosophising that seeks to uphold its unadulterated cultural identity, cling to what it identifies as its "original ideas and thoughts" and uses these against what it perceives as external intrusion, manipulation and oppression in view of making itself heard and remaining influential within the ambit of global philosophy. The danger in this type of undertaking is that epistemology is easily brought into direct relationship with folk's ideological politics of power struggle, just as Aristotle brought Metaphysics into direct relationship with folk's ideological philosophy of domination. Kimmerle's allusion to making African conceptual schemes "active and influential in present debates", while referring to Wiredu's grand project, is very reminiscent of the motives behind Aristotle's ideological grand project in his "Metaphysics". Besides, the context of struggle against colonialism that gave rise to Wiredu's thinking, it may still be necessary to stress that his idea of conceptual decolonisation rests on other questionable epistemological pillars that make it overhaul worthy.

Here, I have in mind Wiredu's penchant, usually, to associate deeply with well-known proponents of an exclusivist bifurcating type of philosophy of the empiricist analytic tradition. These are those philosophers who go about boasting that metaphysical statements are nonsensical and as such are in need of total elimination. A typical example is A. J. Ayer. In other words, understanding his position has to proceed not only from its socio-ideological dimension, but more so from its epistemological and ontological affiliation. Here, that aspect that has to deal with conceptual and theoretical fidelity can be attributed to the fondness of some African philosophers to ally themselves with theoretical models that have deep-rooted dualistic and polarising character. Here, Wiredu's grand project of conceptual decolonisation qualifies as one. It is one of those philosophical models fashioned after the basic assumptions of logical positivism with its exclusivist excesses. This approach in its theoretical formulation shares a common weakness with all types of hegemonic absolute reason masquerading as localised rationality in their inherently dualistic tendencies. They are reminiscent of a milieu that is very antagonistic to the complementary comprehensive structure of being in history, as is typical of positivist rejection of metaphysical knowledge.

In African philosophy, this dualism surfaces in the excessive concern, which its major protagonists show in their preoccupation with the issue of language analysis.

In all, one can say that African philosophy, as so-called African logical positivists clearly understand, entails some sort of linguistic analysis. However, it does not subsist in only linguistic analysis, as Momoh sharply sees (Preface, xvi). The impression that African philosophy consists of the analysis of African concepts can be considered as one of those unfortunate consequences of the raw importation of extreme forms of logical positivism into African philosophy. This style of philosophising seeks to ignore the important position, which the totality of indeterminate forms of intuition takes in the formation of our ideas. The impression that is created by this form of philosophising is that the more data we have about an event, in its original habitat, the nearer we are to the truth and the more influential we become. In other words, the more we try to analyse our ideas and concepts, as to get at their original meanings, in the sense of proving beyond all reasonable doubt that they are ours wholly and entirely, without relations and indebtedness to anyone, that is also the moment we are nearest to the truth of African concepts, conceptual schemes and experiences. It is at this point that its theoretical concern matches its ideological worries, in that it seeks to use its positivist theoretical inheritance to foster and consolidate its ideological claims. What this means is that armed with the positivist tools of analysis, as this concerns language, thought and meaning, so-called African neo-positivists now seek to emancipate African concepts and ideas from the clutches of colonial amputation and distortion. The unfortunate thing is that in trying to do this, they find themselves almost at the same point of polarisation and superimposition characteristic of what they have come to identify as colonial domination. More serious still, they fall deeper into the empiricist extreme position of separating form from content, in which case, they assume that the origin of ideas and thoughts can be conceptualised in a non-relational absolute form, as if matters and forms do not have internal relationship to each other. This is the empiricist illusion. This empiricist burden dates back to the mindset underlying its excogitation, as we have this in the bifurcating ontologies of both Plato and Aristotle, in their thoroughgoing dualism, which they misunderstood both as idealism and realism. This is that type of mindset that has lingered on in all philosophies that have imbibed the spirit of these early philosophers. Most especially, Aristotle's elitist extremism finds deafening echoes in Wiredu's philosophy. More often than not, he makes recourse to Aristotle's sharp distinction between substance and accidents. This bifurcating approach to reality stays definitely at variance with the basic ontology of many traditional African philosophical systems of thought, most especially with the complementary comprehensive type, which many of these theorists think that they are salvaging.

One can say that such approaches, in their thoroughgoing polarising tendencies, run contrary to what authentic complementary African ontology stands for. In this case, it is questionable if one can subscribe, without serious objection, to this form of approach, even if one wishes to uphold one's identity in the face of what might be adjudged colonial excesses, bearing in mind its divisive consequences. Many, with diverse reasons, have even shown deeper apprehension as to the wisdom behind the raw importation of logical positivism into African philosophy. Thus, with special reference to Wiredu, Anyanwu (The Problem of the Method in African Philosophy 57-73) together with Azenabor (Schools of Thought 40), have raised serious questions, in this regard, as it concerns the analysis of language. These apprehensions are justifiable if one considers the exclusivist heavy load overburdening its basic assumptions (Asouzu, Method 415). The African neo-logical positivists might be tempted to answer to these worries by insisting that they consider themselves real patriots who are fighting a just cause in joining hands to salvage African languages and conceptual formations from colonial impositions. If these worries were to be carried to Wiredu's doors today in view of his grand project of conceptual decolonisation, he would very probably acquiesce that he is a patriot of aforementioned type. Here, he and his conceptual comrades may be right, but they have to do it correctly lest they find themselves fighting a losing battle. Evidently, they appear to be acting out of goodwill, but these people of goodwill we all are, and this is why we have to put heads together to find good solutions to some of the complications that might arise were we to subject ourselves unduly to the temptations of excessive zeal and optimism.

To start with, searching for original African thoughts and ideas in a non-relational manner can hardly be said to be in the interest of Africans themselves for reasons that shall be given later. Wherever this type of philosophical attitude is in place, we would always hear such comments as colonialism "simply ignored and even despised the whole values and civilisation of a people" (Okolo, Problems of Philosophy 14). The so-called values and civilisation of a people are not immutable raw data that can be considered solely on their own merit, such that they are perpetually immune to positive changes. We do not just hang on to such conceptual schemes and values because they are our own. Faced with problems of this kind and those issues we think concern us most, a pertinent question should always be: How do we react to them as philosophers? Certainly not as insiders who take sides pejoratively. In all matters of this nature, the inquirer, as a philosopher, is not an uncritical preserver, informer, describer or presenter of the culture of his people. It is for this reason that we have to bear in mind always that all inquirers are both *insiders* and *outsiders.* So seen, *the inquirer is* thought thinking itself and reality at the same time. It is in this critical reflective attitude that the greatest challenge is placed on the thinker, which entails trying to represent reality as it actually is, even as "insider". This task should never be misconstrued as one of re-establishing the objective world of my cultural milieu as my raw primary cognitive ambience. It is more than this. This objective world as belonging to my raw primary cognitive ambience attain its true worth only within my complementary cognitive ambience, which transcends every moment of reflection. All those philosophers who seek to clinch to their raw primary cognitive ambiences as the only true world accessible to them do so at the risk of pursuing mere shadow, since such a raw world in its originality devoid of relations does not exist. This is the case with many versions of hermeneutics as these are being pursued in African today. Here, hermeneutics is being misunderstood and misapplied as all the processes needed to dig out original pristine meanings and concepts in view of analysing, restoring, reconstructing and commenting on them. Language in its dynamism gets richer and gathers momentum as critic of common sense experience enshrined in the collective localised modes of understanding affixed to them. Thus, what Wiredu designates as "the locative concept of existence found in the Akan language" (The Need For Conceptual Decolonization 30) can be cited as a typical example of localising meaning beyond the type of transformation ensuing from a more universal complementary usage of concepts. Meaning ensues in a broader self-conscious criticism bearing in mind the mutual complementary interrelatedness between all concepts and ideas. It is in such a critical process that we address the theory-ladness of language, which can impinge on its growth and narrow down our perspective of the world. Outside of this self-conscious critical stance, which has a universal complementary connotation, all localised meanings turn inherently subjective. If the way we use terms and ideas is merely local, we render meaning stagnant and can even kill it.

Not even as a historian or as a chronicler of cultural events is it possible for a thinker to dig out unadulterated meaning enshrined in events. In seeking to decolonise African conceptual schemes, ideas and meanings, and to state or extract original meaning, we give new meanings, our most sincere efforts notwithstanding. In matters of this nature, we all are colonisers of meaning. In the case of Africa, this is applicable most especially to those who have appropriated foreign languages and mentality, as tools for their research efforts. As interpreters, even of those ideas we think belong to us originally and in those cases where we think that we are insiders, we are not free from those impositions we fear and abhor. In this matter, everything is open, and here, philosophy comes in with its critical function of questioning beyond given meanings. It performs this critical function within the framework provided by the complementary structure of reality. With regard to those philosophers who are obsessed with warning us against "uncritical assimilation" and in view of depicting thought, ideas and conceptual schemes exactly as they are found in their given localities, and bearing in mind the fact that we are all potential colonisers of ideas, a pertinent question arises: Who will protect or emancipate us from the conceptual de-colonisers themselves? This is why it is essential, in the spirit of true philosophising, that a given philosopher makes efforts to represent his ideas in a way that makes it intelligible as his personal idea, but within the framework of the totality. In this matter, as in all matters dealing with past events, not only the outsider, but more so the African is subject to the challenges of error of transposition. In matters of African worldviews, the African philosopher is still more liable to this type of error because of his overconfidence in believing that he is the one most qualified to tell us what his people have in mind, because he is an insider. This type of overconfidence can lead to undue dogmatism. In this dogmatism, he can easily forget the complementary dimension of philosophy, as an ambient reflection constituted of all the actors and factors that enter into the idea of the philosopher.

Hence, those conceptual schemes we designate as African can be conceptualised, be thought of, only within the framework of all the actors and factors that enter into their excogitation. Philosophy does not have two subject matters that are differently pursued by different peoples of the world. As a science of the ultimate nature of reality, it seeks to consider being in its most dynamic relational essentiality. In this way, it seeks to grasp and articulate being in diverse modes of its relative fragmentary historicity, as missing links that are in infinite mutual complementary relationship and in anticipation of a totality that offers the foundation for their harmonisation.

It is for this reason that all attempts at working out original ideas, thought and conceptual schemes, in any section of human culture, are bound to be difficult, because being can only be grasped within the framework of the totality of reality. Besides, worldviews are in constant dynamic mutual complementary relationship such that the more we strain ourselves to get at those thoughts we consider locally original, the more we are alienated from the truth that sustains them. All forms of hegemonic reason often lay claim to special characteristics and rules that make them different and original. They are instances of human reason seeking absoluteness, oblivious of its relative characteristic, which makes it dependent on all missing links for its ultimate authentication. These modes of expression of reason as specialised types of rationality are moments of our fundamental passion for exclusiveness, as this rests on the fallacy of "the nearer the better and safer". If there is any form of original thought, it is better articulated as a complementary type of thought, where the very logic of discourse turns out to be a complementary logic of discourse, which distinguishes itself from all forms of special absolute and ideal forms of rationality masquerading as localised rationalities. This complementary rationality seeks to lay the groundwork for the logic of discourse as the arena for mutual enrichment of thoughts beyond impositions and unwarranted influences.

iii) Some difficulties posed by a project of conceptual decolonisation in philosophy

Having now tried to shed some light on some background issues that must be considered in discussing matters of this nature, it suffices to focus my attention directly to Wiredu's grand project of "conceptual decolonisation" as the philosophical variant of this wide-ranging project. In indulging in this type of strenuous undertaking, I feel somewhat uneasy having to scrutinise a project whose basic tenets many have almost come to regard as an accepted dogma in African philosophy. In this uneasiness is rooted the initial weakness of my position, since it shall have to contend with what appears to be hardened prejudices. This notwithstanding, I hope I would be amply rewarded having exposed the weaknesses of a doctrine whose basic tenets, though highly cherished by many, appear not to have been well understood. In this sense, exposing some of the dangers inherent in this doctrine, as an epistemological and developmental paradigm, justify the expediency of this undertaking, which many may be inclined to adjudge unwholesome, considering Wiredu's towering eminence in African philosophy. For these reasons, prudence obliges me to submit myself to the guidance of those who are better acquainted with his ideas, lest I be accused of having misunderstood him, as Kimmerle appears to be instigating, when he claims, "To decolonise the mind does not mean to go back to traditional ways of thought, but to make them active and influential in present debates." It may be useful to read Kimmerle's caution from the background of an unhealthy air circulating in African philosophy today. This is that situation, where many assume that the canons of African philosophy are now known and fixed. For this reason, the books closed. Hence, anyone who dares ask a pertinent question, by challenging the opinions of those well-established thinkers rated as orthodox or canonical, is immediately suspected of heresy. To salvage my submission from falling on deaf ears, and to create an acceptable ambience for fruitful discussions, I have decided that in a sensitive matter of this kind that has almost the character of a canon, those who know more should advance, so that I can cautiously follow them. This is precisely one of the main reasons I have decided to be guided by the expositions of those whose understanding of this thematic best reflects the target of my criticism. This is the case with Olusegun Oladipo, a zealous admirer of Wiredu, who has spent some time now studying him and promoting his ideas. In his carefully articulated view on this issue, Oladipo teaches: "By conceptual decolonisation Wiredu means two complementary things. On the one side, the negative side, it means 'avoiding or reversing through a critical conceptual self-awareness the unexamined assimilation in our thought (that is, in the thought of contemporary African philosophers) of the conceptual frameworks embedded in the foreign philosophical traditions that have had an impact on African life and thought.' And, on the positive side, it means 'exploiting as much as is judicious the resources of our own indigenous conceptual schemes in our philosophical meditations on even the most technical problems of philosophy.' The two sides of the meaning of conceptual decolonisation given by Wiredu are complementary. They involve the 'comparative utilization of different languages in philosophical thinking', with a view to guarding against the uncritical assimilation of conceptual schemes embedded in foreign languages and cultures and, at the same time, promoting an adequate understanding of the intellectual foundation of African culture." (Kwasi Wiredu's Idea of African Philosophy 42; cf. Philosophy and the African Experience 19-20). For Wiredu, the bone of contention centres around such concepts that he thinks are in need of decolonisation: "Reality, Being, Existence, Thing, Object, Entity, Substance, Property, Quality, Truth, Fact, Opinion, Belief, Knowledge, Faith, Doubt, Certainty,, Statement, Proposition,, Sentence, Idea, Mind, Soul, Spirit, Thought, Sensation, Matter, Ego, Self, Person, Individuality, Community, Subjectivity, Objectivity, Cause, Chance, Reason, Explanation, Meaning, Freedom, Responsibility, Punishment, Democracy, Justice, God, World, Universe, Nature, Supernature, Space, Time, Nothingness, Creation, Life, Death, Afterlife, Morality, Religion" (The Need for Conceptual Decolonization in African Philosophy 23). Having given us the above comprehensive catalogue, Wiredu generously also gives us the clue as how to go about decolonising: "In regard to all these concepts the simple recipe for decolonisation for the African is: Try to think them through in your own African language and, on the basis of the result, review the intelligibility of the associated problems or the plausibility of the apparent solutions that have tempted when you have pondered them in some metropolitan language." (The Need for Conceptual Decolonization in African Philosophy 23).

Now that we have heard from Wiredu and his people, let us try to look into some of the implications of their position. That all human beings have those conceptual schemes and systems of thought that enable them communicate effectively is something any person can understand without difficulties: Here, I quite agree with Wiredu on the need for "comparative utilization of different languages in philosophical thinking". However, in this comparison, we must bear in mind that inherent relationship existing between all conceptual schemes such that the issue of "guarding against the uncritical assimilation of conceptual schemes embedded in foreign languages and cultures" would arise only in very special case. In this case, it becomes necessary to mount such guards in view of the type of corruption that could arise in mutual assimilation of inimical ideas directed against the overall interest of those concerned. If this is what Wiredu intends, then there is no need picking issues with him. However, I do not believe that most of the concepts he outlined above qualify as some of those dangers threatening humanity, and Africans in particular, as to warrant mounting critical guards against assimilating them. In this case, there are indications that he has other things in mind, while demanding that we mount guards in view of forestalling assimilation of concepts of the type he outlines. One can assume that his list would have continued if not for limitations imposed by space. Depending on the way one sees it, and in keeping with Wiredu's concern, one would expect such words as "is", "was", "and", "this", "that", "they", "rat", "rabbit" etc to qualify for acceptance into this list, as things worth guarding against, when it comes to "foreign languages". If this is the case, the consequences are obvious.

To start with, we cannot pretend that there are fixed and immutable meanings assigned to so-called "conceptual schemes", to our ideas, and thought patterns for which reason we must mount guards in view of upholding their purity. As an instance of ethnocentric reduction and imposition, a project of this nature easily induces actors to undue acts of competition of the eliminative divisive type, most especially when it views culture as a veritable means of becoming "influential" within the ambit of global philosophy. Not even if one were to adopt African "conceptual schemes" only, if we have such, is the mode of understanding the genesis of ideas as something complementary abdicable.

No one can deny the fact that human beings are different in many respects and that they have localised conceptual schemes that determine the way they use certain words and ideas. However, they are different within a framework of mutual enrichment and mutual dependence in the genesis of their thoughts and ideas. Where this understanding is in place, the general attitude would be to reach out to each other in view of appropriating from other conceptual schemes as much as may be deficient in my conceptual scheme and in view of enriching it. Defective and insufficient conceptual schemes and concepts can be rectified and augmented in the process of mutual encounter and not when each person stays as his or her sentinel post. Failure to reach out in this way might amount to lack of foresight. In this case, the overall attitude would also be that of reaching out in view of knowing what is deficient in the conceptual schemes of others and by so doing, one is in a position to take needed precautions. This we do, not because others are alien, but because they belong to the same framework of meaning. Where an inquirer proceeds in this way, chances are that he or she would seek to understand such ideas as democracy, truth, essence, nothingness etc. with a view of retaining them, if they are useful in understanding reality in general and not necessarily because they do not belong to my conceptual scheme as something outside the range of the totality. They belong to my conceptual scheme the moment I encounter them as aspects of the totality of reality. In this way, the mind becomes forward looking and expansive and not only backwards looking and ungenerous.

Hence, if one were to consider the fact that all ideas are complementary in their genesis and development, the issue of "guarding against the uncritical assimilation of conceptual schemes embedded in foreign languages and cultures", would definitely not arise. The same is applicable to the need for "a cross-cultural comparison of 'different languages and cultures in relation to their philosophical prepossesions'" (Oladipo, Philosophy and African Experience 19). One of the major effects of complementary approach to the world is that it creates the freedom of association. In keeping with this freedom, an individual, as an autonomous free subject, is not condemned to undue vigilance against anything. The more we guard against new concepts and ideas, the more we evolve new conceptual schemes from which we must protect ourselves. How can a person spend his life in such an enterprise of negative ceaseless sentinel?

The only type of vigilance that is worth cultivating, at all moments is that with regard to the ambivalent nature of all existential situations that can instigate the mind to guard only against its own interests outside of the legitimacy provided by all missing links. Here, the type of vigilance that is recommended as it relates to the use of concepts and conceptual schemes can definitely be said to be in harmony with what it means to be. For complementary reflection, to be is not to be alone (*ka sọ mụ adina*), but to be in mutual complementary relationship with all missing links. Where a selective, restrictive attitude is adopted as a paradigm of epistemology, it might probably lead to a custodial compulsive type of neurotic epistemology. This is why I said that Wiredu's list might have continued, if not for lack of space. In matters of this nature, it is important to remember that being in its dynamic essentiality gets full force and expression in complementary mutuality, such that differences have meaning only within such a framework. Where this exposition has been well understood, issues such as "conceptual decolonisation", "guarding against uncritical assimilation of conceptual schemes" etc, as the magic pill for African philosophical revitalisation and self-determination, would definitely not arise.

Generally, all forms of interpretation, even of those ideas we think belong to us originally, are not free from those superimposition we dread and seek to decolonise. We are never the same human beings. When now we come to think of it that even the proponents of conceptual decolonisation arm themselves very well with colonial categories, mentality and strategies, as they urge us on, one is bound to ask the pertinent question: qui custodiat custodiens (who will guard the guards themselves)? In other words, who will protect us against the superimpositions of the conceptual de-colonisers themselves?

Wiredu's lucid use of the English language is highly commendable, let us hope that he does not consider this a heavy colonial burden that must be relegated soon to junk pile of conceptual decolonisation. In this case, many would miss him greatly if he were to return soon to full use of his Akan language, as his choice means of communicating his ideas. Should he succeed in doing this soon, then he is a free individual according to his own understanding. All human beings are colonised "new" individuals and we colonise in decolonising all at the same time. This is all the more the case when we are decolonising within a complex new world situation, with all the unintended associations underlying our thinking. For those who think that the idea of colonisation is something between oppressive aliens it is important to remark that the yoke of slavery does not become less cumbersome or sweeter just because it has been affixed more carefully and properly by a fellow kinsperson. In matters of this kind, indigenes sometimes, turn out to be some of the worst colonisers of their own people. It is in this connection that one can better appreciate the type of contradiction and difficulties such persons place themselves in when according to Masolo, in spite of their criticism of colonialism, they insist on "accepting the colonial categories of 'traditional' and 'modern'" (Karp and Masolo, African philosophy as Cultural Inquiry 6).

This inherent self-contradiction merely goes to show that some of the protagonists of this type of philosophising are not fully acting in bad intention. On the contrary, they can be absolved if we come to think of what unintended ethnocentric mindset can do to a thinking subject. However, the sooner they see into their difficulties, the better for African philosophy, which they can easily drag into their confusion. The same is valid for all who think that we can restore the old way with categories of thought borrowed from the new and still have the old way intact. There is nothing wrong in seeking to penetrate the old way through the new way, but we have to bear in mind always that what results is an unending new horizon of meaning ensuing from the fact of enduring mutual complementary relationship between all missing links.

Those thoughts we designate as original can be thought of only within the framework of all the actors and factors that enter into their excogitation, since the horizon needed to be and exist is complementary in determination. Our rights to our personal ideas get their character within this horizon; such ideas can be defined, vindicated and validated only within this horizon. It is in this sense that a philosopher should feel free to use the words, concepts and thoughts he finds in other cultures, with clear conscience, as veritable tools for his own personal reflection. Such materials are definitely no dangers worth guarding against, as Wiredu appears to be insinuating. Should African philosophy be preoccupied with penetrating African conceptual schemes and languages, so is the ultimate target not definitely the excavation of African meaning alone. The illusion that the target of such efforts is African meaning is caused by the fallacy of "the nearer the better and the safer". It is in this sense that people seek to find "original African thought" that would make them "influential in present debates". It is for this reason also that many have come to believe that African philosophy never changes and never progresses since it is congenial to an "African thought" stowed away somewhere in the past.

In all matters dealing with thought, philosophy seeks to break with all forms of narrow-minded tendencies and impositions. In this sense, it is a general meta-critique or meta-analysis with the aim of ultimate excogitation of meaning. It is not a localised form of analysis that aims at excogitation of what concepts designate locally. At this critical meta-analytic plane, all forms of thought resemble themselves, insofar as they are things worthy of excavation in view of the ultimate meaning establishing them. Where we pretend that the meaning, which concepts have within their given ambits, is the most appropriate meaning they can ever have, then we are merely under the influence of unintended ethnocentric mindset, which seeks to present raw data as they are and mistakes them for the thing in itself.

Concepts and ideas enshrine meaning, but not all meanings are meaningful enough. Hence, all conceptual schemes, ideas and meanings are critique worthy, at all levels of excogitation. The excogitation of what concepts actually designate takes place at a transcendent meta-plane, where the philosopher scrutinises their adequacy, or inadequacy and applicability from the background of ultimate complementary determination. Here, philosophy has an unmistakable absolute ontological commitment, which serves as the ideal of reason seeking full expression and authentication. The project of conceptual decolonisation would be a grand project if it were to be located within this ontological bracket and not degraded to a local preoccupation.

In this case, we are probing the adequacy of these localised meanings and allegedly original conceptual schemes towards ultimate representation of meaning beyond ethnic biases. It is at this level of articulation that they can become influential. Here, what the meaning of a thinker intends may not be adequate to reflect fully what is enshrined in reality, even if the inquirer thinks otherwise. Thus, representation of facts and grasping of reality are two things that can be articulated at diverse planes, but which must be seen as aspects of the overarching tendency of the mind to penetrate reality ultimately. Each person represents reality as it occurs to him or her, but our different perceptions do not give us what is actually intended, not even collectively. We are all potential victims of the tyranny of commonsense experience, and the tyranny of the ambivalence of our situations. In all cases, when are bound to allow the raw facts and data to speak. However, beyond this more needs to be done in view of grasping what is ultimately intend. Here all inquiries are subject to the same truth and authenticity criterion, as this offers us the condition for their validation. Hence, what is intended can only be grasped within the framework of a comprehensive complementary whole, in a future related manner, since reality does not evince itself in singular instances only, but seeks to reveal itself in a comprehensive complementary sense. Our capacity to represent reality accurately from our diverse backgrounds is very limited, such that the limits of our worlds are the limits of our complementary capacity and vice versa.

This lengthy exposition is worthwhile, if one considers the type of influence a thought or project of this nature can have in an emotion-charged debate of this kind concerning matters colonial. I say this bearing in mind the fascination, which the idea of conceptual decolonisation has on many young African minds. A typical example is Ogunmodede, who enthusiastically identifies himself with all the shortcomings of Wiredu. Bearing in mind some of the most severe consequences of Wiredu's position in this matter, one is yet to understand fully in what sense Ogunmodede considers himself lucky to be considered a progressive along line Wiredu's thinking. This is when he claims with enthusiasm: "The progressivists or Africanists believe that all forms of colonial legacy which are inimical to the development of the African people should be removed. These include European language as the media of the philosophical thought of African people. Kwasi Wiredu who sounded a note of caution initially on the matter champions now this cause. He has even gone ahead to consider the use of African languages in every conceivable area of human endeavour in his article, "Formulating Modern thought in African Language. Some Theoretical Considerations (1984)" (Ogunmodede, African Philosophy in African Language 21). Here, Ogunmodede is alluding to what he describes as new Wiredu, not knowing that the germ of this backwards-looking way of perceiving reality had already taken firm roots in Wiredu's thinking as far back as June 1980 when he first "advocated a program of conceptual decolonisation" (Wiredu, The Need for Conceptual Decolonization in African Philosophy 22).

What is striking in this advocacy is that Ogunmodede targets "European language" as one of the colonial legacies inimical to development of the African people. What I find disturbing in the idea of these zealous advocates of a philosophy of disengagement is their penchant to incite others to follow a false route which, by every indication, they carefully avoid or have no courage to tread. This is why I had earlier on remarked that although Wiredu advocates conceptual decolonisation, this "surprisingly, did not begin with him" (Asouzu, The Method and Principles 230). To be consistent in this type of advocacy, one has to take the bull by the horns as Ngugi did. Thus, Ngugi said that he would stop writing in English and would continue to write in his native Gikuyu only. He does this now and his works are being translated to other languages. Let us also hope that he would soon stop answering to questions posed in foreign languages. I would say that all who advocate the use of African languages, as a medium of dissemination of information, should follow suit and be consistent by showing this in their use of these languages in their literary works. This would definitely help strengthen their positions. The general practice so far is that they are saying one thing and doing another. It is in this sense that Moses Oke sets out to show the implausibility of their position, as this concerns Makinde, a passionate advocate of the use of African languages in literary creation. Here, Oke calls our attention to the fact that Makinde is of the opinion that Wiredu does not qualify to be called an African philosopher because Wiredu writes in foreign language. Concluding Oke says, "If this turns out to be the case, then, Makinde too is not to be known as an African philosopher, after all. This is because he is yet to start writing on and teaching African Philosophy in an African language" (Modelling the Contemporary African Philosopher 30). I feel Oke makes a point that is very pertinent in a matter of this kind.

34. On conceptual decolonisation as a universal critique of hegemonic absolute reason

i) Positive integration and assimilation

The idea of conceptual decolonisation serves definitely some positive function, if viewed as something designed towards a universal critique of ideology and of human reason itself. This is all the more the case if one remembers that human reason has the inherent capacity to be hegemonic and absolute, anywhere and anytime. Where one approaches the matter in this manner, there is every likelihood that one would be in a position to tap fully into the potentials of this coinage. This is when as a philosophical epistemological thematic the idea gets a universal relevance, both practically and theoretically. Where this happens, such a project would be relevant, not only for African philosophy, but more so, for all philosophies and all human situations, insofar as the human subject has the tendency to colonise and persecute others to submission. By taking such a non-parochial outlook, such a critique can then pave the way for an ontology that has a broader horizon, where the interests of all stakeholders are taken into consideration, without discrimination and ethnocentric reduction. Such a universal approach is very much aware of the immensity of opportunities characterising being in its diverse modes of expression. It is by adopting this universal approach that while being critical of the excesses of colonialism, for example, the inquirer does not foist his attention only on the negative impacts of this phenomenon. On the contrary, the inquirer seeks to tap immediately into some of its major benefits. It would be absurd to think that colonisation has no positive benefits. Those who think this way are definitely not being sincere to themselves. As a force that brings positive changes in the live of the colonised, it is an ambivalent phenomenon. Should we approach the matter in this manner, then decolonisation would turn out to be a more pragmatic process needed to approach such a complex phenomenon. This is when such a process of decolonisation does not take the negative connotation most of its vanguards ascribe to it, but turns out to be a process that can help tap into some of the positive benefits accruing from the multidimensional character of reality itself. Where this differentiated understanding and approach to this process is lacking, it can easily be degraded to an ideological tool towards the preservation of one's private interests, culture and identity, in the face of what one perceives as external agents of destruction and as external agents of destruction and manipulation.

It is indeed gratifying to note that even Wiredu himself seems to have seen some of the difficulties enshrined in his earlier position, as to try to align his project of conceptual decolonisation more properly to a universal direction, as to be defined within a context of mutual complementing units. This is at least the impression one gets when reading his new agenda for African philosophy: Thus, "the agenda for contemporary African philosophy must include the critical reconstructive treatment of the oral tradition and the exploitation of the literary and scientific resources of the modern world in pursuit of a synthesis" (Wiredu quoted by Oladipo in "Conceptual Decolonisation in African Philosophy" 2). It is in this sense, that Wiredu recognises the fact that African culture "is a product of 'interplay between traditional modes of life and thought, Christian and Islamic customs and ideas along with the impact of modern science, technology and industrialization" (Oladipo Conceptual Decolonisation in Africa 2). It seems to me that by taking this stand, he appears to have realised that human achievements can only be articulated within the context of all missing links, of all actors and factors that enter into their genesis. This is the way it should be. Taking this stand is a completely new and highly commendable way of looking at the problematic.

Therefore, there is need to embark on conceptual decolonisation, but in the positive sense of freeing one's self from self-imposed constraints and inhibitions. This is what Africans need and this can be achieved when actors realise that they share a certain common horizon of appropriation that makes them active free agent. This is that horizon sought in new complementary ontology, by reason of which all missing links are mutually indebted to each other in the genesis and further development of their ideas and resources. Where actors always think within the brackets of division and segregation, they are bound to create strange worlds, values and strange personalities. This is when they start to encrypt and create encrypted conceptual schemes, languages and phenomena that are in consistent war with each other and with the world. Such conceptual asymmetries are the very breeding ground for diverse forms of complexes of both the superiority and inferiority type. Such an atmosphere easily gives rise to feelings of achievers and underachievers, the superior and inferior, master and slave. Indeed, all assumptions that give the impression that human achievements are not complementary, in both genesis and development, are the very breeding grounds for all forms of reduction and impositions, including those arising from what most opponents colonialism view as colonial excesses. In this sense, I quite agree with Azikiwe that "By mental emancipation, I mean the eradication of fear in the mental make-up of the African" (229). However, it is highly doubtful if this can be achieved through the process of "psychological aggression" of self-affirmation as he proposes (My Odyssey 229). It is this type of negative self-affirmation, borne by "psychological aggression", that is at the foundation of most theories of conceptual colonisation. It is a type of compulsion that easily rebounds on the actor. Hence, there is need to liberate the mind from the forces of self-imposed delimitations by having it fully integrated into the totality of which it is a part. This can be achieved not through negative actions that can boomerang. On the contrary, this can be achieved when actors are open to changes in a way that does not discriminate against persons or along ethnic lines; this is that type of mindset that sees all missing links, including itself, as an integral aspect of all the processes that enter into historical changes, because of the mutual complementary link between all stakeholders. Such an equilibrated mindset does not suffer under undue feeling of inhibition or constraints against any persons or institutions. It is when one approaches matter of our common humanity with suspicion and little mindedness that the issue of mounting guards "against the uncritical assimilation of conceptual schemes embedded in foreign languages and cultures" arises.

We can mount such guards creditably not with regard to protecting African meanings and conceptual schemes only, but when there are dangers of rendering meaning obscure, due to the intrusions of private motivated interests. Were we to mount such vigilance only with regard to safeguarding African meanings and conceptual schemes, then, the essence of "comparative utilization", as Wiredu himself foresees, would be grossly undermined. In view of such avoidable difficulties, all matters of conceptual decolonisation, in the sense of warding off what might be perceived as external aggressors, appear to me to be backwards looking, self-delimiting, non-dynamic, non-progressive, unduly conservative, custodial and negative.

One of the most important questions of life is, and would ever remain, how do we react effectively to our ambivalent existential situations, to which belong such phenomena as colonialism, external influences, conceptual schemes embedded in foreign languages and cultures? Here, I would say that the awareness of the mutual dependence and interdependence in complementarity between all missing links serves as a veritable tool towards addressing such matters. Where we think this way, chances are that we approach burning issues not with the mindset of people who are strangers to each other or who are at daggers drawn to each. On the contrary, we shall approach each other as partners who need each other in their insufficiency and potentialities. In a situation of this kind, what is demanded is openness to positive ideas and conceptual schemes, such that stakeholders have the obligation to expunge only those ideas that do not augur well for the harmony and wellbeing of all whose interests are at stake. These repugnant ideas and values are the only things worth guarding against. In other words, if there is anything worth guarding against, it is the assimilation of those values, including languages and conceptual schemes that impinge on the growth and welfare of the human family. Here, all missing links have the same obligation to guard against such, be they Africans or non-Africans. In this case, I do not consider it wise, as philosophers, merely to focus on those things we think are exceptional about our cultures and use these as the only basis for self-actualisation. This is still questionable, when we use such as the criterion for judging others, or even as the only basis for converting, indoctrinating or persuading them. This is the very thing almost all critics of colonialism seem to recognise as being deficient about colonial strategy and mentality and most especially with regard to the colonial penchant to be influential based on preconceived paradigms. Adopting the strategy of conceptual decolonisation, in the way Wiredu proposes, or in the mood of "psychological aggression" of self-affirmation, one would be forced to adopt those strategies one criticises and rejects.

This is that situation where one seeks to be influential based on the dictates of one's conceptual apparatus only. Were we to adopt this strategy, the whole issue of oppressors and oppressed, exploiters and exploited would continue unabated. I guess, this is definitely not what the theorists of conceptual decolonisation wish.

Colonialism as an ambivalent phenomenon has to be approached with utmost caution. This is why I quite agree with Ugwuanyi that, "Going by the hegemonizing ideals of colonialism …there is no doubt that decolonisation has both moral and political justification. However, this again should not be an end in itself. The end should be that of careful indigenous search for an African alternative to the western paradigm of development which in the first place creates difficult conditions for African developments and in an even more disturbing intellectual plain, creates the impression that African development begins when Africa jettisons all her cultural achievements, even those that provide the basis for self-worth and self-belief" (12). In other words, conceptual decolonisation should be a process of positive self-affirmation, that is enriching and not one that is negatively delimiting. It has to be read as the processes needed to free the mind from the forces of narrow-mindedness, in view of attuning the mind to positive changes. This is relevant, not only for African values, but also, for those values that make humanity great. Within such a process, there is hardly any point guarding against any ideas, except those that impinge against global peace and harmony. If we consider some colonial strategy in their discriminative highhandedness to be deficient and wrong, one wonders how justified we would be in adopting restrictive strategies to address issues that touch on our humanity. Hence, it would be a tragedy to adopt such deficient strategies as tools of social dynamics and engineering. What this means is that those theories that advocate negative self-affirmation are not only self-delimiting but also contradictory. To forestall relapse into such difficulties, there is need for positive self-affirmation borne by the spirit of mutual dependence and interdependence in complementarity.

It is within this context that Onah's observation becomes relevant that "whatever one man in any corner of the globe has thought out and expressed publicly should be regarded as a common patrimony of the entire human race and each group of people should [feel] free to appropriate and apply such thoughts to their particular circumstances, if it suits them to do so." (Concept of Man for a developing Continent 181).

It seems to me that this suggestion is relevant, not only with regard to those things belonging to the inside, but more so, to those that have to do with the outside. In other words, we grow through positive appropriation and not through undue inhibitory negative self-delimitation. The capacity for missing links to be in mutual complementary relationship opens up possibilities and is the catalyst for positive changes. Unless African philosophy is emancipated from unintended ethnocentric reasoning, as is enshrined in those attitudes that are only interested in "guarding against the uncritical assimilation of conceptual schemes embedded in foreign languages and cultures", it would hardly attain the level of refinement that gives it full forcefulness.

It is in this spirit of positive unprejudiced assimilation that Njoku avers that "in using the language of the coloniser, Achebe sees himself free to add his cultural touch and intuitions. Thus, he employs a 'new English' with which he carries his experience and in which he artistically weaves African proverbs, traditions, conversations and songs". (Njoku, Essays in African Philosophy 122). He would not have achieved this if he considered such conceptual schemes as things worthy of guarding against.

To this, one can say that within any given framework, reality evinces itself in a way that each individual has equal claims to it. It is on account of this freedom and feeling of mutual universal belongingness that the ego can excel and do those things that surprise and enrich us all. It can do this only from the perspective of the joy of being, which challenges it to wholeness and comprehensiveness and not in the act of negative inhibitory self-delimitation that is characteristic of the negation of this joy. Here, we appropriate critically, mutually and in a transcendent joyous manner those conceptual schemes, ideas, languages, values and resources that help us grow and represent reality in its most authentic form. We do this bearing in mind that being always seeking full actualisation and expression in history, in the form of missing links. This will not happen where we spend our lives timidly "guarding against the uncritical assimilation of conceptual schemes embedded in foreign languages and cultures". Here, the Igbo adage holds sway that *ejigi ntufu abụ ọgaranya* (we do not become richer by throwing things away unnecessarily).

ii) African languages and philosophy

What is clear from Wiredu's position, as Ogunmodede further informs us, is that he advocates the notion of conceptual decolonisation by reason of which he discourages the use of "European language as the media of the philosophical thought of African people". Due to the obvious grievous implications of his position for any philosophy geared towards positive transformation in Africa, it is essential to review his position from the background of the position of language in philosophy. I had earlier on handled this matter in this book very briefly. I wish to go into it once more bearing in mind its importance, but from a perspective that makes my position still clearer. Hence, this section has to be read in conjunction with my position above concerning the relationship between language, philosophy and expression of meaning. Without underrating some of the advantages that might accrue, were Africans to write and communicate their ideas in their own mother tongues always and consistently, it would certainly still not be opportune if in our zeal to achieve our petty ideological gains, we find ourselves en route to conceptual underachievement. I think this option of underachievement and underdevelopment of our own conceptual frameworks is something unavoidable for any project that discourages the use of "European languages as the media of philosophical thought of African people". This is obvious because any tactic that has an implicit moment of negation of the mutual complementary relationship existing between entities has also an implicit moment of self-delimitation.

When handling matters of this nature, there are certain realities that one should never forget. These are those realities that stare many Africans on the face, due to their historical condition. One of the most obvious is the heterogeneous composition of most African nations in matters dealing with language, culture and other social arrangements. In the face of these *facts*, a realistic approach in matters of this kind is not an advocacy that seeks to define personal autonomy as if it is a value that can be had outside of the legitimacy accruing from the totality. Where we try to achieve such autonomy, it would naturally boomerang. In the case of most African countries, with the obvious constraints associated with diversity of languages and dialects, a pertinent question would always be how to present one's thought in good conscience effectively and without much inhibition. To answer this question creditably, it is important to note that beyond the linguistic and intellectual technicalities involved in the use of language and in communication, there are other non-cognitive dimensions that must be present such that meaning remains intact and communication effective. It is therefore, very important to bear in mind these non-cognitive dimensions of communication and meaning. Contrary to the fears of those purists who imagine that the use of the mother tongue gives us a perfect picture of the world, and the meaning intended, it is important to remember that in all situations of communication, as acts involving human beings in their insufficiency, there is always something left out un-communicated and unattended to. This does not make communication incomplete or undesirable. It rather portrays communication as a human act, where all matters of meaning have an anticipatory character that can be grasped fully within the context of the totality and in future reference. Where communication consciously targets curtailment of those forces that aid the mind at attaining meaning, it immediately distorts meaning and can even create unintended strange meanings. In this case, a good communication using language is like a good story, where we always want to come back with the desire of hearing more. Such a good story arouses passion, which connects the storyteller with the hearers. It is this passion that is one of the most important elements that help to bridge our individual subjective worlds and enables us to share a common horizon on account of which what is communicated has a personal touch. What this means is that beyond language itself, there are other things that enter into the success of what is communicated and which help to make what is communicated clearer and sustain interest. This is the personal dimension of all forms of communication. Here, we are thinking of that dimension of language in communication that it shares with *obinwanne* (vicarious feeling of compassion). Remove this dimension from communication, it loses its flavour, likewise, meaning becomes obscure, even if interlocutors share the same mother language.

In this case, the dimension of *obinwanne* (vicarious feeling of compassion) is indispensable should what is communicated through language become evident. Where the use of language in communication loses this inter-subjective personal dimension, it becomes sterile and uninteresting. Hence, in all matters of communication, communicators should intend to tell a good and interesting story and not ones that kill the joy of being. In such a good story, all stakeholders are capable of sharing fully the meaning communicated no matter how obscure and no matter the language adopted. This is why, when we are confronted with a good story, we have the capacity to anticipate what comes next. When the storyteller finally relates his tale, we are happier still, when what he or she wishes to communicate corresponds with what we anticipated, even if the languages used are dissimilar. When the story takes a different and quite unexpected new dimension, it adds more to the embellishment of the story, and shows that we are listening and interested. This is the character of all forms of communication, whose most important dimension remains the anticipated joy of being, that draws all stakeholders together more intimately. This is the joy that is imbedded in what is left uncommunicated. This joy carries and sustains all forms of communication, and it makes meaning accessible. This joy of being, in anticipation, is what gives language its dynamism and makes it interesting as carrier of meaning enshrouded in symbols. These symbols, as they represent our diverse linguistic modes of expression, should not be sources of distraction, but reasons for attraction due to the joy of being they contain.

This mode of understanding the matter is applicable to the use of language at all levels of determination. Hence, the mindset with which we approach issues of this kind is very decisive. Where the mind remains internally polarised, obdurate, sceptical and suspicious, it would invariably block the flow of communication, even if interlocutors speak the same language. Where the mind, on the other hand, has learnt that all missing links stay in mutual complementary relationship, it would be most disposed relate to the world around it in the most natural joyous way. Where this happens, recourse to all the languages in vogue, as veritable linguistic ingredients that can be blended into the way we express our views, becomes a natural viable option. This is why within such a context, one can write in known popular languages, even if these are "foreign" and still interject one's ideas with key concepts drawn from local languages and from one's mother tongue.

Approaching the matter in this natural manner is very different from the approaches of those who despise their mother tongues and prefer foreign languages only. The same can be said of those who scorn at other languages and seek to hang on to unadulterated mother tongues. Many who advocate communicating in one's mother tongue only have one major fear to contest with; this is the fear that recourse to other languages, other than the mother tongue, renders meaning obscure. Over and above all, they imagine that by recourse to means of communicating meaning other than one's mother tongue, some important moments of communication gets lost. These are unfounded fears that can grossly impinge on the joy of being.

Hence, all forms of understanding are possible when we try to situate them within a complementary comprehensive future referential framework. As such, what is communicated does not get lost just because one has not written or spoken completely in the mother tongue. What is communicated becomes evident within the totality of the context from which meaning ensues. Meaning and what is intended go beyond mere linguistic symbols, and can easily get lost where we to hang on to mere symbols and where we seek to inhibit communication because of biases. Understanding and meaning become possible when we remain open to what is communicated to us irrespective of the means adopted to do so. This does not imply in any way that the means of communication are not important. On the contrary, these must be viewed in conjunction with the comprehensive framework of understanding to get their true worth. The very character of meaning, and quality of understanding likely to accrue from a given communication situations, are likely to be compromised, grossly minimised, and can even get lost, if we become too sensitive about the vehicles employed in communication. Here, we have to bear in mind that there is hardly anything that is called a perfect communication condition or a perfect end result of communication. Those who pursue such perfect communications, often create the impression that only insiders can tell us what is communicated, and where the opinion of the insider is not available, then the meaning sought is not only inaccurate but also obscure. If this were the case, then we would hardly rely on any translations concerning ancient texts and other sources whose meanings are not always too clear. In all situations of communication, we are dealing with imperfect translations and mere approximations. In this way, translations cannot be equated with meaning; they merely seek to approximate what is intended. This does not mean that translations do not convey meaning; they do, but on the condition that translators have mastered some basic skills needed in the art of translation. Since most communication situations can be likened to situations of translation, the success of communication does not only lie in the dexterity of translation, but more so on the readiness of the receiver of the message or the listener to trust that what is being communicated makes a meaning. When this happens, the listener is disposed to accept what has been communicated in its relative insufficiency as something useful. Where this readiness is not given, no meaningful communication can take place. What this shows is that we can never have perfect meaning delivered to us in any communication condition. All matters of meaning are imperfect but they have a future referential dimension by reason of which they acquire further richness.

Hence, the issue of the use of mother tongue in writing or in other forms of communicating meaning appears to me to be an artificial problem at certain levels of articulation. This is an issue that has to be handled realistically. Should it be possible to write fully in the mother tongue sometime soon, I would still consider this a very welcome development, but this is not a necessary condition for determining the truth worth, value or quality of what is communicated. Generally, understanding and communication of meaning are possible, even in the most mixed linguistic communication conditions.

Over and above all, it is important to stress that understanding of very difficult and complex meanings needs some extra effort. In some cases, this cannot be achieved without extra training. However, in goodwill and in consideration of the joy of being that is the foundation of all modes of communication, most linguistic problems can be handled naturally.

In matters of this kind, those who are open to other conceptual schemes appear to be at an advantage when compared to those who are over sensitive about outside influence. A simple example suffices to illustrate what is meant: The English language, as we know it today owes much of its greatness, strength, dynamism and growth largely to its ability to assimilate and integrate other languages and conceptual schemes. This has been its character right from antiquity, when it first came into contact with colonial impositions. Here, Tacitus, one of the eminent "cultural anthropologists" of his time informs us that "instead of loathing the Latin language they [the Britons] became eager to speak it effectively" (Tacitus, The Agricola and the Germania 72-73). This eagerness never left these Britons, until they used what is best in the Latin language, and other sources, to bring the English language to its present grandeur, as one of the number one global languages of choice today. Here, Tacitus is referring to the attitude of the colonised Britons to their perceived tormentors, the Romans, their language and traditions. It is instructive that these Britons had no written literary traditions before they came into contact with the civilised Romans. In other words, they were illiterates the way some traditional African societies were barely 200 years ago. The same is applicable with most Roman colonies of the time including Germany and Gaul, the lands of some of our admired great philosophers, and this is barely about 2000 years ago. The ability of these once backwards cultures to assimilate the good things from almost all advanced cultures in view of much needed improvement can serve as a lesson to those who are looking for an effective way of casting off the yoke of oppression and colonialism. These people who have mastered the internal dynamics of this type of positive casting off of the yoke go about their business of integration quietly. They do not make undue noises and shout about conceptual decolonisation. Rather, most of them go ahead even to claiming all the good fruits arising from such synthesis as their own ingenious inventions, which are now tagged Western civilisation. Does it surprise anyone when they associate with the Greeks and all nice peoples of the world, fight tooth and nail to prove their common cultural heritage and affinity in almost everything, to the bewilderment of all of us?

As unbelievable as it may seem, we are informed, that most of the concepts the Greek philosophers made their own, were "photocopies" of Egyptian ideas and conceptual schemes as Onyewuenyi and many others claim they are (The African Origin of Greek Philosophy 224-287). They are not the only ones who think this way. Even Aristotle in the Metaphysics informs us, in view of buttressing a very important point that ".the mathematical arts were founded in Egypt; for there the priestly caste was allowed to be at leisure." (Metaphysica Book A, 1). If there is any lesson we can learn from all these, it is the fact that what we call Greek philosophy, and with it European history and conceptual schemes, would hardly have developed to their present stage had they gone about shouting "conceptual decolonisation". No, like most sensible people, they keep their mouths shut because they have realised early that no human achievement can progress where the units do not reach out to others. This is the way most advanced and civilised cultures get matters resolved, even to this day. I think that they are doing the most natural thing, because no one has a prerogative of any conceptual schemes in a world of mutual complementarity of idea. For mere mortals, creativity or originality does not entail creating out of nothingness. When a person becomes creative and an inventor, we all know, since as Igbos say, we know the ripe corn by seeing it (*eji anya ama ọka chara acha*). Those who spend their precious time and energies guarding critically against external influence and those who are "guarding against the uncritical assimilation of conceptual schemes embedded in foreign languages and cultures", would definitely reap the bountiful fruits accruing to night watchmen and women. We all know how meagre the wages of these can be. This is why, I consider culture an ongoing process "which subsists in our ability not to reinvent the wheels, but in our dynamic ability to turn the wheel to the demands and exigencies of our situation and in full consciousness that we are turning the wheel in a manner that would bring positive changes in our lives and society" (Method and Principles 268).

In this sense, it appears to me that those backward peoples Tacitus was writing about learnt early to internalise the fact that anything that exists serves a missing link of reality in view of the joy of being. It is due to this insight that they were able to turn apparently bad colonial conditions into a source of joy. Thereby, they allowed the limitations of being to be the cause of their joy. This struggle to associate with all nice peoples and to be open to new ideas and conceptual schemes must be global to be complete. The same can be said of some of the simple tricks needed to succeed. These are some of the fruits of positive complementary mutual relationship that have always characterised human development.

In view of the above observations, I maintain that in pluralistic multilingual contexts as we have it in the world today, "*the onus does not so much so lie in constructing or adapting a common language but making people understand that all languages, actions, values, norms of persons and societies serve a missing link of which every individual is a part." (Asouzu, Multilingualism, 33).* In human interpersonal relationship, the tendency to negate this mutual complementary relationship of all stakeholders can have very grievous consequences, as it stems from our natural instinct of self-preservation, which fires our passion for exclusiveness. It is in keeping with this primitive instinct that we seek those things that are original based on which we seek to influence those outside of the range of the little world we have carved out for ourselves.

ii) The problem with the "philosophy of stolen legacy" and "copycat philosophy"

Any attempts that view thought systems as if these are destined to be in mutual competition in view of each demonstrating its superior position is bound to remain divisive. The same is applicable to any attempt to make one thought system influential in relationship to others by mere reference to what one thinks is his or her original conceptual schemes or ideas. Such approaches can very easily expose a claimant to ridicule, if one remembers that the mutual complementary character of all ideas in their genesis and further development. This is valid, not only for African philosophy, but also, for all philosophies and ideas. The same is applicable most especially to those intransigent ethnocentrists, whose major preoccupations entails laying claims to the achievements of some distant hidden wisdom in the past belonging to their ancestors. Granted that it is a part of being human that one should be proud of one's past and heritage, if this pride entails only extolling the achievements of one's dead ancestors, it remains empty. As the saying goes, whoever has nothing to show other than the achievements of one's dead ancestors has already the best part of himself or herself in the grave.

In the case of Africa, this concerns most especially proponents of that brand of extreme Afrocentrism, who make reference to a distant Ancient Egyptian culture as the cradle of human civilisation and most especially as the cradle of what many have come to regard as the classical Greek civilisation. The same can be said with regard to all those Eurocentrists, who make adamant claims to a distant Greek culture, which is for them the very source of all thinkable human achievements. Authentic commonsense, which is not common anyway, shows that both the ancient Greeks and Egyptians were mere mortals, whose ideas could not have arisen out of nothingness and devoid of any form of mutual relationship with other ideas. Even at the most elementary level, the teacher is dependent on the students and vice versa. The type of intellectual combat we are witnessing, most especially with regard to the origin of philosophy, is what happens when human beings fail to grasp some fundamental issues with regard to the character of the origin of our ideas, which is complementary. The same is applicable to further development of all ideas and what constitutes human civilisation. These can be thought of only within the context of all the actors and factors that enter into their genesis and further development. Hence, the relevance of Africa or Europe does not need to be proved by recourse to some distant primeval cultures, where human beings had all it took to generate their ideas without any outside influences. We do not need to prove self-evident facts, as these concern the insight that all missing links are involved in the process of self-affirmation of being in history. In this case, the relevance of Africa, Europe or any human legacies does not require any proof. On the contrary, this has to be grasped as an integral part of the totality of determinations driving our world and reality already. I feel that this should continue to remain an authentic aspect of our experience of reality in the age of globalisation and multi-causal determinations, where our achievements can be assessed positively as a result of complementary mutual enrichment between diverse cultures. The same can be said of its failures.

Cultures do not become influential because of their claims to be the most original and supreme. What makes a culture original, and in what her supremacy consists, is rooted, in what the culture in question puts in place to represent reality truly and authentically, as a shared complementary affair. Wherever one mistakes originality for authenticity, tension is bound to arise and endure. In the search for truth and authenticity, all philosophies and ideas are subject to the same truth and authenticity criterion, as this is an integral part of the principle of non-contradiction. Matters of who is responsible for what, and who takes credit for what are not such issues as to be subject to empirical proofs only. Such matters are grossly also dispositional psychological matters. This is why those who think that they are victims of a "stolen legacy", be they Africans or Westerners, for example, are as liable to the same mistakes as the alleged "thieves" themselves, since their position would amount to a negation of the obvious mutual dependence between all missing links in the process of self-actualisation of being in history. I say this bearing in mind those who accuse Westerners of having stolen Egyptian ideas and those Westerners today who appear to be so bereft of ideas that their only preoccupation is searching for those who copy or are echoing what they identify as Western ideas. One thing stands out clearly, no human culture and achievement arose out of nothingness.

The moment researchers lose sight of the mutual complementary relationship between all missing links, that is the moment they become undue nuisances and embarrassments, not only to themselves, but more so, to others. In all our research efforts, it is important to bear in mind always, that all ideas in their origin and further development are related in a mutual complementary way. In most situations of life, human beings are subject to similar, and in some cases, even identical experiences and challenges, around which they anchor their philosophical thinking. This arises from the fact of human beings sharing a certain horizon of being commonly. Our responses to most of these challenges and experiences are often fundamentally similar irrespective of times and places. This is all the more the case, when we consider the fact, that most of these challenges are deeply rooted in our fundamental instinct of self-preservation and human feeling of insufficiency. Among those major existential challenges and experiences that sustain philosophical reflection include, the fear of the unknown, human innate desire for honour and recognition, excitement about life, joy in success, ambition, the desire to excel, human desire for immortality, phenomenon of death, misfortune, sickness, uncertainties and vagaries of existence. Others are such experiences as love, acceptance, disappointment, rejection, failure, hatred, sadness, success, competition, envy etc. These phenomena and experiences are among those that form the themes of most folklore, both in cultures with and without literary traditions. In some cases, not only the content of our reflection, but even our style of presenting them can overlap. These facts are not mere coincidences. On the contrary, they go to confirm that we are human beings who share certain things in common including some sources from which we draw our inspiration, meaning and have our being.

In the midst of these similarities, there could be some differences ensuing from new insights, due to the future referential dimension of all missing links. This future is open to all actors, irrespective of their backgrounds, and has to be harnessed in consideration of all the actors and factors that cohere to sustain our being in mutual complementary way. Hence, there is always room for surprises arising from any of the units that enter into this complementary relationship, anywhere and anytime. To imagine that there is no more room for the new insights is to negate existence itself. It is in this connection that this comment from a preface to Plato's Dialogues can be instructive. Here, Frost Jr. avers, "The philosophy of Plato is coextensive with the world. Referring to the universality of Plato's work,

Emerson exclaims, 'Burn the libraries; for their value is in this book'. Indeed, there is hardly a subject of human interest that Plato did not touch upon in his pilgrimage of thought. The brotherhood of man, eugenics, socialism, communism, feminism, birth control, free love, free speech, the double and the single standards of morality, the public ownership of wealth, of women, of children –these are only a few of the problems that he discusses in his dialogues" (4). Should we go by what is depicted here, as the universal character of Plato's themes, then there is no point talking of any new ideas after Plato. However, this can hardly be said. Human beings can arrive at new insights and offer better solutions for their problems irrespective of times and places. That human beings arrive at similar and identical conclusions merely shows how in spite of the immensity of reality, all share certain things in common. For this reasons, most daunting problems of humanity can be addressed when all stakeholders complement their efforts bearing in mind that *ibuanyidanda* (no task is impossible for *danda* the ant) In other words, the assumption that any set of peoples or cultures must steer a course quite removed from the general human experience is quite uncalled for.

Quite different from "the philosophy of stolen legacy" and "copycat philosophy", complementary reflection is committed to the insight that a person can steal from himself only at the risk of self-negation and contradiction. Where the ego is cognisant of this danger, it can only see itself as a unit in complementary service to all missing links of reality, since anything that exists serves a missing link of reality. It is with this frame of mind, that we are in a position to avoid doing those things that would put us on a collision course with other missing links, bearing in mind that where we pursue only our interests consistently, we jeopardise optimal realisation of the same interests. This is why we say that consistent or consequent self-interest is anti self-interest. Hence, anything aimed at undermining the units outside of the legitimacy provided by the whole, will always rebound on the actor. Likewise all actions undertaken by the units to enhance the welfare of the whole would amount to enhancing the welfare of the units. This is the ontological boomerang effect enshrined in the Igbo aphorism *egbe bere ugo bere nke si ibe ya ebena nku kwaa ya* (let the kite perch, let the eagle perch, whichever denies the other the same rights let its wings break). Where this complementary approach has been internalised, the mind learns to see missing links in their relativity, as pure means or pure dynamic essences that have the capacity to evoke the joy of being.

35. On some personal internal challenges of African philosophy

African philosophy has had to attain its recognition as a discipline through very strenuous efforts. A greater difficulty relates to what it takes to uphold this recognition. This can only happen through sustained constructive efforts to make it attractive. By every indication, this appears not to be the case always going by the state of philosophy in most institutions of higher learning in Africa today. This may be what Makinde had in mind in his paper "Whither Philosophy in Africa?" which he presented during the 20th World Congress of Philosophy.

In that paper, Makinde sought external intervention in view of salvaging African philosophy from what he identified as its present state of desolation. He ended his solicitation on a sad note by adding: "My fear, however, is that although we know why such an intervention is necessary for bringing philosophy back to life in Africa, or some parts of Africa, I must confess we really don't know what form such an intervention would take, and how it would be accomplished. We can only hope, though not without doubt, that philosophy in Africa would not suffer the same fate of many African Journals, which existed in one moment and went out of existence the next moment. It is very unlikely that the continuous existence of philosophy on the African continent would in any way be guaranteed by God, as Berkeley said of material objects. This, then, is the totality of my submission to the world congress of philosophy about the condition of philosophy in Africa. As of now, the question is apposite: Whither philosophy in Africa, on the eve of the 21st century?" (http://www.bu.edu/wcp/Papers/Afri/AfriMaki.htm).

Evidently, solutions to human problems have to be sought in the true spirit of mutual complementary dependence; here one has to commend any moves thus motivated. However, in his solicitation, Makinde seems to assume that solutions to the state of philosophy can be resolved through outside intervention only without due regard to what Africans can do themselves. Thus, his solicitation is reminiscent of Anyanwu's remark that some "philosophers in Africa are asking us to go to Greece and England, France and Germany to ask the thinkers of those nations what is true or false in African culture" (Anyanwu, The Problem of Method in African Philosophy 61). Unless we seek to explore the input of all the actors and factors needed to bring about desired effects, our efforts would remain ineffective. Certainly, what Makinde sees as the precarious state of philosophy in Africa is not something that can be rectified when the World Congress of Philosophy embarks on an emergency philosophical rescue mission to Africa, as he seems to assume. Philosophy is not like natural disaster where international agencies send their delegates and relief materials. For African philosophy to attend that level of dynamism, which Makinde thinks is lacking, it has to have its doors open and not have it closed. We do not achieve this in the spirit of double-dealing where we reach out to the outside only when we think that we are in trouble. This attitude of double-dealing is typical of those Africans who, in very precarious situations, submit that salvation comes from the West, but they go about rejecting the West by any given opportunities. This is typical of Makinde's strategy, who, according to Oke, is now campaigning that Wiredu should be de-recognised as an African philosopher just because "Wiredu writes in foreign language". With this type of divided mindset, African philosophy would definitely be condemned to crisis. The problem is that many do not know exactly what they want. Even if some of the issues, which Makinde has in mind, might be genuine, his approach is definitely unsatisfactory. We salvage African philosophy by doing it, since a person becomes a worker by working.

Coming now to what might be regarded as some of the major causes of the difficulties that saddle African philosophy, as a discipline, one can say that they are of a rational and a quasi-rational nature. To start with, philosophy, as a discipline, is often approached with prejudices, which range from the incomprehensible to the absurd. It is often seen as a time consuming preoccupation; this relates mostly to what some see as the penchant of its practitioners to indulge in unending arguments, hair-splitting distinctions and over sensitivity to issues that may not strike a common observer immediately. That is to say, many feel rather frustrated and irritated dealing with philosophers, who claim to see differences and nuances where the matter should be clear to any "normal" person. In most cases, many approach philosophy, as a discipline, from a utilitarian point of view. This is when people are doubtful if by studying philosophy, they can be in the position later to make ends meet in life. Here, the policies of our governments do not seem to be helping matters when they lay more emphasis on technological oriented education and create the impression that the humanities are less important (Asouzu, Humanistic Education, Technology and National Development 68-73). In an age where many believe that what a student studies by far determines his or her prospects in life, many parents are hesitant to support their wards who entertain such ambitions as studying philosophy. Today, in Nigeria, many parents would consider their wards doing philosophy as a last option. Even then, they would expect them to attach something more concrete and rewarding goals to such ambitions as studying philosophy. One of the best prospects in this sense is where philosophy is seen as a handmaid of those studies leading to a career that is materially rewarding.

In addition to this, is the prejudice about what many have come to see as philosophy's strange-to-life outlook. Here, many seem to see philosophy as an abstract discipline with hardly any practical usage. When this prejudice is targeted at African philosophy, many appear to see it as debates about old customs and cultural heritages, about dead ancestors and antiquated traditions. In this case, it is a preoccupation reserved only for exotics and never-do-well. We can then understand why some students intending to study in institutions of higher learning, use philosophy as a stepping-stone to gain admission. These are mostly those students who are fearful of making the requisite grades needed to get such admission. Bearing in mind that not many students study philosophy, they register philosophy as their first choice of study. However, they do this with the intention of changing their course of study later and the moment they have been admitted. This gamble often pays off, when one remembers that the entry requirements for those courses they identify as more rewarding are usually very stringent. Once registered in the university, they can all the easier change courses. To complicate matters, the nature of the curriculum of studies at the elementary and higher school levels is such that most Nigerian children are hardly instructed in a way that arouses passionate interests in the cultural heritages of their people. They are often carried away by what they see in the mass media. Going by the information being fed by the new film industry, Nollywood, for example, one can say that most children are victims of circumstance. To study those old customs and artefacts that have come to symbolise backwardness, in the minds of most youths, would be very presumptuous.

Where such impressions exist, they are not totally out of place because more often than not, philosophy is done in many seminars in the spirit of feeding the listener with what has been identified as the much-needed information that is lacking. In this case, some philosophers go about their business describing traditional values and mores, talking about marriage customs and other cultural practices, as Amaku clearly captured this mood. This they do in the name of critical philosophy. This informative, descriptive type of approach, which concentrates on extolling the significances of the past with her myths, symbols and antique objects, often reduces the listener to a mere consumer who once informed is expected to concur being satisfied with the excellent cultural achievements of his people. Unfortunately, most youths are often not interested in such information, because they can have access to even better antique objects via the internet at E-Bay without being subjected to long rigorous hours of listening to boring tales in classrooms.

One of the most adverse effects of this consumer oriented approach is that there is hardly any efforts to articulate knowledge in a systematic methodological way as to make it challenging, evoke lasting interest and drive intellectual curiosity beyond known clichés. Hence, one must admit that the discipline has been plagued by the near absence of very attractive theories and systems of thought comparable to what is obtainable elsewhere, as to stimulate sustained debates. Where such are at all present, there is often lack of interest among practitioners of philosophy themselves. In this case, prospective theoreticians are discouraged due to lack of patronage.

Besides, there is near absence of serious reading culture beyond newspapers publication. Where philosophical texts of substance are available, within the limited circles of intellectual elites, there is still the problem that not all have the strong teeth to chew strong philosophical texts directly from the primary sources. In this case, there is noticeable near absence of sufficient serious secondary sources needed to break down hard materials for the comprehension of non-experts and some scholars of philosophy alike.

Coming back to what happens at the elementary and secondary levels, chances are that these youngsters have heard of some names of philosophers other than Africans. To consider philosophy as a study option means going for it in view of learning about those figures they easily associate with certain types of values and expectations. This is one of the reasons some of these students come into the university and have their minds already set as to the nature, the type of philosophy and philosophers they want to be acquainted with. Considering how some of our philosophy students get admission to study philosophy itself, as people who could not get a chance in the disciplines they have always wanted to study, most of our philosophy students show their true colours mostly at the tail end of their second year in the university. This is when they start showing appreciable amount of self-confidence with regard to philosophy as their discipline. This is the moment also when they can associate freely with their peers as people who are also studying something worth talking about. Fortunately, many students who have completed their studies in philosophy are ever grateful having made the correct decision by choosing to study it.

Coming back to a more serious issue, that I have just hinted at briefly, one can say that there is virtually near absence of philosophical traditions and systems of thought that can sustain fruitful debates, and on which researchers can anchor their thoughts on African philosophy credibly. Here, I quite agree with Ogbogbo, a historian, who equally bemoans this unwholesome situation of near lack of systematic theoretical traditions in philosophy (Explaining the Crisis of Relevance in African Philosophy, 59-65). In his observation, Ogbogbo takes Ozumba's comment a step further, who holds that "a philosophical work is hardly complete or successful if it lacks systemacity" (A Review 133). Here, commitment to a clearly identifiable methodological systematic approach becomes indispensable should African philosophy evolve to those types of philosophies we have come to admire and study. Even amongst those really committed to African philosophy, the mood of the moment appears to be one where each person is on his own, analysing, interpreting and trying to presenting the worldviews of his people, in the manner he or she understands best. There is virtually nothing wrong in this approach, which goes by diverse names under hermeneutics of culture, but it has to be done in a manner that does not reduce philosophical research to ethnological studies. With the excitement generated by the great debate about the existence or non-existence of African philosophy, African philosophy appears to be marking time around these ethnocentric motivated themes, whose content is philosophically very wanting. Such an approach can at times be very boring. This appears to be what Ralph Dumain has in mind when writing about African philosophy he observes, "By now there must be dozens of readers in African Philosophy in English alone, all of them overlapping considerably and repeating the same tiresome themes. Even those who reject the notion of a philosophy categorically African (ethnophilosophical) in content—an essentially obscurantist ideological project—are caught within a tedious identity crisis which has long outlived its time." (http://www.autodidactproject.org/my/blog-culture-0612.html). As this matter concerns some of the works presented as African philosophy, the remark of Peter King on his review of the book "Readings in African Philosophy" edited by Safro Kwame (Lanham: University Press of America, 1995) informs: "The problem is that a collection of readings in African philosophy only makes sense if there's something distinctive about such philosophy -- otherwise it makes no more sense than a collection of papers written on Tuesdays, or by red-headed philosophers." (http://users.ox.ac.uk/~shil0124/mystuff/africa-2.html). These remarks and observations go to underscore the near lack of exciting themes prevalent in African philosophy as to elicit interest.

Within the rank and file of African philosophers themselves, many are yet to make up their minds about what is expected of African philosophy as a philosophy in keeping with academic tradition. I say this bearing in mind the fact that even some, who are trained philosophers, contest the usefulness of devotion to clearly worked out systems in philosophy. Others do not even believe that there is need for philosophy to follow any specific methods, since for them, philosophy should be a free enterprise. As typical anti-system thinkers in African philosophy today, one can cite Theophilus Okere and Eze Emmanuel, who have the penchant to scorn at the important role which systems and methods play in philosophical inquiry. For Okere commitment to system is likely to alienate philosophy from its practical and humanistic vocations (Philosophy, Culture and Society in Africa 70). On his part, Eze shares Okere's strong passion in this regard, but for a totally different reason. For Eze such a commitment easily exposes philosophy to the dangers of being lost in an absolute type of ontologism (In Search of Reason's Traces). Contrary to the positions of these two eminent philosophers, I quite agree with Solomon that it is in the commitment to system that we can distinguish "great metaphysicians from lesser philosophical technicians" (84). What he designates as "philosophical technicians", I call "patchwork philosophers".

With regard to the indispensable role which systems and methods play in the mode of our thinking, we can still learn much even from anonymous traditional Igbo philosophers for whom system-building translates to bridge building (*ikwa ogwe*). It is for this reason that these philosophers insist that *onye kwaa ogwe amara uche ya* (when a person builds a bridge we know his mind). In other words, for them, methodological systematic approaches are indispensable towards clear and distinct presentation of reality. In this point, their opinion is quite consistent with those of most systematic thinkers the world over. Philosophy and learning become interesting mostly when we have such systems and methods on which the mind builds, as it strides on its way to certainty. A situation where Africans indulge only in ethnophilosophic themes, and thereby supply others with the requisite raw data for system and theory building, can merely succeed in impoverishing African philosophy. This is when it keeps marking time. Furthermore, it would hardly endear African philosophy to the hearts of the younger generation; what more to the world that is in search of much needed alternative paradigms to combat some of the challenges of our time? Contrary to the pretension of those who scorn at system building, such well-crafted systems and methods do not come per chance but are fruits of very hard work based on facts.

Commitment to systems and methods has always belonged to the character of the human intellect in its tendency towards truth, clarity, unity and universality. We should not equate this striving with possession of absolute knowledge; even if there is often the temptation to substitute one's opinion with what is intended. Where such substitutions do occur, we can say that *absus non tolit usum,* misuse does not invalidate the mores. Hence, the important position, which system-building takes, in any attempt to get at the thing in itself, can never be underrated even if people can hide behind systems to dogmatise on issues. It is the function of philosophy to expose such misuses when they occur.

If there is anything that systematic methodological approach to issues does, it is to give us accurate information on the stand of the thinker about issues beyond guesswork. In this case, we know what has been affirmed or denied, and we know what to accept and what to reject. It is in the systematic methodological commitment of the mind to the complex art of constructing a bridge (*ikwa ogwe*) that we know what this mind is up to. This methodological systematic merely indicates the freedom to strive towards an end in the process of which the mind reveals its character. In this, is rooted the autonomy of the subject and defines equally the autonomy of others to disagree. In this case, it merely helps us grasp the nature of the mind concerned in its striving to certainty. In other words, the presence of diverse systems in our inquiry shows how diverse and varied thinking subjects can be. It is not an indication that subjects are condemned to despotism and dogmatism. Since these systems rest on carefully crafted ways of doing things, they offer us a variety of choices that can complement themselves in our search for truth.

In this sense, the appearance of complementary reflection as a system of thought, which Kimmerle justifiably designates as a "new approach to African philosophy as a whole" is timely. Among other things, it is one of the numerous efforts by scholars of African philosophy designed to fill one of the yawning gaps in African philosophy that have hitherto hindered its growth. It seeks to achieve this by trying to supersede all forms of ethnocentric reduction and impositions and by so doing make philosophy a universal undertaking including African philosophy. Commitment to a clearly worked out system, saves us the embarrassment of hiding behind the general worldviews of peoples, which we never tire of describing, informing about and thereby, dogmatising about.

To forestall retrogression and lack of creativity in African philosophy, therefore, a change of strategy has become inevitable. Here, the classical approach that entails the study, only of known western philosophers and their methodologies, must be complemented with studies of works and systems of African philosophers if such are available. These would serve as models for criticisms and reviews since they already contain clearly identifiable paradigms around which individual reflections can be anchored. Progress and stagnation of African philosophy depends largely on the attitude of Africans themselves who have the primary duty to patronise and promote it. In our institutions of higher learning, a conducive atmosphere has to be created for the promotion and patronage of ideas, systems and methods of African philosophers in view of promoting African philosophy. That is to say, the thoughts of regional philosophers should be studied and made available to students and should be brought to compete with each other. All forms of escapist tendencies with regard to things African kill African presence in the age of globalisation. I say this bearing in mind some allied difficulties in this regard. The first is that occasioned by laziness of the mind to embrace African philosophy as a challenge. Some who have studied western and other philosophies all their lives, seem to find it difficult to adjust to the demands of this new trend. Besides, since some of the major issues are raised by their colleagues and are as such locally brewed, they tend to view them as lacking in merit and elegance. To these I would say, it is never too late to be wiser.

Behind this attitude is that lack of enthusiasm for things made in Africa. This is what I have identified as the phenomenon of practical existential pessimism and scepticism, as this pertains to the attitude of most Africans to scorn at things African. (The Method and Principles 262-273). Not even in the academia is this a less violent scourge. Here, it surfaces in diverse forms of which the flair and taste for the exotic is the most pronounced. This is when students are more likely to take notice of expression arising from foreign languages, than those of African origin. They write down any phrases arising from say, Greek, Latin, German, French etc, but would vehemently refrain from writing those expressions of African origin. It may even be seen as lack of erudition, philosophical sophistication and elegance, by some students, when one is trying to expound philosophical ideas in their known African idioms and expressions. Since they are not used to having philosophical ideas expounded in their native dialects, they find such attempts as presumptuous, strange and embarrassing. This is mostly the case in classes with mixed ethnic composition, where such can be misconstrued as tribalistic imputations. Generally, there is every indication that most teachers and students of philosophy in our institutions of higher learning take less pride in identifying with African philosophy, as a discipline. As most things African, many prefer other brands of the product and most especially, the imported types. The irony is that some of those vanguards of African heritage and tradition, compromise their position when it matters most and when their most cherished interests are at stake, just as we have seen in the case of Moses Akin Makinde. Here, many who apparently advocate African philosophy do so only for the purpose of attaining some ideological gains. In their writings and research efforts, their claims are hardly reflected by their references and sources, which grossly contradict what they hypocritically profess. More often than not, they carefully avoid the works written by eminent African philosophers in those themes where they should have been consulted. Making allowance for ignorance and laziness of the mind, more work in this regard needs to be done should African philosophy take that enviable position that we all cherish.

Generally, one can say that a typical African academic and practitioner of philosophy is not always convinced that locally made and brewed knowledge is something very fulfilling. It is always fashionable and a way of showing modernity, learning and erudition, a way of demonstrating beyond reasonable doubts that one has arrived and is abreast with latest happenings in philosophy, if one talks very loudly about those theories brewed and hatched by say, European and American philosophers. Naturally, one is bound to recognise, in all honesty, the enormous contributions these have made in philosophy. However, any sheepish attachment to Western philosophers and paradigms can kill creativity in African philosophy. Here, we forget that philosophy, like so many areas of human knowledge, has its own ideological underpinnings, which a person can easily manipulate to his or her advantage. It is often amazing that it is easier, surer and quicker to get a book written by an African philosopher from European or American library or sources. It is often an exercise in futility trying to search for works of fellow Africans in African libraries, be this at the universities, research institutes, departments, and seminaries. Non-availability of fund is only a part of the problem. More often than not, Africans hardly treasure the works of fellow Africans and would hardly give these serious considerations, even when the funds are available. The same is applicable to collecting them, promoting them and documenting them. By purchase of new books, journals and publications, we often mean in Africa, those books published not by local writers. From here derives the lukewarmness when it comes to speaking out to have African philosophy as the fulcrum of any curriculum in philosophy, when the need arises that new courses should be introduced. Over and above all, there is lack of the spirit of adventure and risk-taking in view of a discipline whose future is not fully determined.

African philosophy must be freed from all forms of passive and active indoctrination to retain its value. Here, many Africans indulge in this type of passive indoctrination, which makes them victims even in their own things. To counter this form of passive indoctrination, Africans and most especially African scholars should take pride in studying, understanding, and internalising the ideas of African philosophers, as an integral part of human intellectual heritage. In doing this, the African has to learn to assert himself and his ideas positively. He has to learn to make claims to his ideas doggedly, bearing in mind the mutual complementary relationship between all missing links. This is a simple trick that many have mastered, but often wrongly, when they doggedly give the impression that they are the originators of all ideas. The African has to avoid this exclusivist approach. Mastering this simple trick correctly and in a positive sense has great implication most especially for the way we study philosophy in our institutions of higher learning. This time, we must not do it the old way of claiming everything for ourselves, because of the obvious mutual complementary relationship between all human achievements. In other words, our efforts should not aim at enhancing our prestige only, but must be geared towards providing genuine insights and solutions to human problems beyond local needs.

It is gratifying to note that the overall attitude of today's youth to the world can modestly be designated as more positive, open and tolerant. Many of them who have access to the Web spend some time chatting with their peers around the globe. In view of these positive changes, it may be worthwhile, as philosophers, to emphasise those matters that enhance this positive attitude more, than those that discourage it. Without prejudice to the important position historical records play in our lives, it does not always pay to concentrate only on negative themes. There is often the wrong assumption that all matters of African philosophy must begin and end with colonial legacies. This can boomerang, since there are far more positive experiences that can compensate enormously for a gloomy past. Hence, over sensitivity to certain themes, be it violence, reason, sex, emotion, race etc. are not always to the best interest of anyone. Not all forms of curiosity are philosophically rewarding. Definitely not the type that kills the cat. Most philosophical issues, to be rewarding, need the type of moderation and modesty that is characteristic of wisdom. I think, in most contentious matters, positive examples would continue to speak louder than mere theories. Here, most theoreticians and leaders in Africa need to do more by matching words with deeds. In this way, our theories could have more inspiring values, lasting impacts and elicit patronage.

36. On some challenges of African philosophy within the context of world philosophy

Some African practitioners of philosophy lack tact in their public relationship with non-Africans. Due to their methods of approach that focus more on form than on content, they tend to scare away those interested in African affairs. This is when such African practitioners of philosophy tend to see non-Africans who delve into African affairs as uninvited intruders. In some cases, the works of some of these well deserving non-African scholars are targets of unsubstantiated criticisms. The impression is given that such works are unserious curious enquiries interested in gathering specific types of sensational information meant to feed curious audiences, mostly in Europe and America. This is the impression one gets when the works of such well deserving and serious anthropologists and scholars, as Basden, are easily dismissed as mere "traveller's tales" (Ekei 48). With this, the impression is created that the insider or the native is all knowing and only himself or herself has the prerogative to tell all the truth about African experience. This is the foundation of most false theories propounded by African scholars themselves, who give African philosophy the character of age group engagement.

The attitude of some foreigners helps to cement such prejudices, since some of them snare at matters relating to African philosophy as if these do not deserve serious academic merit; indeed, they assume that African philosophy is mere pretence. In an E-mail I received from Prof. Jürgen Hengelbrock of the University of Bochum, Germany, on January 15, 2006, a part of which I am publishing with his permission, he has this to report: "Ich weiß sehr wohl um eine gewisse Arroganz unserer Kollegen hier, die meinen, eigentlich könne man nur in Deutsch oder Griechisch richtig philosophieren, und die anderen Kulturen seien in Sachen Philosophie höchstens Entwicklungsländer" (*I know some of our arrogant colleagues here who are of the opinion that it is only in German and Greek that one can philosophise in the true sense of the word. Other cultures are, in matters of philosophy, merely developing countries.* Translation from the German original by me). Naturally, I made it clear to Prof. Hengelbrock, in very strong terms, that I disapprove of any form of narrow mindedness, by any serious scholars, in matters so grievous. Argumentum ad hominem, has always constituted one of the main stocks in trade of ethnocentric jingoists, anti-intellectual fanatics and anarchists who are good for nothing except glorying in a collective achievements of some distant ancestors; mostly the dead ones. In the case of those Westerners who glory in Greek heritage, the irony is that many of them appear to be ashamed of the achievements of their own indigenous ancestors. The beauty of philosophy is that it is wisdom. As wisdom, it gives people the opportunity to say the truth. Unfortunately this has not always happened. Because of philosophy, many have refused to answer their father's names. Instead of answering their ancestral names, many tell us that Aristotle is their father. The same is applicable to those who are claiming that Egypt is their ancestral philosophical home. This is *ibuarụ* of unknown magnitude. Fortunately, we know were many come from and what their ancestors were capable of achieving, and how they excelled philosophically by recourse to their indigenous cultural backgrounds.

Prejudices, whether they come from Africans or from non-Africans, are certainly not to the best interest of research. Scientific integrity is upheld where scientists are devoted to the search for truth, which does not discriminate and does not draw artificial boundaries. Here, both "insiders" and "outsiders" are necessary complements to each other, as they unite to give us a true picture of reality. One of the major consequences of this biased attitude as it relates to African philosophy is that it has yielded a debate that appears to be found only within African philosophy. This is the debate concerning who qualifies to be considered an African philosopher. Such debates are reminiscent of George Orwell's "Animal Farm" where the criterion for being an animal is captured in "the essential principle of Animalism" consisting of the maxim, "Four legs good two legs bad" (31). The moment human beings reduce the essence of their being to a few cheap maxims, that is the moment they forfeit their right to a higher form of collective definition. Paradoxes ensuing from such forms of reductionisms, easily give the impression that African philosophy is a special type of undertaking, a club, with her own sets of special rules and conditions for admittance. It is precisely due to misconceptions of this kind that many have come to regard African philosophy as a strange type of scientific undertaking. When now because of such prejudices, spiteful comments are directed at African intellectuals, such comments often have the desired effect. This is when some less-determined African scholars become conditioned, and actually start to think that theirs must be another type of reflection. Indeed, many often assume that theirs is the crudest form of philosophy and philosophising. It is for this reason that some of these conditioned individuals seek escape routes in matters dealing with esoteric tales and fables, indeed in matters dealing with some special cultural patrimonies and mythological narratives that they call their own. Based on this type of reductionism, the temptation is to place special types of expectations on the works that bear the tag "African philosophy". Where the works of African practitioners of philosophy do not meet these marks, they are immediately dismissed as either copies or mere pretensions. The overall effect is often devastating. One of these is that the more systematic and methodological works of African practitioner of philosopher become, the more their intellectual tormentors raise suspicion and red alert signals concerning what they deem imitation, and the less such works stand to gain in merit and recognition.

In such situations, it does appear as if African thinkers are destined and condemned to supply the social anthropological and ethnological raw materials from which authentic philosophical theories are produced. Indeed, it appears to be the expectation determining demand and supply of, not only economic commodities, but of late also, of intellectual cooperation between African scholars and some of their Western counterparts. Here, I quite agree with Oladipo who quoting Hountondji calls this phenomenon "displacement of knowledge" (Knowledge and African Renaissance 11). This attitude shows itself even in the publications of research materials of African practitioners of philosophy. Here, those philosophical research works of African scholars are more likely to be published in international journals that exhibit the type of expectations carried towards them. Hence, the more narrative and abstruse the materials, the more unheard-of the pretensions become, the more likely they have the chances to see the light of the day. When now such materials are grudgingly published, they are acclaimed and labelled "original African thought", for the world to see and be entertained. Since the researcher wants his work to be accepted for publication in international journals, many easily succumb to the temptations of this *demand and supply mentality.* This is that situation where the African supplies the intellectual raw materials, while others evolve the theories that should be binding even on Africans themselves. However, it has to be remarked that this trend is to be found mostly within the ranks of promotion-driven or promotion motivated scholars. This is not likely to stop soon, since as the saying goes, an empty stomach does listen. Thus, the level of economic empowerment of most African scholars can help to define the level of their academic freedom vis-à-vis their peers elsewhere. Good philosophising can hardly be divorced from economic empowerment. Here, Aristotle is right when he reminds us that ".the mathematical arts were founded in Egypt; for there the priestly caste was allowed to be at leisure." (Metaphysica Book A, 1)

Just like those African scholars who concentrate on showing where the ideological divide between Africa and the rest of them stands, other non-African practitioners of philosophy when dealing with matters African seem to concentrate more on those themes, which they think mark African philosophy out for what it is. If they are not comparing different type of sciences, they are indulging in themes concerning different types of reason and emotion as these relate to diverse cultures. Even if we cannot legislate about the themes that researchers have to embark upon, having our research efforts determined by ideological considerations is hardly to the interest of scientific objectivity and healthy coexistence between peoples. This is why, I insist that unintended ethnocentric commitment is a deep scourge that has eaten into the way we do science and philosophy. For this reason, it deserves the serious attention that it merits. Where this is not done, we would see ourselves exhausting our energies solving fake puzzles in the name of philosophy and science.

These difficulties notwithstanding, there are very clear indications that African philosophy is taking a completely new turn that is complementary in articulation. Even if there are reasons to worry due to lapses here and there, most positive efforts to sustain the growth of African philosophy through diverse channels such as, increasing local and international conferences, modest good publications, growing number of students and philosophy departments and constructive debates are definitely not signs of impending disaster, contrary to Makinde, whose apprehension seems exaggerated. I would say that these efforts are very clear indications that academic philosophy in Africa is here to stay. For African philosophy, this new complementary turn as a part of African intellectual heritage has to be sustained in the face of globalisation. Here, one must cherish and nurse the good things one has in order to be effective. Our diverse intellectual heritages are the very ingredients of globalisation as it touches us as philosophers. These are the very things we make available to others in a world tending to universality. For Africans this is the question concerning the rediscovery of African philosophy in the face of global challenges in its complementary dynamism. African philosophy in the age of globalisation has the sacred duty of making philosophy relevant from the ambience of African existential living. This is the attempt of bringing African experience of the world to bear on the problems facing our world today. This challenge is a comprehensive challenge, which addresses all the actors and factors that condition the mind of the African philosopher. Hence, any form of one-sided approach to African philosophy today, is bound to present enormous difficulties. Not everything can be heaped at the door steps of politicians and planners of our diverse nations. These, at times, need well-formulated principles, systems and method, which the academia must offer.

37. On what African philosophy has to offer the world in the age of globalisation

The harder the struggle and the more fierce the battle the sweeter the victory. Hence, her many woes and troubles notwithstanding, African philosophy has much to offer the world. Here, I have identified the phenomenon of globalisation and the idea of *Ibuanyidanda* as credible horizons within which an ontology that is universal in articulation can be expounding. It is within this turbulent horizon that some of the gains of African philosophy can be situated. For this reason, one of the main challenges of African philosophy within a horizon of this kind is rooted in probing into the conditions necessary for conceptualising reality such that all missing links stay mutually harmonised in a universal comprehensive complementary way. In practical terms, this is a challenge to inquire into all forms of assumptions, methodologies, principles and theory formulations as to determine their adequacy or inadequacy towards upholding the co-existence of units in the face of their inherent tendencies towards universality, totality and comprehensiveness, in a future related perspective, their relativity notwithstanding. In other words, the contributions of African philosophers and African philosophy become more credible if these were to be defined within a more embracing framework as to transcend their localised settings. It is in view of this new task, that I insist that African philosophy has more to it than preoccupation with ethno-centric ideas aimed at showing how such ideas are peculiar to African framework of meaning. These so-called peculiar or ambient issues must be articulated and schematised within a wider framework. This is important since all inquiries get their full meaning when they are related to all missing links and not when they recoil to their raw primary cognitive ambiences.

The way this matter is understood, goes a long way in determining the type of philosophy we pursue, the type of relationship we enter into, the type of world we build, the type of idea of freedom, justice, international relations, government, development, morality, responsibility etc. we are capable of advocating. Therefore, one can say that an African philosophy, articulated around an ontology whose horizon is global in constitution, has the same sacred task as the one that binds all philosophers everywhere and every time since the philosophical thematic and subject matter is timeless as it seeks to expound the nature of being as being in its relational essentiality . It is in strict adherence to an objective of this kind that African philosophers can contribute their quota in helping the content enshrined in the active and passive force that is globalisation to materialise fully for the benefit of all stakeholders.

Now, when we talk of the scope of African philosophy within this global ontological horizon, certain things come to mind. One of the fine ways of determining the scope is by reference to the subject matter itself. In this case, we bring the subject matter of philosophy, being in its relational essentiality, to bear directly on the issue in question. Within the framework of complementary ontology, I have identified globalisation as both a hidden force and an ongoing process that sustains all historical events (Asouzu, Ibuanyidanda 378). As that force that spans our understanding of human history, it is as old as human history itself. In keeping with this understanding therefore, when we think of African philosophers and philosophy within this global context, we are thinking of a contribution that spans the past and the present marching into the future. For this reason, we are thinking, first and foremost, of the contributions that African philosophers have already made in order that this process is sustained. Again, we think of some of the contributions African philosophers are still making, as this process keeps unfolding. Furthermore, we think of some of the contributions expected of African philosophers within the context of this process.

When we think of the contributions African philosophers have made and are making, we are referred to the history of philosophy, as to think of some of the contributions, which African philosophers have always made towards the evolution of those ideas that are visible manifestations of the hidden force that we consciously identify as globalisation. While and whenever we are thinking of this, our minds should always be focused on the complementary structure of this evolution, which is a matter of mutual dependence and indebtedness of all missing links. In this history, we must bear in mind that there is a real and ontological complementary mutual relationship between human ideas because of the intricate mutual dependence and indebtedness between the units that constitute the whole. We profit from the ideas of others and others profit from our ideas because of our extended natural rights and responsibilities. The fact of our extended natural rights states that there is an infinite ontological mutual relationship of rights, privileges and responsibilities in any sets of relationship. The reason for this is that every idea is coextensive in a way that makes it an integral part of other ideas within a whole, since anything that exists serves a missing link of reality. We can then say that all human achievements are because of this mutual complementary dependence of ideas, which can concretely be grasped in the sense of mutual co-founding, co-inventing, co-evolving and co-authenticating. This process at times takes very definite and radical shapes in the achievements of those individuals whose contributions to this evolution of ideas become most striking and significant.

When this happens, we start thinking of concrete historical individuals and groups whose ideas have helped to shape our lives and destinies in very particular ways. It is in this connection that we start thinking of the contributions of those Africans who belong to what I call "the other Africa" that is often forgotten in matters of this kind (Asouzu, The Method and Principles 273-276). This other Africa is a residue of those achievements that can be credited to the insights of some forgotten Africans in the course of the history of ideas from antiquity through the ages even unto our own modern digital age. In this connection, one has to think of the numerous research works being undertaken by African academics and scholars towards finding lasting solutions to the problems of Africa and the world in general. Not to be forgotten are the efforts being put in place by numerous Africans of repute, and even less known individuals, in view of making the world a better place for all. These Africans are innumerable to mention in the areas of politics, international relations, science and technology, business and management, sports etc. Special mention needs be made here of some of those major philosophical ideas with clearly worked out teachings, systems and methods that have very much impacted on the lives of many not only in African but beyond. Here, one thinks of philosophies built around such concepts as Ubuntu, Communalism, Ujamaa, Consciencism, etc, the difficulties they present notwithstanding. Within this context, hardly anything can be said without highlighting the enormous contributions and the influence of the ideas of anonymous traditional African philosophers of the complementary system of thought. These, just like the ancient Egyptian philosophical tradition, bequeathed to the world what has come to be called the complementary conceptualisation of the world, which offers one of the most formidable tools towards addressing some of the major issues of globalisation.

Inspired by these thinkers, I have articulated what has come to be known as complementary reflection within the context of contemporary African philosophy as a veritable tool towards addressing some of the challenges posed by the paradoxes ensuing from a globalising world. Here, complementary reflection draws from the ambience of African philosophical tradition and explores veritable ways of reconciling the tension arising from coexistence of peoples in pluralistic multi-cultural and multi-ethnic context in their heterogeneity, similarities and differences. It studies the complex nature of this coming together and identifies the nature of the tension arising from there and views this not merely as a socio-political or economic challenge, as is being assumed in many quarters. On the contrary, it sees this as a comprehensive challenge of our humanity in the depth of its ambivalence and as a challenge that goes to the very foundation of our being. Confronting this challenge entails the resolve to put selfishness on its head, as that parasite that keeps sapping the world, in the process of globalisation, of the much-needed energy to cohere as system of units within the framework of the whole. Here, selfishness is identified as a wrong response to the dictate of our natural instinct of self-preservation. It is because of an ignorance of a special type that this primitive drive threatens some of the main positive gains of globalisation. This is the existential ignorance ensuing from lack of insight into the fact that consistent or consequent self-interest is anti-self interest. Complementary reflection helps elucidate and understand the character of this ignorance and its cause. It is by so doing that it calls for a massive global enlightenment about the threat, which such ignorance poses to world peace and security, for the development of the world, even at the private levels and as nations. This is that type of ignorance that seeks to monopolise, as matters of pure personal insight, and achievement, those lofty goals and dreams that individuals and groups have always cherished for themselves. As an aspect of African philosophical heritage, complementary reflection deals with the perfectibility of our potentialities, as the condition for mutual and harmonious exchange within a globalised and globalising community. In this capacity, its basic assumptions are still directed towards the needs of Africa and Africans in particular, most especially in her search for identity, self-definition and rediscovery, as a condition for fruitful encounter with the rest of the world. Naturally, it does this within a global framework, such that its method and principles are not for local African consumptions only, but more so, for human beings everywhere who are fundamentally challenged by the same problems.

In this way, complementary reflection, as a pedagogy of reason in asymmetrical situations, helps to bring the world still nearer to all stakeholders in very significant and insightful ways. It seeks to probe into the conditions needed to bring about radical changes in the mind as to make it amenable towards seeking harmony in all contentious situations of life. While not overlooking the fact that human beings see the world differently, it emphasises the need for each unit to sift out what it needs most, but in view of upholding harmony among all stakeholders. In other words, complementary reflection seeks to demonstrate that in spite of the plural character of the world, all stakeholders can be richer by drawing from the immensity of opportunity resulting from differences when each gives the other a chance. Within such a context, the insufficiency and fragility of the units become clearer to them and draw them to each other and challenge them to complement their efforts in a way that makes them better human beings, better communities and global citizens whose destinies can only be articulated within a comprehensive complementary framework. In this way, it offers us some of the useful tools needed to confront the obvious paradoxes and tensions that becloud globalisation as a process aimed at returning units to the foundation of their being.

In view of this objective, complementary reflection makes it clear that globalisation must not be a burden, as many unfortunately have come to conclude. On the contrary, it can be a joy if we understand ourselves as beings destined for the future and for comprehensiveness. In our determination for comprehensiveness, we tend towards other beings beyond ourselves and this can only happen within a global setting where each unit explores those things that characterise it best for the growth and betterment of all in the evident insight that service rendered to others is service rendered to self either directly or indirectly. In this way, it sees globalisation as the life we live, the completion we seek in our search for meaning and the measures we take to stay alive in the face of challenges that involve many. In this process, the perfection of each unit is a task involving all. It all then means that each unit should direct its energies towards doing those things that it can do best towards enriching all. Pushing this insight through is one of the greatest challenges of African philosophy today as this insight is deeply enshrined in the ideas of anonymous traditional African philosophers of the complementary system of thought. Here, African philosophy has lots to offer the world from the preceding conditions of its African background.

If there is anything that is fascinating in a plural context, it is the capacity of units to explore means towards the enrichment of all stakeholders in the evident insight that *ibuanyidanda* (in complementarity, we endure). It is this thought that enters into most unions that characterise our world today in our bid to master hardship, misfortune and misery and in our bid to do our best for our children, our peoples and ourselves. Thus, some of the major gains of globalisation turn out to be the possibility of harnessing the best opportunities offered by the world as veritable tools of making the world a better place for all. It is within this context that most bodies, organs and ideas that drive globalisation as visible instance of being seeking full expression in history can be assessed creditable. This is the case with such concepts as UN and her many organs, capitalism, democracy, diverse local, national, international and multi-national organs and cooperation as these institutions and concepts form indispensable and substantial part of our existential experiences in the world imbued with alternative paradigms. These concepts and institutions can still serve the aim establishing them without these constituting stumbling blocks to peace, harmony and prosperity for all. It is quite unfortunate that some of these bodies and organs have come to represent and be associated with the very evil arms of globalisation, as some are wont to criticise. However, not all these bodies and similar ideas, that have been devised to keep the tempo of our world in motion, are intrinsically evil in themselves, as many have come to assume. Where these bodies are misused against the ends establishing them, that is not immediately indicative of their innate negative constitution. On the contrary, this is indicative of the innate human capacity to misuse or mismanage opportunities due to the tension that is characteristic of human consciousness in its ambivalence.

In the incapacity to manage this ambivalence successfully subsists the moment where these institutions and bodies can revert to those things we dread. This is the moment also where the fundamental human tendency to universalise and globalise, as is characteristic of our being and as is expressed by these bodies, is automatically put into jeopardy. In this case, what is needed is not a complete eradication of these agents of human self-actualisation in history. On the contrary, what are needed are the requisite insight, wisdom and courage to translate those positive objectives enshrined in them into practical results for the good and betterment of all. It is in this capacity to transform that we say that a human person is *being-in-control.* In doing this, we should never forget that all stakeholders themselves are embodiments of mini-paradoxes that challenge our being even at personal private levels. For this reason, no individual is immune from the errors arising from the challenges of selfishness.

Therefore, what is important in all cases is to bear in mind always that in a system of interests, what is needed to uphold personal interest is equally what is needed to subvert it. Should we desire that the interests of all stakeholders be intact, then all must work hard towards upholding the common good, which offers the framework for the realisation of all interests. Where one seeks to subvert the common good and in the process puts his or her own interest into jeopardy, such is a demonstration of lack of insight and in the worse case scenario, a demonstration of foolishness. However, this situation is very characteristic of our world today, where many, in their blind zeal to secure only their interests, put the optimal realisation of the same into serious jeopardy. This is the existential tragedy that goes with the global paradox and in most situations puts the rationality of our actions into very serious question in as much as we claim to be one of the most enlightened generations that humanity has ever known. We can then understand that, when those organs of global process are put to the wrong use, they automatically become self-contradictory and counter intuitive in constitution. Many, who have adopted these organs as means of demonstrating vile forms of empowerment, merely demonstrate a form of poor and weak intellect. A world spent in subverting the interests of others is a world spent against one's own interests, since consistent seeking of one's interests is a form of anti-self interest in its most radical form.

Generally philosophy, as the love of wisdom and science of pure knowledge and essences, insofar these become evident through missing links, has the sacred duty to make this hidden insight evident and here, African philosophy in a complementary perspective, in the age of globalisation, has much to offer. It keeps us awake to the ignorance that makes even our own lives cumbersome and insecure as we experience this daily where most acts of injustice are reciprocated in manners that make the optimal attainment of desired advantages improbable, remote, if not impossible. In most of these cases, the actors are engulfed in the worst form of ignorance. The effect of this ignorance is at the root of the backwardness that we experience in a world marked with material affluence of unimaginable proportions, but which unfortunately and paradoxically also experiences human misery and deprivation in an inconceivable magnitude. It is because of this ignorance that the fundamental human tendency to globalise and universalise can be misconstrued as an opportunity to exploit and dominate, to grab and destroy, to despise and denigrate, most especially in asymmetrical situations.

One of the greatest challenges of African philosophy today is to reverse this trend concretely through recourse to its rich tradition that is inherently complementary in constitution. This tradition must be reflected in the way of life of any average African to be credible. It is by so doing that African philosophy would forestall its relapse into a *philosophy of the living dead* in the real sense of the word. Here, the world has much to learn from complementary reflection as further exposition of the African complementary conception of the world.

References

Abanuka, B. *Philosophy and the Igbo World.* Spiritan Publications, Onitsha, 2004.

Achebe Chinua. "'Chi' in Igbo Cosmology". In: *African Philosophy. An Anthology.* Edited by Emmanuel Chukwudi Eze, Blackwell Publishers Ltd, 1998.

---------------------*Things Fall Apart.* African Writers Series 1. Heinemann, London, Ibadan, 1982.

Adler, Jerry. "Unlocking Minds". In: Newsweek, March 19, 2007.

Aghamelu Fidelis, Chuka. "African Development: Contribution of African Philosophy". In: *Ogirisi: A New Journal of African Studies*, vol. 1 No. 1 2003.

Akogu, Peter O. *Why Anthropology. Basic Facts about the Anthropological Science.* Futuretech Publishers, Awka 1999.

Amaku, E. E. "Philosophy and African Culture". In: *Academia. ACIP Journal of Philosophy,* Vol. 1 No. 1. June, 2003.

Anyanwu, K.C. "The Problem of the Method in African Philosophy". In: *Substance of African Philosophy,* edited by C. S. Momoh, African Philosophy Projects' Publication, Auchi 2000.

--------------------- "The African World-View and Theory of Knowledge". In: *African Philosophy. An Introduction to the main Philosophical trends in Contemporary Africa.* By Prof. E. A. Ruch, Omi and Dr. K. C. Anyanwu. Catholic Book Agency – Officium Libri Catholici Rome, 1981.

Arinze, Francis. Sacrifice in Ibo Religion. Ibadan University Press, 1970

Aristotle. *Metaphysica,* Translated into English under the editorship of W. D. Ross, M.A., Hon. LL.D (Edin.) Oxford. Vol. VIII, Second Edition, OXFORD at the Clarendon Press 1926. Online Edition.

Asouzu, Innocent. "Humanistic Education, Technology and National Development". In: *Journal of Education and*

Peace, Vol. 2, Nos. 1 , November 1996.

-------------------- "The Impact of Pseudo-legitimate Strategies of Survival on Systems and Institutions". In: *Classical Journal of Research in Education,* Vol. 2. No. 1, 2000, 102-114.

-------------------- "Multilingualism, Interest, Transcendence of Meaning and Principle of Harmonious Complementation". In: *Global Journal of Humanities, Vol. 1, No. 1, 2002*

-------------------- "Method as Disposition. Challenges of Philosophy in a World of Relativity". In: *Calabar Journal of Religious Studies, Vol. 1. No. 1. November 1999.*

--------------------*From Nise to Arondizuogu and to the World. Nmelonye Family History 1819-2004.* Edited by Innocent Asouzu, Chedal *Global Prints Ltd. Aba, 2004.*

-------------------- *Ibuanyidanda. New Complementary Ontology. Beyond World-Immanentism, Ethnocentric Reduction and Impositions.* Litverlag, Münster, 2007.

Ayer, A. J. "The Impossibility Of Metaphysics". In: *Science, Faith,and Man . European Thought since 1924.* Edited by W. Warren Wagar, London, 1968.

-------------------- "Demonstration of the Impossibility of Metaphysics": *Mind* XLIII (July 1934) 334-345.

Azenabor, Godwin. *Understanding the Problems in African Philosophy.* First Academic Publishers, Lagos, 2004.

-------------------- "Schools of Thought in Contemporary African Philosophy". In: *Substance of African Philosophy* edited by C. S. Momoh, African Philosophy Projects' Publication, Auchi, 2000.

Azikiwe Nnamdi. *My Odyssey. An Autobiography.* Spectrum Books Limited, Abuja, Benin City, Lagos, Owerri, 2004.

Balogun, A. Abiodun. "The Role of the Gods and Theoretical Entities: An extension of Natural Explanations in Traditional African Thought". In: *West African Journal of Philosophical Studies (WAJOPS). Vol. 8, December, 2005.*

Basden, G. T. *Among the Ibos of Nigeria.* Frank Cass & Co. Ltd. London, 1921.

Beck, Heinrich. "Europe-Africa-Asia. The Creative Proportion Between The World Cultures". In: *Thought and Practice in African Philosophy,* edited by Gail M. Presbey et al. Published by Konrad Adenauer Foundation, Nairobi, Kenya, 2002.

Brown, Lee M. African Philosophy. "Understanding and Ontology in Traditional African Thought". In: *New and Traditional Perspectives,* edited by Lee M. Brown, Oxford University Press, 2004.

Caesar Julius. *The Gallic Wars.* Translated by W. A. McDevitte and W. S. Bohn. Online Edition.

Congregation of The Holy Ghost Province of Nigeria. *Short Life of Bishop Shanahan C.S.Sp.* A Spiritan Publication, Onitsha, 1996.

Copleston Frederick. *A History of Philosophy*, volumes 1-9. Image Books, A Division of Doubleday and Company, Inc. Garden City, New York, 1977.

Dukor, Maduabuchi. "Philosophy and Scientific Paradigms: The Concepts of Space and Time In African Philosophy and Quantum Gravity". In: *Philosophy and Praxis. Journal of Nigerian Philosophical Association.* Vol. 1, 2005.

Ekei, John C. "Is there an African Moral Philosophy? (A Hermeneutical Investigation into African-Igbo Ethics)". In: *Understanding Philosophy.* Published by Pope John Paul II Seminary, Okpuno , Awka, 2003

Ejizu C. "Religion and Politics in Nigeria: The Perspective of The Indigenous Religion". In: *The Nigerian Journal of Theology. Vol. 1. No. 6, May 1991.*

Eliade, Mircea. *The Sacred and the Profane. The Nature of Religion. The significance of religious myth, symbolism, and ritual within life and culture.* Harcourt, Brace & World, Inc., New York, 1959.

Esu, Thomas Ejemot. *The Dialectics in Asouzu's Complementary Reflection and The Principle of Contradiction. A Cri-*

tique. Unpublished M.A. Thesis submitted to The Graduate School, University of Calabar –Nigeria, March, 2006.

Ekwunife A. N. O. *Meaning and Function of "INỌ ỤWA" (Reincarnation) in Igbo Traditional Religious Cuture*. Spiritan Publications, Nigeria, 2000.

Ekwuru, Emeka George. The Pangs of an African Culture In Travail. Ụwa Ndi Igbo Yaghara Ayagha (Igbo World in Disarray). Owerri 1999.

Frost Jr. S. E. ed. *Masterworks of Philosophy* Vol. I, McGraw Hill Books, New York, 1972.

Gmainer-Pranzl, Franz. "zu: I.I. Asouzu: The Method and Principles of Complementary Reflection in and beyond African Philosophy". In: *Polylog, Zeitschrift für interkulturelles Philosophieren,* Nr. 15 (2006), 90-93.

Heidegger, Martin. *Die Technik und die Kehre*. Verlag Günther Neske Pfullingen 1962.

Hengelbrock Jürgen . "The stranger between oppression and superiority. Close encounter with Heinz Kimmerle." http://home.concepts-ict.nl/~kimmerle/ceheng.htm.

Igwegbe, R. O. *The Original History of Arondizuogu From 1635-1960*. International Press Aba, 1962.

Iroegbu, Pantaleon, *Metaphysics. The Kpim of Philosophy*. Owerri, 1995.

Iwuchukwu, Oliver. "African Cultural Anthropology: The Quest for a Grounding Principle". In: *West African Journal of Philosophical Studies, Vol. 1 Nr. 1* September 1998.

Isichei, Elizabeth. *A History of the Igbo People*. The Macmillan Press Ltd, London, 1976.

Janz, Bruce. "Alterity, Dialogue, and African Philosophy". In: *Postcolonial African Philosophy. A Critical Reader*. Edited by Emmanuel Chukwudi Eze, Bucknell University, Lewisburg, PA, 1997.

Kant, Immanuel. "The Metaphysical Foundation of Morals". In: *The Enduring Questions . Main Problems of Philosophy*, arranged by Melvin Rader, Holt, Rinehart and Winston, New York, 1976.

Kimmerle, Heinz. "Response to Jürgen Hengelbrock by Heinz Kimmerle". http://home.concepts-ict.nl/~kimmerle/ceheng.htm.

Kresse, Kai. Kresse, Kai. "Towards a postcolonial synthesis in African Philosophy – Conceptual Liberation and Reconstructive Self-evaluation in the Work of Okot p'Bitek". In: *The Third Way in African Philosophy,* edited by Olusegun Oladipo, Hope Publications Ltd, Ibadan 2002

-------------------- "Towards and Anthropology of Philosophies: Four Turns, With Reference to the African Context". In: *Thought and Practice in African Philosophy*, edited by Gail M. Presbey et al. Published by Konrad Adenauer Foundation, Nairobi, Kenya, 2002.

Makang, Jean-Marie. "Of the Good Use of Tradition: Keeping the Critical Perspective in African Philosophy". In: *Postcolonial African Philosophy. A Critical Reader.* Edited by Emmanuel Chukwudi Eze, Blackwell Publishers, Cambridge, Massachusetts, 1997.

Makinde, Moses Akin. Whither Philosophy in Africa? http://www.bu.edu/wcp/Papers/Afri/AfriMaki.htm

Masolo, D. A. *"The Concept of the Person in Luo Modes of Thought".* In: Brown, Lee M. editor *African Philosophy. New and Traditional Perspectives.* Oxford University Press, 2004.

Massoni, Marco "Mutato nominee, de nobis historia narrator?" In: *African Philosophy and the Hermeneutics of Culture. Essays in Honour of Theophilus Okere.* Edited by J. Obi Oguejiofor and Godfrey Igwebuike Onah. Studies in African Philosophy, Münster 2005.

Momoh, C. S. "Nature, Issues and Substance of African Philosophy". In: *Schools of Thought in Contemporary African Philosophy*, in: Substance of African Philosophy edited by C. S. Momoh, African Philosophy Projects' Publication, Auchi 2000.

-------------------- "Nature, Issues and Substance of African Philosophy". In: *Metaphysics, Phenomenology and African Philosophy.* Edited by Jim I. Unah FADEC Publishers Lagos, 2004.

---------------------"Preface". *Substance of African Philosophy* edited by C. S. Momoh, African Philosophy Projects' Publication, Auchi 2000.

Ngugi wa Thiong'o. *Decolonising the Mind. The Politics of Language in African Literature.* Heinemann London, 1986.

Njoku, Francis O. *Essays in African Philosophy. Thought and Theology.* Owerri, Enugu, Lagos, 2002.

--------------------- "The Originality of African Philosophy as a Hermeneutical Problem in Okere". In: *African Philosophy and the Hermeneutics of Culture. Essays in Honour of Theophilus Okere.* Edited by J. Obi Oguejiofor and Godfrey Igwebuike Onah. Studies in African Philosophy, Münster 2005.

Nkrumah Kwame. *Consciencism. Philosophy and Ideology for De-Colonisation*, Kwame Nkrumah and Panaf Books Ltd, London, 1964.

Nwigwe, B. E. "Causality in Selected Igbo Cultural Novels: Perspective in Igbo Meatphysics". In: *West African Journal of Philosphical Studies (WAJOPS). Vol. 7, December 2004.*

Nwala, Uzodinma T. *Igbo Philosophy.* Lantern Books, Lagos 1985.

---------------------"The Concept of Traditional African Philosophy". In: *Philosophy, Science & Society, An Interdisciplinary, International Journal of Concerned African Philosophers,* Vol. 2. 2005.

Nwoga, Ibe Donatus. *Nka na Nzere. The Focus of Igbo World View.* Ahiajoku Lecture 1984. Published by Culture Division, Ministry of Information, Culture, Youth and Sports and Printed by the Government printer Owerri.

Nze, C.B. "Uncovering Logic in Igbo Language and Thought". In: *West African Journal of Philosophical Studies (WAJOPS). Vol. 1, No. 1. September 1998.*

December 2002.

Obi, A. C. "Senses of Being in Igbo Metaphysics". In: : *West African Journal of Philosophical Studies (WAJOPS). Vol. 5, December 2002.*

Oguah, Benjamin Ewuke. "African and Western Philosophy: A Comparative Study". In: *African Philosophy. An Introduction.* Edited by Richard Wright, Lanham, New York, London, 1979.

Ogugua Paul I. "Understanding Deities in Igbo-African World: A Religio-Philosophical Perspective". In: *Essence. Interdisciplinary-International Journal of Philosophy, Vol. 2, 2005.*

Ogunmodede Francis. "African Philosophy in African Language". In: *West African Journal of Philosophical Studies,* Vol. 1, No. 1 September 1998.

Oguejiofor, Obi. J. *Philosophy and The African Predicament.* Hope Publications Ltd, Ibadan, 2001.

-------------------- "The Universal and the Particular in Igbo Concept of Ala". In: *West African Journal of Philosophical Studies (WAJOPS). Vol. 5, December 2002.*

-------------------- *African Philosophy and the Hermeneutics of Culture. Essays in Honour of Theophilus Okere.* Edited by J. Obi Oguejiofor and Godfrey Igwebuike Onah. Studies in African Philosophy, Münster 2005.

-------------------- "Ethnophilosophy and Hermeneutics". In: *African Philosophy and the Hermeneutics of Culture. Essays in Honour of Theophilus Okere.* Edited by J. Obi Oguejiofor and Godfrey Igwebuike Onah. Studies in African Philosophy, Münster 2005.

Oke, Moses. "Modelling the Contemporary African Philosopher: Kwasi Wiredu in Focus". In: *The Third Way in African Philosophy*, edited by Olusegun Oladipo, Hope Publications Ltd, Ibadan, 2002

--------------------"Cultural Nostalgia: A Philosophical Critique of Appeals to the Past in Theories of Re-Making Africa". In: Nordic Journal of African Studies 15(3):

332-343, 2006.

Okere, Theophilus. *African Philosophy: A Hermeneutico-Historical Inquiry into the Conditions of its Possibility*, Lanham, University Press of America, 1983.

---------------------"African Culture: The Past and the Present as an Indivisible Whole". In: *Identity and Change. Nigerian Philosophical Studies*, I. Edited by Theophilus Okere, Washington 1996.

Okolo, B. C. *Problems of African Philosophy And one other Essay.* Cecta (Nigeria) Limited, Enugu, 1990.

Oladipo, Olusegun. *Conceptual Decolonization in African Philosophy. Four Essays By Kwasi Wiredu.* Hope Publications, Ibadan, 1995.

---------------------*Philosophy and the African Experience. The Contributions of Kwasi Wiredu.* Hope Publications, Ibadan Nigeria, 1996

---------------------"Kwasi Wiredu's Idea of African Philosophy". In: *The Third Way in African Philosophy*, edited by Olusegun Oladipo, Hope Publications Ltd, Ibadan, 2002

---------------------"Rethinking Yoruba World-View and Ideals of Life". In: *The Third Way in African Philosophy*, edited by Olusegun Oladipo, Hope Publications Ltd, Ibadan, 2002

---------------------"Knowledge and the African Renaissance". In: *WAJOPS, West African Journal of Philosophical Studies,* Vol. 2, December, 1999.

--------------------- *Core Issues In African Philosophy*. Edited by Olusegun Oladipo. Hope Publications, Ibadan-Nigeria, 2006

Oluwole, Sophie, B. *Philosophy and Oral Tradition. ARK Publications, Ikeja, Lagos, 1999.*

Onah, Godfrey. "Concept of Man for a developing Continent" in: *Africa. Philosophy and Public Affairs. Proceedings of an International Conference held at Bigard Memorial Seminary, Enugu from April 29-May 3, 1997.* Edited by J. Obi Oguejiofor. Delta Publications, 1998.

Onyeocha, Izu M. "Africa's Idea About the Nature of Reality". In: *Journal of the Humanities, Vol., No. III, September, 2000.*

Onyewuenyi, Innocent C. *The African Origin of Greek Philosophy: An Exercise in Afrocentrism.* University of Nigeria Press, Nsukka, 1993.

-------------------- *African Belief in Reincarnation:* A Philosophical Reappraisal. Snapp Publishers, Enugu 1996.

Orwell, George, *Animal Farm.* Penguin Books, Middlesex, England, 1980.

Otto, Rudolf. *Das Heilig.* Munich, 1947

Ozumba. G. O. "A Review of Kwasi Wiredu's ‚How Not to Compare African Thought with Western Thought". In: *Footmarks on African Philosophy,* edited by A. F. Uduigwomen, Obaroh & Ogbinaka Publishers Ltd, Lagos 1995.

Pannenberg, Wolfhart. *Anthropologie in theologischer Perspektive.* Göttingen 1983.

Serequeberhan, Tsenay. "Colonialism and the Colonized: Violence and Counter Violence". In: *African Philosophy. An Anthology.* Edited by Emmanuel Chukwudi Eze, Blackwell Publishers Ltd, 1998.

St. Augustine, The City of God Christian Doctrine. Online Edition. Translated by The Rev. Marchs Dods, D. D. of Glasgow. T&T Clark WM. B. Eerdmans Publishing Company Edinburgh Grand Rapids, Michigan.

Stegmüller Wolfgang. *Main Currents in Contemporary German, British and American Philosophy,* D. Reidel Publishing, Dordrecht, Holland, 1969.

Sunday Sun, September 17, 2006.

Ugwuanyi, Ogbo. "Decolonisation, Development and Modernization in Africa". In: *Sophia, An African Journal of Philosophy,* Vol. 6, No. 1 September, 2003.

Umorem, Grace. "African Traditional Cosmological World-View

and Western World View: Conflicts and Adaptations". In: *Sophia. An African Journal of Philosophy,* Vol. 3. No. 2, April, 2001.

Unah, Jim I. "The Nature of African Metaphysics", in: *Metaphysics, Phenomenology and African Philosophy,* edited by Jim I. Unah. FADEC Publishers, Lagos 2004.

Winch, Peter. *The Idea of a Social Science*. London, Routledge & Kegan Paul, 1958.

Wiredu, Kwasi. "The Need for Conceptual Decolonization in African Philosophy". In: *Conceptual Decolonization in African Philosophy. Four Essays by Kwasi Wiredu, Selected and Introduced by Olusegun Oladipo*, Hope Publications Ibadan, 1995.

Index:

Studies in African Philosophy

hrsg. von Prof. Dr. J. Obi Oguejiofor (Enugu/Nigeria), Prof. Dr. Godfrey I. Onah (Univ. Urbaniana, Rom), Prof. Dr. Mogobe Ramose (Univ. of Pretoria, Südafrika)

Josephat Oguejiofor (ed.)

Philosophy, Democracy and Responsible Governance in Africa

The essays presented in *Philosophy, Democracy and Responsible Governance in Africa* set out to explore various aspects of the issue of governance and to reflect on how governance in Africa can be made to be more responsible. All the contributors exhibit clear awareness of the stupendous problems confronting governance in Africa, and make different suggestions aimed at obviating the difficulties. The volume is a timely and welcome contribution to the never-ending discussions about Africa, its problems, its leaders and managers, and the possible ways of drawing it out of the quagmire into which decades of bad governance, in addition to many other factors, have thrown most countries of the continent. Very Rev. Dr. John I. Okoye Rector,
Bigard Memorial Seminary,
Enugu.

Bd. 1, 2003, 640 S., 49,90 €, gb.,
ISBN 3-8258-7105-3

African Philosophy and the Hermeneutics of Culture

Essays in Honour of Theophilus Okere. Edited by J. Obi Oguejiofor and Godfrey Igwebuike Onah

Although Theophilus Okere´s book *African Philosophy* has made remarkable impact on African philosophical scholarship, many may not be aware of the way he tried to apply his preferred method to other areas of the philosophical investigation in Africa and to overcome the risk of relativism through the promotion of intercultural dialogue in philosophy. The essays published in this volume bear testimony to the multivalent character of Okere´s contribution to African philosophy. Most of the essays are about Okere´s hermeneutics of culture. Some of the authors examine the method in itself, while others focus attention on its application to specific philosophical themes.

Bd. 2, 2005, 376 S., 39,90 €, gb.,
ISBN 3-8258-8217-9

Ukoro Theophilus Igwe

Communicative Rationality and Deliberative Democracy of Jürgen Habermas: Toward Consolidation of Democracy in Africa

Comunnicative Rationality and Deliberative Democracy of Jürgen Habermas: Toward Consolidation of Democracy in Africa, investigates critically Habermas's attempt to develop communicative conception of human rationality. It explores Habermas's fundamental commitment to the practical import and ramifications of communicative rationality in the field of African political philosophy. Within this context, Habermas's ambitious project to reconcile law, justice, and democracy is wide-ranging. This work explores how it is, among other things, that deliberative institutions can become more democratic through, as Dewey put it, "*improvements in the methods and conditions of debate, discussion and persuasion*".

Bd. 3, 2005, 520 S., 29,90 €, br.,
ISBN 3-8258-7908-9

Innocent I. Asouzu

The Method and Principles of Complementary Reflection in and beyond African Philosophy

Questions relating to types of philosophical trends within African philosophy can be very decisive for any idea of African philosophy. In this strikingly novel approach to African Philosophy, the author explores a complementary philosophical trend that goes back to those he calls *anonymous traditional African philosophers*. Based on their thoughts, he articulates a distinctive variant of the principles, method and imperative of complementarity *(Ibu anyi danda)* around which he builds his

LIT Verlag GmbH & Co. KG Wien – Zürich

Auslieferung Österreich: Medienlogistik Pichler-ÖBZ GmbH & Co KG
IZ-NÖ Süd, Straße 1, Objekt 34, A-2355 Wiener Neudorf, Postfach 133
Tel. +43 (0) 2236/63 535 - 290, Fax +43 (0) 2236/63 535 - 243, e-Mail: bestellen@medien-logistik.at

Auslieferung Deutschland: Fresnostr. 2 48159 Münster
Tel.: 0251 – 62 03 222 – Fax 0251 – 23 19 72
e-Mail: vertrieb@lit-verlag.de – http://www.lit-verlag.de

system. He anchors his reflection on such ambient concepts as *the joy of being (jide k' iji), fragmentation, wholeness, and future reference.*
vol. 4, 2005, 536 pp., 49,90 €, br.,
ISBN-DE 3-8258-8578-x, ISBN-CH 3-03735-127-6

Vernantius Emeka Ndukaihe
Achievement as Value in the Igbo/African Identity: The Ethics
Perspectives in the light of Christian normative/value systems. Nachwort von Prof. Peter Fonk

Achievement seems to be a first-class value in our world today. With the ongoing global debate on what constitutes identity, can we include achievement as one of the constituents? In the Igbo/African identity, the achievement instinct is basically innate. The ethics of this phenomenon needs an evaluation, aimed at improving the status quo. What is the plight of the Igbo/African „achieving" in the face of modern capitalistic tendencies? What has become of the many other values in her identity, which has been her pride as a race? How is her religiosity (which is inseparable from daily living) affected by „modernity" and its new trends of the achievement ethos? These are some of the issues, which the autor addresses in this book with the conviction that theology, achievement and identity, are continuity.
Bd. 5, 2006, 448 S., 29,90 €, br.,
ISBN 3-8258-9929-2

Hermann Fechtrup; Friedbert Schulze; Thomas Sternberg (Hg.)
Wissen und Weisheit
Zwei Symposien zu Ehren von Josef Pieper (1904 – 1997). Mit Beiträgen von Charles Taylor, Hans Joas, Ludwig Siep u. a.

Zum 100. Geburtstag Josef Piepers wurden 2004 zwei Symposien veranstaltet, die hier dokumentiert werden. Erstmalig wurde der Josef Pieper Preis verliehen. Die Vorträge des Preisträgers Charles Taylor und seines Laudators Ludwig Siep geben Einblicke in Denken und Themen des kanadischen Philosophen. Grundsätzliche Erörterungen der Philosophie in ihrem Verhältnis zu Theologie, Sprache und Ethik werden in den Beiträgen von Hans-Martin Gauger, Hans Joas, Karl Lehmann, Annemarie Pieper und Richard Schaeffler dokumentiert. William Hoye, Jörg Splett und Berthold Wald beleuchten Grundthemen Josef Piepers neu.
Bd. 6, 2005, 240 S., 24,90 €, br.,
ISBN 3-8258-8527-5

Schriftenreihe der Josef Pieper Stiftung

hrsg. von Dr. Hermann Fechtrup, Friedbert Schulze und Dr. Dr. Thomas Sternberg

Josef Schmidt; Martin Splett; Thomas Splett; Peter-Otto Ullrich (Hg.)
Mitdenken über Gott und den Menschen
Dialogische Festschrift für Jörg Splett

Jörg Splett ist einer der bedeutendsten Vertreter des christlichen Philosophierens. Die Gewißheit, daß Glaube und Vernunft eine unauflösliche Zwei-Einheit bilden, buchstabiert er anspruchsvoll argumentierend in einer Verknüpfung von philosophischer Anthropologie und Gotteslehre aus. Die Festschrift anläßlich seines 65. Geburtstags versammelt Beiträge zu Spletts Hauptthemen, die sich explizit mit seiner Position auseinandersetzen. Eine ausführliche Replik des Jubilars setzt die dialogische Anlage des Buches fort. Stimmen zu Spletts Wirken in Fortbildung und Seelsorge sowie zu künstlerischen Kontaktfeldern beschließen es. Ein Anhang enthält die vollständige Bibliographie Spletts.
Bd. 2, 2001, 312 S., 25,90 €, br.,
ISBN 3-8258-4947-3

Aloysius Obiwulu
***Tractatus de legibus* in 13th Century Scholasticism**
A Critical Study and Interpretation of Law in Summa Fratris Alexandri, Albertus Magnus and Thomas Aquinas

Whereas the Summa Halensis saw natural law as a created order as such that is applicable

LIT Verlag GmbH & Co. KG Wien – Zürich
Auslieferung Österreich: Medienlogistik Pichler-ÖBZ GmbH & Co KG
IZ-NÖ Süd, Straße 1, Objekt 34, A-2355 Wiener Neudorf, Postfach 133
Tel. +43 (0) 2236/63 535 - 290, Fax +43 (0) 2236/63 535 - 243, e-Mail: bestellen@medien-logistik.at
Auslieferung Deutschland: Fresnostr. 2 48159 Münster
Tel.: 0251 – 62 03 222 – Fax 0251 – 23 19 72
e-Mail: vertrieb@lit-verlag.de – http://www.lit-verlag.de

to all beings according to the view of Ulpian, Albert the Great refuses to take account of any thing other than human reason: man is man for no other reason than his possession of intellect. The research of Aloysius Obiwulu points out in a considerable way what is at stake in this decision of Albert, which was transmitted to Thomas Aquinas and all subsequent political thinkers. Natural law is concerned about man himself to the extent that by his reason, he has innate in him the seeds of all juridical order, exactly as he possesses in himself the principles of geometry and metaphysics. The full merit of this book of Aloysius Obiwulu is this: to show that other utterances of law are possible and by that to be able to re-evaluate the present and to turn toward the future with determination and lucidity. *P*rof. Jean-Michel Counet, Institut Supérieur de Philosophie, Université Catholique de Louvain (U.C.L), Belgium.
Bd. 4, 2003, 352 S., 29,90 €, br.,
ISBN 3-8258-7065-0

Münsteraner Bioethik-Studien

hrsg. von Prof. Dr. Ludwig Siep (Universität Münster) in Verbindung mit Prof. Dr. Antonio Autiero, Prof. Dr. Kurt Bayertz, Prof. Dr. Bernd Holznagel, Prof. Dr. Dr. Peter Hucklenbroich, Prof. Dr. Bettina Schöne-Seifert und Prof. Dr. Heinz-Dietrich Steinmeyer

Ludwig Siep; Michael Quante (Hg.)
Der Umgang mit dem beginnenden menschlichen Leben
Ethische, medizintheoretische und rechtliche Probleme aus niederländischer und deutscher Perspektive
Neue Erkenntnisse im Bereich der Biologie und Medizin sowie die damit verbundenen technischen Fortschritte rücken vielversprechende diagnostische und therapeutische Möglichkeiten im Umgang mit den frühesten Formen menschlichen Lebens ins Blickfeld. Die Diskussion um die Nutzung menschlicher embryonaler Stammzellen und die Frage der Zulassung der Präimplantationsdiagnostik sind dabei die in Deutschland gegenwärtig prominentesten Beispiele für den gesellschaftlichen Diskussions- und Regelungsbedarf in diesem Bereich. Dabei lassen sich in den europäischen Ländern unterschiedliche Einstellungen zu den ethischen und rechtlichen Problemen feststellen. In den Beiträgen, die in diesem Band versammelt sind, werden die verschiedenen Aspekte dieses Themas aus deutscher und niederländischer Perspektive beleuchtet.
Bd. 1, 2003, 184 S., 24,90 €, br.,
ISBN 3-8258-5951-7

Christian Lenk
Therapie und Enhancement
Ziele und Grenzen der modernen Medizin
Bd. 2, 2002, 304 S., 20,90 €, br.,
ISBN 3-8258-5837-5

Peter Hucklenbroich; Richard Toellner (Hg.)
Symposium 20 Jahre Ethikkommission Münster – 15 Jahre Arbeitskreis Medizinischer Ethikkommissionen
Erfahrungen – Probleme – Perspektiven
In den Münsteraner Bioethischen Studien erscheinen Schriften zu aktuellen und grundlegenden Problemen der Bioethik, die im Kontext der Forschungsstelle Bioethik der Westfälischen Wilhelms-Universität Münster entstanden sind. Ziel dieser Schriftenreihe ist eine sachliche und angemessene Diskussion zentraler bioethischer Fragen, nicht die Formulierung einer einheitlichen weltanschaulichen Position. Vielmehr verstehen sich die Münsteraner Bioethischen Studien als Plattform für eine interdisziplinäre, konstruktive und offene Diskussion.
Bd. 3, 2002, 80 S., 15,90 €, br.,
ISBN 3-8258-6153-8